Letters of the
Queens of England
1100–1547

Letters of the Queens of England 1100–1547

Edited by Anne Crawford

ALAN SUTTON

First published in the United Kingdom in 1994 by
Alan Sutton Publishing Ltd
Phoenix Mill · Far Thrupp · Stroud · Gloucestershire

First published in the United States of America in 1994 by
Alan Sutton Publishing Inc · 83 Washington Street · Dover NH 03820

British Library Cataloguing in Publication Data. A catalogue record for this book is
available from the British Library.

ISBN 0-86299-726-7

Library of Congress Cataloging in Publication Data

Crawford, Anne.
    The letters of the queens of England, 1100–1547 / Anne Crawford.
    Includes bibliography references
    ISBN 0-86299-726-7
    1. Great Britain–History–Medieval period, 1100–1485–Sources.
    2. Great Britain–History–Tudors, 1485–1547–Sources. 3. Queens–
    Great Britain–Correspondence. I. Title.
DA170.C73   1994
942–dc20   93-33709
                                                              CIP

Typeset in 11/14 Baskerville.
Typesetting and origination by
Alan Sutton Publishing Ltd.
Printed in Great Britain by
The Bath Press, Bath, Avon.

Contents

Acknowledgements

My greatest debt in compiling this book is to those two great pioneering historians of the mid-nineteenth century, Agnes Strickland and Mary Anne Everett Wood. My thanks are also due to Elizabeth Stuart, Elizabeth Hallam, Kevin Barrett and Eric Poole for their work on the translations.

Introduction

The letters in this volume are those of the wives of the medieval and Tudor kings of England, from William the Conqueror to Henry VIII. The earliest letter dates from *c.* 1103 and there are none from William's queen, Matilda of Flanders, yet to have omitted her and the few other queens for whom there are no letters from the study would have been to unbalance the whole, and therefore a brief portrait of each has been included to preserve continuity. In addition, four royal ladies who were all mothers of kings, yet not queens themselves, have been included: the Empress Matilda, who should have been the first English queen regnant, and who was the mother of Henry II; Joan of Kent, Princess of Wales, who would have been queen but for the death of the Black Prince before his father, and who was the mother of Richard II; Cecily Neville, duchess of York, mother of Edward IV and Richard III; and Margaret Beaufort, countess of Richmond and Derby, mother of Henry VII. After the death of Henry VIII in 1547 there were no queens consort for nearly sixty years during the reigns of his three children, Edward VI, who died unmarried, Mary I and Elizabeth, who were queens regnant. The last letter dates from 1554 and was written by Henry VIII's fourth wife, Anne of Cleves, who survived him by several years.

Many of the letters have been in print for a long time, some since the publication of Rymer's *Foedera* in the early eighteenth century. The majority, however, first appeared in Mary Anne Everett Wood's three-volume work, *Letters of Royal and Illustrious Ladies of Great Britain*, published in 1846. Others have appeared in more specialist works relating to a particular subject or reign. Most of these works are now only available in specialist libraries and details are set out in the Sources. Most of the original letters are now in the British Library or the Public Record Office, a few in the Vatican or other ecclesiastical collections. In some cases the originals have not been traced and the letters are only known from their printed version. The survival of the letters has been, for the most part, because of their official nature. Thus the majority have been preserved among the records of the royal chancery or exchequer, and this accounts for the high proportion of letters addressed to the Chancellor. Probably the greatest number of letters sent by any queen would have been to her own officials, particularly those not resident at court, her bailiffs, parkers and receivers in all her many estates. Inevitably, the letters which would have been of most interest to modern readers, those of a personal nature to family and friends, are those least likely to have survived. For some of the queens, I have been unable to trace any letters at all; Matilda of Flanders, Adela of Louvain and Matilda of Boulogne are so early that perhaps it is more surprising that any have survived for their contemporaries than that none have survived for them. From the mid-twelfth century, letters exist for all the queens until the late fourteenth century. There are none for Richard II's little queen, Isabella, nor for her sister, Katherine, wife of Henry V. Thereafter, only Anne Neville, Richard III's queen, is unrepresented. Inevitably the sixteenth century produces the most riches in terms of letters that reflect the feelings or emotions of their writers, but over 120 letters survive for Eleanor of Provence in the mid-thirteenth century and many of them are written in the queen's remarkably modern, chatty style.

The selection of the letters has not always been easy. For some queens so little survives that any letter, no matter how brief or official, has been included. For others, there are so many letters that only the most substantial, in political, personal or characteristic terms have been included. Until the late fifteenth century, all the letters were written on behalf of the queen by a secretary. This certainly does not imply that the queen herself was unable to write, any more than a modern letter dictated to and typed by a secretary means a businessperson cannot write. It does however mean that evidence of the literacy of queens is harder to come by. Certainly in the early part of our period, many nobles could read but saw no point in learning to write. Yet in the late thirteenth century, Eleanor of Castile was ordering tablets for her daughters to write on, which hardly suggests that she was herself unable to write. The earliest use of a signature was that of Joan of Navarre in the early fifteenth century (see p. 116); until that date all that was required to authenticate a letter was the queen's seal. The first holograph letter in this collection, written entirely by the lady herself, is one from Margaret Beaufort in 1497.

The languages of the letters are chiefly Latin, French and English. Until the late thirteenth century, all were in Latin, the common language of Christendom which was used for all official purposes. From then on, a combination of French and Latin was used by the two Eleanors, of Provence and Castile. It is not always easy to decide what determined the language. Latin was used for more formal documents, or any sent to ecclesiastics, French for more personal letters or for semi-official correspondence with officials, but some officials handled both languages with apparent ease. The last queen to use French was Joan of Navarre, but nothing survives for her French successor, Katherine of Valois. Two decades later, Margaret of Anjou had mastered English sufficiently well to use it in all her correspondence, a reflection of usage in the country generally. Elizabeth of York, however, writing to Queen Isabella of Castile, reverted to the use of Latin, since neither could be expected to be familiar with each other's language. Some of the most personal letters of all, those written by Katherine of Aragon as the widowed Princess of Wales to her father, Ferdinand, are in Spanish.

The choice of a wife was the most important single decision ever made by any medieval king. The ability to produce from her a male heir was his most important responsibility. For her to bear this son in time for him to be of age when his father died was scarcely less essential. The astonishing dynastic longevity of the Capetian kings of France (from 978 to 1328) and of their successors, the Valois (from 1328 to 1498) is a remarkable testimony to the virility of the kings, the fecundity of their wives and their sense of timing. With the exceptions of Louis IX (St Louis), king at fourteen, and Charles VIII, king at thirteen, there were no significant minorities in the French monarchy over a period of some 500 years and, except in 1328, there was no lack of a direct male heir. The English royal families over a similar period were rather less fortunate.

Four kings of England, William II, Richard I, Richard II and Richard III, died without an heir of their body to succeed them. William Rufus and Richard the Lionheart were succeeded by brothers, Richard II by a first cousin and Richard III by a man with only a remote connection with the royal line, who promptly married the late king's niece. Henry I's only son died during his father's lifetime, leaving as the king's heir his only daughter, Matilda. Her succession was contested by one of the king's nearest male relatives, his nephew Stephen. The civil war which followed left Stephen in possession of the throne, but the ultimate succession went not to his son, but to Matilda's. The second civil war of our period, the Wars of the Roses, also had dynastic problems as one of its root causes. Long minorities, as with Henry III and even more with Henry VI, might prove deeply damaging to the authority of the Crown. Not only the production of a royal family, but also its management was of critical importance to a reigning king. Strong-willed or self-interested queens, particularly if they tried, like Eleanor of Provence or Elizabeth Woodville, to advance members of their own families, could create deep internal discord. Unruly sons, such as those of Henry II, or as in Edward IV's case, an unruly brother, could cause equally severe disturbance.

The supreme example of the political complications caused by dynastic concerns is, of course, Henry VIII. The whole history of his reign is in many ways an explicit commentary on the central significance of such matters to a king, but it is a significance which only becomes apparent when the king has no direct male heir. Given the importance of these dynastic concerns, it is surprising that it has been so neglected by historians as a theme in English medieval history. It was certainly in no danger of being overlooked by contemporaries. The prime importance of the succession to titles and lands was recognized by the entire landowning section of the English community, from the richest peer down to the yeoman with a few acres to his name. Yet between them and the king there was one essential difference – he had to have a son, for there could be no division of the kingdom among co-heiresses as so often happened to family estates lower down the social scale. By great good fortune, no king in our period died leaving only daughters but no sons, except Henry I, and even in his case, Matilda had no sisters. For many years the succession to Henry VIII remained in doubt, while the king wavered between two daughters, each in turn declared his heiress and then illegitimate, and an illegitimate son. He was saved by the timely birth of a legitimate son, but on more than one occasion he had the succession settled by act of Parliament.

How, then, did a medieval king of England set about finding a suitable wife? Until the beginning of the fifteenth century at least, the primary consideration was diplomatic. With very few exceptions, the queens of England came from France's royal family or one of its great feudal houses. This was because for centuries one of the prime considerations of the English Crown was the safe-guarding of its territorial possessions in France. The person and character of the prospective queen, or indeed the fertility of her family, was rarely considered, provided she was not known to be simple-minded, cross-eyed or hump-backed. Such is the magic cast by the word 'princess' that most of the queens were described as beautiful at one time or another, but public opinion seems to have been generally united in regarding Eleanor of Aquitaine, Isabella of Angoulême, Margaret and Isabella of France, Katherine of Valois and Margaret of Anjou as truly fair to look upon. The first verbal description of a queen that has survived in detail is that of Philippa of Hainault by Bishop Stapleton of Exeter, who helped to negotiate her marriage. He pictures her as of medium height, brown of hair and complexion and pleasant enough. Clearly Philippa was not a beauty. Although a number of queens are depicted in manuscript illuminations or in church effigies, the first portrait of a queen which can be accounted a natural likeness is that of the first English queen, Elizabeth Woodville (see p. 131), also considered a beauty by the standards of her day.

While beauty in the wife who presided over his court might be a bonus for any king, it was supremely unimportant compared with her fertility. While the tender age at which many queens were married meant that in a number of cases it was several years before they bore their first child, only a few of the queens in our period proved barren. Adela of Louvain, whom the ageing widower Henry I married after the death of his son, bore him no children, but had them by her second husband. Berengaria of Navarre had no children by Richard I, who despite recent suggestions that he was homosexual, certainly had an acknowledged bastard. Anne of Bohemia and Richard II had no children, and Richard's second wife, Isabella of Valois, was not of child-bearing age during their marriage. Henry IV and Joan of Navarre had no children, though both had issue by former marriages and the succession was secure. Anne Neville, wife of Richard III, bore him only one child, a son who died when he was eleven. The last three of Henry VIII's wives had no children by him.

Despite the high mortality rate of women in childbirth, only two queens died in this fashion, Elizabeth of York, bearing Henry VII's sixth child, and Jane Seymour, bearing Henry VIII's only legitimate son; but Henry IV's first wife, Mary Bohun, died in childbirth and so did Isabella of Valois and Katherine Parr in their subsequent marriages. On the whole it seems queens were a hardy race. While none could equal the physical and intellectual vigour of Eleanor of Aquitaine, journeying across the Pyrennees in winter on royal business at the age of eighty, most queens outlived their husbands. Only Henry I, Edward I and Richard II had two queens, though both John and Henry IV had English wives before they became king, and of course, Henry VIII falls into a class of his own.

Most royal children were married, or at least betrothed, while they were still young. The matches were made by their fathers to seal a new alliance, strengthen an old one or settle a territorial dispute. Many never saw their prospective spouses before their wedding day, and in the case of proxy marriages, not even then. Edward III, if later tradition is to be believed, was lucky enough to be able to choose between the three available daughters of the Count of Hainault, with whom he was staying, but he did not have the option of turning them all down. Although still only a boy, he showed remarkable perspicacity in selecting Philippa, the middle sister and one nearest to him in age, who proved to be one of the best wives and mothers ever to grace the English throne. However, for one reason or another, a number of kings were still unmarried when they succeeded to the throne. Richard I, John (who promptly divested himself of his first, barren wife), Henry IV (a widower), Henry V and Edward IV were all grown men at their accession, while Henry III, Richard II and Henry VI were minors who had their wives chosen by their Council, acting *in loco parentis*. Of the adult kings, there is no reason to suppose Richard I selected Berengaria for any reason other than diplomatic ones. John's motive in choosing Isabella of Angoulême seems to have been a combination of diplomacy and lust. Henry V's wife, Katherine of Valois, had been selected for him as a boy, but he had to conquer half France before he could marry her. He did have the advantage of seeing her beforehand, and according to onlookers was much charmed by her, thus allowing romantically inclined chroniclers to declare it love at first sight and Shakespeare to create one of his most delightful love scenes. His father, Henry IV, who came to the throne with four healthy sons, was the only king in our period in a position to please himself in the matter of a wife. As a usurper he needed a respectable foreign match and as a man he needed a companion to occupy the lonely heights of kingship with him. Although there is no positive evidence, there seems to be a strong presumption that his choice of Joan of Navarre, widowed duchess of Brittany, was based on personal knowledge of the lady. Joan was the first widow to become queen. The second was Elizabeth Woodville, Lady Grey, the personal choice of Edward IV. Edward was the first king to marry an unsuitable woman purely from inclination and Elizabeth became the first Englishwoman since the Conquest to become queen. A century earlier, however, Edward the Black Prince had married his cousin, Joan of Kent, for love. His parents were not best pleased with the match, for Joan was a widow with four children, but they did not prevent it, and as a granddaughter of Edward I, Joan was not unfitted for her new position. Since the Black Prince died in his father's lifetime, Joan never became queen, but their son succeeded his grandfather as Richard II. Henry VIII's first wife, Katherine of Aragon, was a widow when they married. She had spent much of her childhood betrothed to his elder brother, Arthur, Prince of Wales, and was briefly married to him. This marriage, unconsummated as it was, caused unpredictable problems to Katherine as queen.

How successful were these royal marriages? All the participants were brought up to expect nothing other than an arranged match, as indeed was every medieval child at a time when marriages were made for the benefit of the family and community rather than the individual. Yet each couple knew they had to make an effort to make their marriage work in order for life to be tolerable, since the possibility of ending the marriage was remote. Remote, but not impossible. Divorce did not exist in the Middle Ages. Couples could agree to separate while remaining legally married and without affecting the legitimacy of any children. More significantly, the marriage could be annulled on the grounds that it had never been a lawful marriage. This allowed the partners to remarry, but if the marriage had never been valid, how could any children of it be regarded as legitimate? This difficulty was usually irrelevant because much the most compelling reason for annulment was the lack of heirs. If only daughters had been born, they could still be disposed of reasonably satisfactorily with a substantial dowry, because everyone accepted the situation. This happened to Eleanor of Aquitaine's two daughters by Louis VII of France, but they were married into French noble houses and not foreign ones. The two most important grounds for annulment were consanguinity and precontract. Precontract occurs in our period in the cases of Joan of Kent and Edward IV, but generally speaking, consanguinity was more popular by far with the upper reaches of society. From 1215 the Church had settled the prohibited degrees at four; in other words, marriage between third cousins was forbidden. It was, however, prepared to grant dispensation for marriages within these degrees, usually for some form of payment. If no dispensation was obtained, that was grounds for annulment. In many cases such dispensation was deliberately not obtained before the marriage in order to provide grounds for annulment should it ever prove necessary.

In our period, John and Eleanor of Aquitaine rid themselves of unwanted first partners by this means. John ended his childless marriage, made as the youngest son of a king, to his second cousin, the heiress Isabella of Gloucester, immediately upon becoming king. In Eleanor of Aquitaine's case, she had borne her first husband, Louis VII of France, only daughters and Louis needed a son. He was prepared to lose half of southern France to get one, while Eleanor had apparently already selected her second husband. In order to obtain her lands, the future Henry II was prepared to risk the fact that he too, might have no sons by Eleanor. Ironically, Henry VIII should have had no difficulty obtaining such an annulment of his marriage with Katherine of Aragon, save for the uncomfortable political fact that the Pope from whom he required it was under the political control of Katherine's nephew, the Emperor Charles V. By the time he required a second annulment, from Anne of Cleves, Henry was in a stronger position. Her brother, the duke, was far less important diplomatically, and both Henry and Anne were willing to swear that the marriage had never been consummated. He had married his two previous wives for love and was then quite unable to accept the possibility of marriage to Anne without the gloss of romantic love, an attitude which would have amazed his predecessors. In general, however, provided the marriage was fruitful and had produced the required son, the diplomatic repercussions of annulment were such that royal couples who did not get on, simply lived apart. The amount of time a king and queen spent in each other's company varied according to individual inclination. Some were rarely parted, others, if they so wished, could spend as much as six months in every year living in separate households without giving rise to comment. The number of royal residences and the demands on a king's time by progresses throughout his kingdom, visits to overseas territories, military campaigns and the like could be made to serve more personal ends if necessary. Conversely, the fact that the queen was a foreigner and totally dependent on her husband for her position in her new country, and that the king desperately needed a companion who had no political axe to grind and whom he could trust completely, ensured that each marriage had strong grounds for at least moderate success.

On the available evidence and in the eyes of contemporaries, the unions of William I and Matilda of Flanders, Henry III and Eleanor of Provence, Edward I and Eleanor of Castile, Edward III and Philippa of Hainault and Richard II and Anne of Bohemia were particularly happy ones, while those of Henry II and Eleanor of Aquitaine, John and Isabella of Angoulême and Edward II and Isabella of France reached the stage of total breakdown. The remainder of our royal couples reached a tolerable understanding. This is not the mere idle romantic speculation it may appear. Medieval royal children, no matter how fenced about by attendants, were as affected by their parents' relationships as their twentieth-century counterparts, and the formation of a future king's character in turn could affect the politics of a whole reign. Few details survive of the day-to-day lives of the queens and their husbands, but there is the occasional illuminating glimpse: Katherine of Aragon insisting that she make and embroider all Henry VIII's shirts herself, or

Edward I, writing to the physician of his much younger second wife, Margaret of France, after the queen had been ill, giving orders that she was not to be allowed to travel until she was fully well again, and adding 'if you allow her to travel too soon, by God's thigh, you will suffer for it'.

The arrival of a new queen presented considerable problems to the royal finance officers, who had to furnish the means to support the queen and her household. Some queens brought with them a large sum in cash by way of dowry from their fathers, some, like Eleanor of Aquitaine and Isabella of Angoulême, were their fathers' heiresses, or, like Eleanor of Castile, inherited land from some other member of their family (Eleanor inherited the northern French county of Ponthieu from her mother), while others, like Margaret of Anjou, came portionless to their husbands. As part of the marriage negotiations, a sum was agreed upon for the queen's dower; that is, the annual sum settled on her by the English Crown which would support her household during her husband's lifetime and provide her entire income in her widowhood. In the later part of our period, this sum was often largely secured upon dower lands which the queen administered during her husband's lifetime using the income to support herself and her household; earlier, the lands had come into each queen's actual possession only when she was widowed, and had remained in her husband's charge during his lifetime, while he supported her household with the cash equivalent.

While the dower was most satisfactorily secured upon royal lands, such lands were not necessarily available each time a king married, particularly if a queen-dowager was still alive. In the first few years of her marriage, therefore, a queen's income was likely to come from exchequer grants and such temporary expedients as wardships, or episcopal temporalities during the vacancy of a see. Gradually these were replaced by lands as they fell vacant. The queen's purely private expenditure was usually covered by an extra payment from her husband's wardrobe. As long as the English Crown held lands in France, queens might also hold French lands in dower. Richard I, for instance, dowered his queen, Berengaria, on her wedding day with all his Gascon possessions south of the Garonne, together with the reversion of all his mother's dower lands in England, Normandy and Poitou. In 1196 he settled on her additionally the county of Bigorre and town of Le Mans in France, which became her principal residence. Berengaria never set foot in England during her husband's lifetime, the only queen never to do so. Following John's loss of Normandy, the French king, Philip Augustus, granted her the county of Maine, of which Le Mans was the chief town, in compensation for the loss of her dower lands, an extraordinarily generous gesture.

In England, although queens rarely held exactly the same dower lands as their predecessors, many of the same towns, castles and manors passed from one queen to the next: Bristol, Devizes, Nottingham, Rockingham, Langley, Woodstock,

Gillingham, Sonning, Havering, Cookham and Bray, Leeds (in Kent), all feature time and again. On the death of each queen, her successor usually received the bulk of her possessions. Thus, when Margaret of France died in 1318, her niece Isabella, wife of Edward II, was granted most of her lands. On the redistribution of Isabella's lands in 1330, her daughter-in-law, Philippa of Hainault, was the chief beneficiary, and she received more on Isabella's death in 1358. Philippa's dower lands were largely re-assembled for Anne of Bohemia. From the time of Eleanor of Castile to that of young Isabella of Valois, the dower of an English queen was customarily fixed at £4,500 at the time of her marriage. This annual income was sometimes increased to support a growing family of young children or to ease a queen's financial embarrassment. In 1402, when Henry IV married Joan of Navarre, the widowed duchess of Brittany, who also had the income from her Breton dower lands, she received an English dower of approximately £6,500, far in excess of that given to any previous queen. The financing of such a generous settlement was to cause problems throughout Henry's reign and well into his son's and have an unlooked-for effect on Joan's widowhood. None the less, both the next two queens had their dower set at similar levels. Henry V was able to dower Katherine of Valois from his own mother's Bohun inheritance, which was fortunate, because his stepmother, Joan, outlived Katherine by a few months. Margaret of Anjou received a number of the queen's traditional dower lands, but the main part of her endowment came from Duchy of Lancaster lands, including the three great midland honours of Tutbury, Leicester and Kenilworth. Only with the advent of the first English queen, Elizabeth Woodville, who was in no position to argue, did the size of the dower revert to the more reasonable sum of £4,500.

Dower was intended to ensure financial security for the queen in the event of her widowhood. In a number of cases, it failed to provide this security. Berengaria had considerable difficulty obtaining hers from her brother-in-law, King John, and later the Knights Templar in England had to guarantee payment. Joan of Navarre was arrested on a charge of attempting to bring about the death of her stepson, Henry V, by witchcraft, and all her lands were confiscated. It is doubtful if the charge was taken seriously by people at court, since she had nothing to gain from Henry's death, but for three years, until Henry's conscience smote him on his deathbed, the war-impoverished Crown had an additional income of £6,500 p.a. Margaret of Anjou was forced, quite unjustly, to surrender all her rights to dower in England when Louis XI agreed to ransom her from Edward IV in 1475 for 50,000 crowns. Elizabeth Woodville lost her position as queen-dowager together with her dower, when the parliament of the usurping Richard III declared her marriage invalid and her sons bastards. A few months later, as Dame Elizabeth Grey, she came out of sanctuary and accepted an annuity of 700 marks. One of the first acts of Henry VII's parliament was to repeal the former act and restore her to her former title and dignity, but it did not restore her dower. That was left for Henry to determine, and Henry had to provide for his own mother as well as his new wife and her grandmother, Cecily, duchess of York, whose York lands had reverted to the Crown. In these circumstances, he was not ungenerous to the former queen-dowager, restoring many of her original dower lands. Just over a year later, all her lands were granted to her daughter, the queen, and Elizabeth Woodville entered Bermondsey Abbey with an annuity of 400 marks. Her retirement seems genuinely to have been on the grounds of ill-health, for Henry continued to show her marked favour. None the less, for three of the four queen-dowagers of the fifteenth century, their right to dower did not protect them financially for the rest of their lives as it was intended to do. It is, of course, no coincidence that all the queens who suffered thus had no surviving son to protect them.

The queen was the centre of a court and the holder of a landed estate greater than those of all save a handful of peers. Because those estates were scattered throughout many counties, it was by this means that she became known to her husband's subjects and the tone of her administration was set by the queen herself. The king maintained an element of control over her financial affairs, an element considerably greater in the earlier part of our period than in the later, and her chief financial officer, her treasurer, was answerable to the exchequer. If it proved necessary, as in the case of Philippa of Hainault, who fell hopelessly into debt, the king could take his wife's affairs into his own hands, but generally speaking a wide range of her business was subject only to the supervision of the queen and her council. The council, like that of any large landowner, advised, attended to her legal affairs and administered her estates. It was comprised of the chief officers of her household and a number of important outsiders. Her officers had nearly always been trained in the king's household and sometimes moved back to it. How dominant the queen was in the affairs of her council depended entirely on her own interest and personality. Not even the most routine decision was taken without reference to Queen Elizabeth Woodville. In the case of Eleanor of Castile, the Archbishop of Canterbury begged her to improve the behaviour of her officers and, after her death her husband, grief-stricken as he was, ordered an enquiry into the administration of all her lands because of the volume of complaints against her officials. Compensation was paid by her executors to those wronged. The queen had been an active purchaser of land and had also bought up debts owed to the Jews before their expulsion from the kingdom by her husband, a form of early insider dealing which did not endear her to her subjects and gave rise to a popular rhyme:

> *Le Roy cuvayte nos deneres*
> *E la Rayne nos beaus maners*

(the king covets our money and the queen our beautiful manors).

The chief charge upon a queen's income was the financial support of her household. This fell into two distinct parts: the officials who administered her estates and affairs and included her treasurer, chancellor, attornies and all their attendant clerks, together with the stewards and bailiffs who ran the estates and were answerable to the receiver-general; and, secondly, the people who served the queen in her household, her chamberlain, her knights and esquires, chaplains, ladies and master of the horse. The menials who cooked and cleaned were part of the king's household, but during the periods when the royal couple lived apart, sometimes for up to six months in every year, the queen had to pay for her own menials. When dwelling with the king it was customary for the queen to pay a set sum towards the cost of supporting her court, usually about £7 per day. This was not a notional sum, but properly paid and accounted for. Some queens paid it a good deal more regularly than others; in the Merciless Parliament of 1387, there was a petition from the commons that Queen Anne contribute her daily payment to the wardrobe as Queen Philippa had done, or else it should be deducted from her revenues. For the remaining six years of her life Anne's contributions were paid, albeit in a irregular fashion. Although each bride arrived with a train of attendants from her own country, they were usually packed off home at the earliest opportunity. The most she could hope for was to retain one or two ladies of her own nationality. Her senior ladies were in future to be the wives of English peers, the lesser ones often married to her officials.

One considerable, but unpredictable, addition to a queen's income was 'queen's gold'. There is no evidence of its existence before the reign of Henry II when it appeared as an extra 10 per cent levied for the queen's benefit on any voluntary fine paid to the Crown, for instance for a licence or a pardon. Eleanor of Aquitaine was the first queen to receive it, and indeed she continued to receive it throughout her life, for payment of it to her did not lapse after the coronations of either of her daughters-in-law. The queen's interest was safeguarded by the presence of one of her clerks in the exchequer and when the sums were paid it was to officers appointed by the queen. It was never popular and usually difficult to collect, but Philippa of Hainault received £153 during two legal terms, while Eleanor of Castile received the large sum of £4,875 between 1286 and 1289. Collection depended on the vigilance of the queen's lawyers and the vigorous pusuit of claims. Until their expulsion from England in 1290, Jews were the least able to resist such claims. On the death of any Jew, one-third of his possessions was forfeit to the crown, and the queen certainly claimed her share. Nor were the Jews liable for payment only on voluntary fines, for the queen demanded her gold on fines levied on them for transgressions, and the king also agreed that she should have an additional tenth on the tallage or tax of 60,000 marks for which Jewry became liable in 1244. The loss of this source when the Jews were expelled from England in 1290 undoubtedly reduced the amount by which queens benefited from queen's gold, but each successive queen continued to claim what she could from this unpopular source.

Very little is known of the financial affairs of the Anglo-Norman and early Plantagenet queens. Eleanor of Provence is the first for whom some study of the subject is possible. In the course of her long marriage, from 1236 until she became a widow in 1272, she moved from a modest establishment and a role totally subordinate to her husband to having effective control over her extensive resources in a way that radically altered the scale and management of the provision made for English queens. From then on, most, although not all, queens were permitted by their husbands to administer their own estates and income.

For much of the second half of our period it was accepted that the normal size of the queen's household should be approximately 100 persons, perhaps somewhat larger if there was a family of young royal children. In the fifteenth century one of the best sources of information about the queen's household is the series of ordinances for the reform of the royal household. One such was issued in 1445, at the beginning of the married life of Margaret of Anjou and Henry VI. It listed the permitted members of the new queen's household and their allowances. According to its terms the queen was to have sixty-six persons attendant on her, headed by a countess with three female and four male servants of her own. If this ordinance was ever effective, which is doubtful, it certainly did not remain so for long. The next ordinance, issued in 1454, ordered the reduction of numbers in the queen's household to 120 persons, twice the number permitted nine years earlier, and suggesting that Margaret's household in 1454 numbered considerably in excess of 120, a fact confirmed by her household account for 1452–3, which shows that she paid wages to 151 persons, including some twenty men who were clerks and administrators rather than personal attendants. Despite the chronic financial difficulties of the crown, it is clear that Margaret had no intention of keeping her household down to the required level. One of the queen's ladies was to be her successor, and it seems very likely that Elizabeth Woodville learned the importance of solvency from Margaret's inability to achieve it. In 1472 Edward IV caused the 'Liber Niger' to be drawn up, a major work on the running of the royal household. In it the size of household considered suitable for his queen was 100 persons, reverting to time-honoured standards. Queen Elizabeth Woodville kept her household within bounds, and indeed it was smaller than those of any of her predecessors for a century. She also kept it solvent. While she could, and did, spend lavishly on furs, cloth and jewels, she was in general far less extravagant than Margaret, who used her general privy purse expenditure for political purposes, attempting to win friends and influence people by means of gifts and rewards. Elizabeth had several members of her numerous family in her household: her brother John was master of her horse, her sister Anne, Lady Bourchier, was one of her ladies, as was a sister-in-law and the wife of a cousin, but all filled established posts and none received larger than customary salaries.

A royal marriage inevitably gladdened the hearts of London's purveyors of luxuries. A refurbishment of royal apartments, new fashions introduced from abroad, gifts of jewels from the king to his bride, were all very good for business. One of the most significant social factors of the Middle Ages was the relatively small range of what are now termed consumer durables. People with money could spend it mainly on building, plate, jewels and clothes. Horseflesh, hounds and hawks might account for a little and so might musical instruments and books. An interesting illustration to this can be found in the will of our first queen, Matilda of Flanders. Her estates were already settled, but when it came to personal possessions, even she had little to leave. To her abbey of the Holy Trinity, Caen, she bequeathed a mantle embroidered with gold to make a cope, and a tunic, worked at Winchester by Adelbert's wife; two golden girdles, intended to suspend the lamp before the high altar; a large candelabra; her crown and septre; cups in their cases; another cup, made in England; her vessels and all her horse-trappings. In this last item lies the clue to the relative paucity of possessions owned even by a queen. All of them had to be easily and frequently packed and transported, if not on horseback, then in carts. The Bayeux Tapestry is usually, but wrongly, regarded as Matilda's major cultural contribution. The work is not tapestry and was not created by the new queen and her ladies. It was commissioned by her brother-in-law, Odo, Bishop of Bayeux, and is of English embroidery. That embroidery was an area where English workmanship excelled is confirmed by the queen's will, which even identified the craftswoman who worked her tunic.

It would certainly be wrong to see the queen only as a decorative appendage to her husband's court, acting graciously and introducing the gentler arts of music, dancing and embroidery, though doubtless in the military society of the Normans this was one of her roles, but equally it would be wrong to overlook her very important role as leader of fashion. Eleanor of Aquitaine's crusading adventures in the east with her first husband, and Eleanor of Castile's familiarity with the luxurious lifestyle the Muslims had introduced into Spain, influenced their chosen styles as queen. Society in western Europe was greatly influenced by what crusaders saw of the east, and in many ways southern France was the meeting place of two cultures. Four generations of English queen consorts came from southern France or northern Spain. Of Eleanor of Aquitaine's contribution to the cultural life of England and France, whole books have been written. Although she never commissioned a building, composed a note of music or wrote a line of poetry (as far as we know), the court of Henry II and Queen Eleanor was the centre of an intensely creative cultural and artistic life. Eleanor's troubador grandfather, Duke

William IX and her 'eastern' uncle, Raymond of Antioch, gave her a rich cultural background from which she emerged as the inspirational figure for the new type of love songs and romances. She and her French daughters were renowned as patrons of music and poetry, while her sons Richard and Geoffrey were accomplished practitioners. English pictorial art in the second half of the twelfth century is deeply indebted to artistic developments in south-western France. St Denis in Paris, the first northern European church built in the Gothic style, was planned during the period Eleanor was queen of France and owes much to the church of Santiago de Compostella, with which her family had close links. In the years that followed a number of magnificent cathedrals based on its design appeared in the sees of northern France and thence, via William of Sens, architect of Canterbury cathedral, to England.

There is little to suggest that Isabella of Angoulême contributed anything to the cultural or intellectual life of England, but her daughter-in-law, Eleanor of Provence was another matter. She had been brought up at the most sophisticated court of southern France by parents who were highly cultured. It was this background which made her a fitting wife for Henry III. She took to England, in Harvey's words, 'both the less tangible culture denoted by the fine arts, and the material benefits of a highly organised civilisation'. After many years of neglect in the absence of a queen the royal palaces were refurbished, modernized with window glass, wood panelling and improved sanitation. Naturally, where the queen led, others followed. The same was true for personal adornment. Her husband loved rich clothes and jewels and was prepared to spend lavishly on his wife. Her jewellery was supposed to have cost the devoted Henry £30,000. The royal couple's spendthrift ways were undoubtedly good for English merchants and craftsmen if not for the exchequer. Poets and musicians accompanied the new queen to England, and throughout her life she remained in close contact with Provence so that the cross-fertilization of ideas continued. Although the contacts with home were fewer for Eleanor of Castile than for her mother-in-law, she visited the east herself with her crusading husband, Edward I, before he inherited the throne, acquiring a taste for rare and exotic objects. She obtained a licence for her merchant, Giles Martini, to trade in England for seven years and bought raisins, dates, pomegranates, lemons and oranges from a Spanish ship which docked at Portsmouth. The Castilian queen's interest in books of all kinds was considerable. She read light romances, corresponded with an Oxford scholar about one of her books, employed a writer in her household and during the crusade had a translation made for Edward of the Roman manual on the art of war by Vegetius. Her own copy of the *Life of Edward the Confessor* is the most carefully and richly decorated manuscript of all the surviving saints' lives of the period. In many ways, Eleanor's artistic impact on her adopted country was greater in death than life.

The queen died at Harby, near Lincoln and as the cortège moved slowly thence to Westminster, her grieving husband ordered a large decorated cross to be erected at each night's resting place. Only three of these twelve Eleanor crosses now remain, at Northampton, Geddington and Waltham. Where his father Henry III had relied chiefly on French and Italian artists for the creation of Westminster Abbey, by the end of the thirteenth century Edward I found Englishmen capable of executing high-quality workmanship.

Until the mid-fifteenth century, the English court was dominated by French culture; even Philippa of Hainault and Anne of Bohemia had close French connections, and French remained the language of the English court. The first queen to learn English of necessity was Margaret of Anjou. Yet by the late fourteenth century English artists and craftsmen could equal those on the continent – men like Yevele and Herland in architecture, Chaucer in literature and the anonymous painters of the Wilton Diptych and St Stephen's Chapel, Westminster. Froissart, the great chronicler of the Hundred Years' War, was a Hainaulter by birth and followed his lady to England, where he stayed for some time. One of Philippa's ladies, Philippa Roet, known as la Picard from her place of birth, married Geoffrey Chaucer, while her sister, Katherine, became John of Gaunt's mistress, later his third duchess.

If it was as a landowner on a large scale that a queen came into contact with the largest number of her husband's subjects, it was in her role *vis-à-vis* the Church that her impact was likely to be greatest in the earlier part of our period. There is no doubt that the majority of our earlier queens were deeply pious. Matilda of Flanders built the Abbey of the Holy Trinity at Caen, where her daughter, Cecilia, became a nun and later abbess, matching her husband's endowment of another abbey in the same town. Eleanor of Aquitaine's religious interests were centred on the abbey of Fontevrault in Anjou and Berengaria's on her foundation of Espau in Maine. Strangely, though two queens founded nunneries in their husband's French possessions, none founded one in England. It is not without some significance that in the twelfth and thirteenth centuries, the three queens who survived their husbands and remained widows, Eleanor of Aquitaine, Berengaria and Eleanor of Provence, all chose to spend much of their widowhood in religious surroundings. The life of an abbey gave protection and order, not only to queens, but to other gently-born widows who chose to remain as seculars. Eleanor of Provence is the only widowed queen in our period who chose to take the veil, entering Amesbury, which was an English cell of Fontevrault, but she was following a Saxon tradition. Barking Abbey in Essex, one of the few nunneries of any size or wealth, numbered three Saxon queens and two princesses among its abbesses and Matilda of Scotland was brought up by nuns at Wilton, where her aunt Christina was abbess. If none of our queens founded any English nunneries, they were certainly responsible for a number of other religious foundations. Although Matilda's husband, Henry I, founded more than half a dozen monasteries, Matilda was associated with none of them. Her foundation, in 1107, was Holy Trinity, Aldgate, an Augustinian priory. She also founded a hospital in St Giles in the Fields. Her daughter, the Empress Matilda, was associated with her son Henry II in the founding of four Cistercian abbeys, while Matilda of Boulogne and her husband Stephen were co-founders of a Cistercian abbey, Coggeshall, and a Benedictine one, Faversham. Matilda herself founded the church and hospital of St Katherine by the Tower in memory of her two first-born children who died young; it was dissolved because of misgovernment and refounded by Eleanor of Provence. Adela of Louvain founded nothing as queen, but as countess of Arundel was responsible for the small Augustinian priory of Pynham at Arundel. Both Eleanor of Provence and Eleanor of Castile founded friaries. Much has been written of the impact of the religious orders on the spiritual and secular life of England and this is not the place to reiterate it, save to point out the significant role played by the queens in the process. Equally important was their role in the delivery of charity.

To the medieval mind, almsgiving was based on two assumptions. The first was that if a man or woman held property they must assume charity as a charge upon it, and the second that charity must accompany contrition for sin. Because of these assumptions, all classes save the very poorest saw almsgiving as part of their daily lives. In the royal household this took two forms: the customary almsgiving automatically dispensed and the individual acts of charity practised by the king or queen on their own initiative. The term '*elemosina*' covered a wide range of charitable acts, offerings at shrines and churches, contributions towards church-building and repair, support of the mendicant orders and poor university scholars, and general poor relief in the way of food and clothing. '*Elemosina statuta*' first appears as a fixed charge on the revenue of the royal household in the reign of John, when it was set at three shillings per day for the distribution of food to the poor. By the time of his grandson Edward I, varying numbers of the poor were fed at irregular intervals. Towards the end of his reign Edward was, according to his wardrobe accounts for 1299–1302, spending an average of £650 p.a. on meals for the poor, approximately 10 per cent of his income. At the rate of 1½d per head, each pound would feed 160 poor. Yet Edward was not nearly as lavish as his father had been. Henry III usually fed 100 friars and 500 poor at his table every day. On saints' days and special anniversaries literally thousands were fed. Given the itinerant nature of the court, the contribution of the royal family to the problem of poverty up and down the country was quite considerable. It was augmented by the charity dispensed by the custodians of royal residences when the court was absent and by the royal monastic foundations, and it was emulated by noble, gentle and ecclesiastical households everywhere.

The queens usually followed the example of their husbands as far as '*elemosina statuta*' was concerned. Like them, they appointed an almoner who devoted his time to charitable work. Figures are not available before the mid-thirteenth century, but in the period 1264–9, Eleanor of Provence spent a total of £6,928 14s 1d on household offices, of which £102 was spent on alms. Apart from this, the queen devoted £4,017 10s 3d on private charities over a period of eight years. Eleanor of Castile, whose household was smaller and less independent than that of her mother-in-law, was also probably less lavish, but her almoner and alms appear separately in the '*elemosina*' section of Edward's accounts and were an expression of her own charitable views. Alms were likewise paid on behalf of the royal children, and when they were not with their parents, their own officers were responsible.

In general, the piety of the queens in the later part of our period was as great as in the earlier part, but it was expressed in different charitable ways. Queen Philippa, devout as she undoubtedly was, left donations in her will to religious foundations, but more significant is her patronage of Queen's College, Oxford, for she was the first queen to be associated with a scholastic institution. The college was founded by her chaplain, Robert de Eglesfield, who, with a mixture of modesty and cunning, placed it under her protection and that of her successors. Philippa's contribution was small, a yearly rent of twenty marks to sustain six scholar chaplains, but it was an example followed by later queens. Margaret of Anjou, inspired by her husband's devotion to his foundations of Eton and King's College, Cambridge, petitioned to be allowed to found her own college at Cambridge, something no other queen had done. Two of her household, Lords Wenlock and Beaumont, were persuaded to become benefactors of the new college as well, but despite this, her interest did not extend to seeing that the endowment was adequate, with the result that the college might well have foundered without help from her successor, Elizabeth Woodville. Edward IV had little interest in education, but his queen was a generous patron to Margaret's foundation; in 1475 Queen's college, Cambridge received from her a set of statutes as its 'true foundress'. Elizabeth may also have helped Eton, which her husband came close to suppressing. The greatest benefactress of the universities, however, was Henry VII's mother, Margaret Beaufort, a woman of formidable intellect and piety, who founded the great Cambridge college of St John's and the smaller Christ's College.

It seems probable that Anne of Bohemia, or one of the Bohemians in her train, was responsible for the connection between the Czech religious reformer, John Hus, and his English counterpart, John Wyclif. Given Richard II's religious orthodoxy, it is unlikely that Anne openly patronized Lollards, but it is possible that members of her household did. The king's mother, Princess Joan, was certainly interested in Wyclif, and it was she who was responsible for Anne's queenly intervention to save him from the council of Lambeth in 1382. Hus implies, in one of his works, that the queen possessed the scriptures written in German and Bohemian as well as Latin. There can be no doubt at all about Anne Boleyn's reforming interests. She was one of those chiefly responsible for persuading Henry VIII to assert his headship of the Church in England and thus take the initiative in religious change. Of the ten elections to the episcopate during her period of influence, 1532–6, seven were reformers who were regarded as her clients, and who were later described to her daughter, Elizabeth, as 'the evangelical bishops whom your most holy mother had appointed from among those scholars who favoured the purer doctrine of the gospel'. While Anne had obviously not the actual power of appointment, she had pressed very hard for their preferment. Thomas Cranmer himself was one of them. Queen Margaret of Anjou had also a considerable influence on the episcopal bench of her time. No fewer than four members of her household became bishops. Promotions to bishoprics from the royal household were by no means unusual, but they came generally from the king's rather than the queen's household. If nothing else, the clerics concerned had proved their administrative capacities, and Margaret's promotions were talented men, though not necessarily noted for their spirituality. In 1457, when the great see of Durham fell vacant, she recommended her chancellor, Lawrence Booth, to the Pope, despite her husband's previous nomination of his physician, John Arundel. Calixtus III appointed the queen's nominee.

Queens have customarily been seen by historians purely in the shadow of their husbands, often meriting no more than a few lines in the study of a king or reign. In the early part of the period only Empress Matilda, Eleanor of Aquitaine and Eleanor of Castile have had biographers, largely due to the paucity of material, and only from Margaret of Anjou onwards have most queens had them. Contemporaries, however, did not see them as unimportant; they were mothers of the royal heir, landowners, leaders of fashion and a source of much patronage and influence. Such issues are reflected in their letters.

The Norman Queens

MATILDA OF FLANDERS, WIFE OF WILLIAM THE CONQUEROR

Three of the four Norman queens consort and the first potential queen regnant following the Conquest all bore the name Matilda, which does not help in the difficult task of trying to draw a picture of the women concerned. It is virtually impossible to write with any degree of certainty about their personalities or habits. It is like viewing a woman behind a heavy veil; a vague outline is discernable, but there is little chance of gaining more than a glimpse of the real person. Letters, where they exist, can help, but very few survive. None have been traced for either Matilda of Flanders, wife of the Conqueror, or Matilda of Boulogne, wife of King Stephen, and very few for Matilda of Scotland, wife of Henry I, and her daughter, Empress Matilda. Yet the lack of information we have for these women should not lead us to dismiss them as insignificant or unimportant. When William of Normandy embarked on the invasion of England, it was his wife whom he made regent of his duchy, in preference to any male, though it was true that he associated their heir, Robert, with his mother, and she had the support of several senior lords. When, nearly eighteen months after the Conquest, he deemed it safe for her to join him in England, she was crowned queen and hallowed with unction as he had been. Matilda's descent from the illustrious King Alfred had certainly not escaped the king's notice. By 1068 William and Matilda had been married for about seventeen years and had produced three sons and three daughters. Ten months after her arrival in England, Matilda bore her fourth son, the future Henry I. The marriage was by all accounts a happy one, as indeed had been the union of William's parents, unsanctified though it was.

From 1068 until her death in 1083, Matilda divided her time between England and Normandy. One chronicler (Orderic) describes her as very rich, and certainly her religious endowments were considerable. She founded the abbey of the Holy Trinity in Caen, where she was to be buried, as a pair to the one founded by her husband in the same town. When her eldest son Robert, for whom her partiality was widely acknowledged, quarrelled with his father, the queen sent him large quantities of gold and silver. William soon found out and reproached her, but she could only plead love for her son. There is one intriguing clue to her appearance:

Holy Trinity was badly damaged by bombing during the Second World War and her tomb was destroyed. In 1961 a small casket containing her bones was opened and examined. They proved to be those of a woman little more than four feet tall. William the Conqueror's few surviving bones indicate his height was about five feet ten inches. Although the average height of Englishmen has risen over the centuries, the males of the English royal family were noted for their height and several Plantagenets were known to have been well over six feet.

Matilda's second son, William Rufus, to whom her husband bequeathed his new kingdom, never married. He was succeeded by his youngest brother, Henry, who at the time he became king was thirty-two and also unmarried.

MATILDA OF SCOTLAND, FIRST WIFE OF HENRY I

When Henry I came to the throne he was accredited with dozens of bastards but he now required a legitimate heir. The lady selected to be his queen had the important distinction of being descended from the Saxon royal line, through her mother, St Margaret, wife of Malcolm Canmore, king of Scots. The bride had been christened Edith, but at some point after her marriage was given the more acceptably Norman name of Matilda. She had been educated in England by her maternal aunt, Christina, abbess of Romsey. Christina had been anxious for her niece to take the veil, but her father had no such intention, and several matches had been proposed for her before her father and eldest brother were killed invading England. It was five years before her next brother, Edgar, gained his father's throne, and Edith/Matilda and her sisters spent them in England, at Wilton Abbey, where their aunt Christina was by then abbess. They were not wasted years, for from her few surviving letters it is clear that Matilda displayed a scholarship rare among laymen, and quite exceptional among laywomen. When her marriage to Henry I was proposed, objections were raised on the score that she had taken the veil. Matilda always denied it and a council of the Church at Lambeth under Archbishop Anselm found there to be no impediment to the marriage. She and Henry were married on 11 November 1100 at Westminster, and she was crowned the same day.

It seems clear that Matilda brought her husband little in the way of dowry, save her Saxon lineage, but this was to be a priceless asset in assuring Henry the goodwill of his Saxon subjects. Her piety and good works earned Matilda the epithet, the 'good queen', and she became the standard by whom all subsequent medieval queens were judged and most were found wanting. Her piety was almost as deep as that of her saintly mother; she went every day to Westminster Abbey, barefoot in Lent, wearing a hair shirt, uncommon behaviour in a queen. She went further, personally caring for lepers, for whom she built a hospital in St Giles in the Fields. Her good works often took a practical turn. She seems to have been responsible for improvements in the system of roads, and had the first arched bridge in England built over the River Lea. Having herself been in some danger while fording the river, she superintended the building of the bridge at Stratford le Bow, still in use in the nineteenth century, and another smaller bridge over a tributary of the Lea, giving certain manors and a mill as an endowment to keep both bridges in repair. That Matilda had been very generously dowered by her husband is clear from claims by subsequent queens that they should have a dower equal to that of Matilda of Scotland. Little information on the administration of her estates survives, save a complaint that her bailiffs fleeced her tenants to provide the wherewithal for her good works.

After the birth of her surviving son, William, in 1103 (her firstborn died as an infant), Matilda settled mainly at Westminster. She seems to have visited Normandy only once. Whatever their personal relationship, Henry certainly respected her judgement, and during his absences abroad she was usually appointed regent in his place. When Archbishop Anselm went into exile, she corresponded with both him and the Pope, but she knew when not to meddle. In 1105 Henry extracted large sums of money from the clergy, but when representatives came to the queen begging her to intercede for them, she burst into tears but said she could not intervene. She died in 1118 at Westminster while her husband and son were in Normandy; her daughter, another Matilda, had been sent at the age of eight as a bride for the Emperor Henry V. The chronicler, Robert of Gloucester, repeatedly ascribes to Queen Matilda a direct, personal and highly beneficial influence on the condition of England during the years of her marriage, declaring that 'the goodness she did to England cannot be here written nor by any man understood'.

The two letters that follow are the earliest letters by an English queen known to exist. They almost certainly owe their survival to the sophisticated record-keeping of the Church. It must not be assumed that the queen wrote them herself. They would have been written by a clerk at her behest, but the tone suggests that they were quite closely dictated by Matilda. In the first she was addressing Anselm, the leading scholar of his day. Born in Italy and a student of the great Lanfranc, the Conqueror's archbishop, Anselm was his successor as abbot of Bec in Normandy, and was also the most obvious successor to the see of Canterbury. On Lanfranc's death in 1089 William Rufus preferred to leave the see vacant and collect its revenues himself. An illness he feared mortal in 1093, however, frightened him into changing his mind and Anselm was elected. He genuinely seems to have been reluctant to take on the position as the leading advisor of the Crown. There were inevitable difficulties in dealing with a violent, ungodly man like Rufus and, after a few years, Anselm was forced into exile in Rome. On the accession of Henry I in 1100, Anselm was invited back to England but relations with the new king did not continue smoothly. The point at issue was lay investiture, that is, the right of the king to appoint his own bishops, and for any bishops to do homage to the king for the estates they held for the Crown. The recent Lateran Council had issued decrees against lay investiture and Anselm returned determined to enforce them. Henry took his stance on the custom of his kingdom, and Anselm, following the instructions of Pope Paschal II, on the legislation of the Church. In 1503, Anselm, at Henry's insistence, travelled to Rome to try and persuade the Pope to moderate his stance. When he proved unsuccessful, he decided not to return to England and thus entered his second period of exile.

It was during this period that the queen wrote to him. He had been one of the main instigators of her marriage and quite adamant that her period spent at Wilton had not constituted taking the veil. It is hardly surprising, therefore, that Matilda remained devoted to the archbishop and did all she could to bring the two antagonists together. Henry and Anselm maintained a not unfriendly correspondence throughout, and the issue was finally resolved by a compromise in 1107 that in theory satisfied the Church and in practice satisfied the king. Behind the formal rhetoric of her letter, Matilda's personal feelings for her exiled spiritual guide clearly show. In contrast, while the sentiments shown in the letter to the Pope are sincere enough, the florid rhetoric deemed appropriate for their expression in Latin obscures them.

Matilda of Scotland, Queen of Henry I, to Anselm, Archbishop of Canterbury, c. *1103*

To her piously remembered father and worthily reverenced lord, Anselm the archbishop, Matilda by the grace of God queen of England, the least of the handmaidens of his Holiness, wishes perpetual health in Christ.

I give unnumbered thanks to your unceasing goodness, which, not unmindful of me, has condescended, by your letters presented to me, to shew forth your mind, though absent. The clouds of sadness in which I was wrapped being expelled, the streamlet of your words has glided through me like a ray of new light. I embrace the little parchment sent to me by you, as I would my father himself: I cherish it in my bosom, I place it as near my heart as I can; I read over and over again the words flowing from the sweet fountain of your goodness; my mind considers them, my heart broods over them; and I hide the pondered treasures in the very secret place of my heart. Yet, while I praise all you have said, at one thing alone I wonder; that is, at what your discreet excellency has said about your nephew. Yet I do not think I can deal otherwise with your friends than my own. I might say with 'mine' than my own, for all who are yours by kindred are mine by love and adoption. Truly the consolation of your writing strengthens my patience, gives and preserves my hopes, raises me when falling, sustains me when sliding, gladdens me when sorrowful, softens me when angry, pacifies me when weeping. Farther, frequent, though secret, consultation promises the return of the father to his daughter, of the lord to his handmaiden, of the pastor to his flock. I am encouraged to hope the same thing from the confidence which I have in the prayers of good men, and from the good will which, by skilfully investigating, I find to be in the heart of my lord. His mind is better disposed towards you than many men think; and, I favouring it, and suggesting wherever I can, he will become yet more courteous and reconciled to you. As to what he permits now to be done, in reference to your return, he will permit more and better to be done in future, when, according to time and opportunity, you shall request it. But even though he should persist in being an unjust judge, I entreat the affluence of your piety, that, excluding the bitterness of human rancour, which is not wont to dwell in you, you turn not from him the sweetness of your favour, but ever prove a pious intercessor with God for him and me, our common offspring, and the state of our kingdom. May your holiness ever fare well.

(Sancti Anselmi Epistolae, *Liber iii, Epist. xcvi, Latin. Wood, vol. i, letter i.*)

Matilda of Scotland, Queen of Henry I, to Pope Paschal II, c. 1103

To the highest pontiff and universal pope, Paschal, Matilda, by God's grace, queen of the English, trusting that he will so dispense in this life with the apostolic dignity, that he may deserve to be numbered among the apostolic senate in the joys of perpetual peace with the companies of the just.

I give all the thanks and praise I can to your sublime holiness, O apostolic man, for the things which your paternal charity, as though for admonition, has deigned to send to me and my lord the king, both frequently by the words of your legates and also by your own writings. I visit the threshold of the most Roman apostolic seat, and as far as it is lawful and I am able, clasping your paternal knees with my whole heart, my whole soul, my whole mind, praying with importune and opportune petition, I cease not, nor will I cease, to entreat, till I know that my submissive humility, or rather the persevering importunity of my application, is heard by you. Yet let not your excellency be angry, let not the prudent Roman clergy, people, or senate, be amazed at this my rashness, that thus I presume to speak. Once, once, I say, we and the English people, – then how happy! – had, under your apostolic dignity, Anselm, our archbishop, a foster-child of the Holy Ghost, the most prudent counsellor and pious father of us and the aforesaid people. From the most opulent treasures of his Lord, wherof we knew him to hold the keys, he took abundantly, and bestowed them upon us more abundantly; for this same faithful minister and prudent dispenser of the Lord seasoned those things which he bestowed with the most excellent salt of wisdom, softened them with the sweetness of eloquence, and sweetened them by the wonderful conceits of rhetoric. And so it was that neither did the tender lambs lack the abundant milk of the Lord, nor the sheep the richest fatness of the pastures, nor the pastors the most opulent satiety of aliments. But now, when all these things are otherwise, nothing remains but that the pastor wanting food, the flock pasture, the young milk, utter forth the heaviest groans. Since, by the absence of the chief pastor, Anselm, each is deprived of something, or rather all of all things. In such lugubrious mourning, in such opprobrious grief, in such deformity and loss of our kingdom, nothing remains to me, stunned as I am, but, shaking off my stupor, to fly to the blessed Apostle Peter and his vicar the apostolic man. Therefore, my lord, I fly to your benignity, lest we and the people of the kingdom of England perish in such a defect and lapse. What good will our life do us when we go down to corruption? Let your paternity take good counsel concerning us, and deign, within the term which my lord the king asks of your goodness, to let your paternal bowels be moved towards us, that we may both rejoice at the return of our dearest father, Archbishop Anselm, and preserve, uninjured, our subjection to the holy apostolic see. I indeed, taught by your most sound and gracious advice, will, as far as woman's strength may suffice, and with the help of worthy men, which I shall procure, endeavour, with my whole power, that my humility may, as far as possible, fulfil what your highness advises. May your paternity enjoy eternal happiness!

(Sancti Anselmi Epistolae, *Liber iii, Epist. xcix, Latin. Wood, vol. i, letter ii.*)

ADELA OF LOUVAIN, SECOND WIFE OF HENRY I

Henry I had continued to seek entertainment outside his wife's chamber during their married life and there would have been very little likelihood of his bothering to marry again, save for the tragedy of the White Ship, in which his son and heir, William, died in 1120. Within three months he had married Adela or Adelicia, daughter of Count Godfrey of Louvain, and known as the 'fair maid of Brabant'. The new queen seems to have been as good and pious as she was beautiful, but she failed in her primary duty as queen, for she bore the ageing king no child and thus remained a political nonentity. She did, however, form a close friendship with her stepdaughter, the Empress Matilda, who returned as a widow to her father's court. On Henry I's death, the widowed queen married William Albini, bestowing on him the late king's gift to her of the castle of Arundel. She promptly bore a son, thus becoming the ancestress of the earls of Arundel. No letters by her are known to survive.

MATILDA OF BOULOGNE, WIFE OF STEPHEN

Despite Henry I's ardent desire to see his daughter and only surviving legitimate child Matilda succeed him on the English throne, it was his favourite nephew, Stephen, who was crowned instead. Stephen was the son of the Conqueror's daughter Adela, countess of Blois, but had spent most of his adult life at his uncle Henry's court. He was married to a niece of Matilda of Scotland, whose sister Mary had married Eustace, count of Boulogne. The latter's only child and heiress was another Matilda. This lady, Stephen's wife, will be referred to as Queen Matilda, while her cousin, Stephen's rival for the throne, will be titled, as she preferred, the Empress Matilda. Like his uncle and grandfather before him, Stephen was fortunate in the qualities of his queen Matilda. She bore him two sons: Eustace, who predeceased his father, and William, who inherited, not England, but his mother's county of Boulogne. It is believed that Matilda was educated at Bermondsey Abbey; her mother was a benefactress of the abbey and indeed had died there. The author of the *Gesta Stephani* described the queen as a woman of subtlety and a man's resolution. That Stephen retained his throne was due in no small measure to the activity of his wife. It was Matilda who, on the outbreak of civil war, took Eustace to France, won French support, securing her son's investiture as duke of Normandy and his betrothal to the French king's sister, Constance. It was Matilda who reconciled her uncle, David, king of Scots, to her husband's cause and persuaded her husband's brother, Henry, bishop of Winchester, to return to his proper allegiance. The queen also seems to have handled troops quite as effectively as her husband, successfully besieging Dover Castle early in the war with naval support from her own county of Boulogne and relieving Bishop Henry when he was besieged at Winchester. When Stephen was captured in 1141, the queen tried vainly to negotiate with the Empress for his release. 'Abused in harsh and insulting language', she then rallied their scattered forces and marched on London, where the Empress had made herself so unpopular that the citizens drove her out as the queen approached. It was only the capture of Robert, earl of Gloucester (Henry I's favourite bastard and his half-sister's strongest supporter), that gave the queen a hostage important enough to exchange for the king.

Stephen's charm and good nature were acknowledged even by his enemies, but of his personal relations with his wife we have no evidence. Contemporaries found nothing but good in the character of his queen, and certainly her unswerving loyalty, good judgement and ability to handle men were decisive elements in winning back his throne. No letters by her are known to survive, so we cannot judge her by her own words, but we know she won the love of her husband's people.

THE EMPRESS MATILDA

Henry I's only daughter had been married at the age of twelve to the Emperor Henry V but had been sent to Germany four years earlier to be brought up at her future husband's court. The Empress Matilda was extremely popular in Germany, and if she had borne children, would have been happy to remain there, but her husband's death and the drowning of her brother brought her home to England. Much of her trouble sprang from the second marriage forced on her by her father. Her union with Geoffrey, count of Anjou, a man ten years her junior, produced three sons but was notoriously unhappy and the couple preferred to live apart. Geoffrey was uninterested in his wife's attempt to gain her English inheritance, though he successfully conquered Normandy for her. While Matilda was intelligent and not without charm, there is no doubt that with her goal almost within reach and her rival a prisoner, it was her own arrogance and mishandling of the situation in London which threw away everything for which she and her followers had worked so hard.

Matilda's real achievement was to keep alive her claim to the throne until her eldest son Henry was old enough to take it up on his own account. She had left England for good after the death of Robert, earl of Gloucester, and the last few years of Stephen's reign were quiet ones. Queen Matilda died of a fever in 1151 and the question of the succession to the throne was greatly eased in 1153 by the death of Stephen's son, Eustace, without heirs. This left the empress's son, Henry of Anjou, to succeed to the English throne, and Stephen's younger son, William, to inherit his mother's county of Boulogne, his father's county of Mortain and those lands in England that Stephen had held prior to his accession. The empress lived until 1167, exercising to the end a strong influence over her son, Henry II. Her more-or-less permanent residence was a palace in Rouen, built by her father. With her death the era of the Anglo-Norman queens comes to an end. We know little of them save for their public acts, but they seem to have set a standard of queenly behaviour which many of their successors found it difficult to live up to.

No letters of Matilda of Boulogne, Stephen's queen, have been found, but the following letter was written by her cousin, the empress, two years before she died. It encapsulates the main elements of the relationship between her son and Thomas à Becket. These are too well-known to need detailed explanation here: Henry's friendship with the talented archdeacon led to his appointment as chancellor of England and when, after eight years of close collaboration between the two, the

The wedding feast of Henry V and Matilda (Corpus Christi College, Cambridge, MS 373, f. 95b)

archbishopric of Canterbury fell vacant, Becket seemed the ideal candidate. Once elected to Canterbury, however, Becket resigned the chancellorship and transferred his allegiance from the king to the Church. The main feature of the struggle between Henry and Becket was the king's determination to limit the powers of the Church courts, which he felt threatened the Crown's own legal powers. He wanted clerics who were convicted in Church courts to be handed over to the secular authorities for punishment. Becket's refusal to accept this demand ended in his retreat into exile in France, where he appealed for protection to Pope Alexander III, who was himself living in exile.

When Matilda wrote her letter to him, Becket had only recently left England. For the next six years attempts were made to reconcile the two former friends. Matilda was not alone in her attempts; Louis VII of France made genuine and frequent efforts to heal the breach. A compromise was reached in 1170 and the archbishop returned to his flock. His first action was to excommunicate the archbishop of York and two bishops who had taken his place at the recent coronation of Henry's son, Young Henry. Henry II's rage on receiving this news led directly to Becket's murder in his own cathedral.

Matilda's influence on her son was regarded as very strong, which is undoubtedly why both the Pope and archbishop enlisted her aid. She had herself been very generous to the Church and had established several Cistercian foundations (which Henry also patronized, particularly after Becket's death) and was therefore an acceptable mediator to both sides. One of Becket's supporter's, Nicholas of Rouen, wrote to the archbishop of the empress in the following terms: 'You must know that the lady empress was ingenious in defence of her son, excusing him now by his love of justice, and now on account of the malice of some of the bishops. She was acute and discreet in comprehending the origin of the church disturbances; she said some things, in which we greatly praise and admire her sense, and made many acute remarks on the plurality of benefices and the idleness and luxury of some of the clergy, who have no fear of being called to account, do what they will; and these statements she illustrated by recent examples.' Matilda's tone in her letter leaves no doubt of her strong support for her son and her view that Becket should be the one to submit.

The Empress Matilda, daughter of Henry I, to Thomas à Becket, Archbishop of Canterbury, 1165

To Thomas archbishop of Canterbury, Matilda the empress.

My lord Pope sent to me, enjoining me, for the remission of my sins, to interfere to renew peace and concord between you and the king, my son, and to try to reconcile you to him. You, as you well know, have asked the same thing from me;

wherefore, with the more goodwill, for the honour of God and the Holy church, I have begun and carefully treated of that affair. But it seems a very hard thing to the king, as well as to his barons and council, seeing he so loved and honoured you, and appointed you lord of his whole kingdom and of all his lands, and raised you to the highest honours in the land, believing he might trust you rather than any other; and especially so, because he declares that you have, as far as you could, roused his whole kingdom against him; nor was it your fault that you did not disinherit him by main force. Therefore I send you my faithful servant, Archdeacon Laurence, that by him I may know your will in these affairs, and what sort of disposition you entertain towards my son, and how you intend to conduct yourself, if it should happen that he fully grants my petition and prayer on your behalf. One thing I plainly tell you, that you cannot recover the king's favour, except by great humility and most evident moderation. However, what you intend to do in this matter signify to me by my messenger and your letters.

(Bouquet's Recueil des Historiens de la France, *vol. xvi, p. 235, Latin. Wood, vol. i, letter iv.)*

The Angevin Queens

ELEANOR OF AQUITAINE, WIFE OF HENRY II

Eleanor of Aquitaine was one of the great personalities of the Middle Ages. A combination of birth, character and longevity allowed her a greater control over the direction of her life than was possible for most noblewomen. She was born in 1122, the eldest child of William, tenth duke of Aquitaine and eighth count of Poitou, and his wife, Aenor of Chatellerault. Her mother and only brother died while Eleanor was still a child and her father chose not to remarry. He died on a pilgrimage in 1137, leaving Eleanor as heiress to his territories. The dominant figure of her childhood, however, was not her father but her paternal grandfather. William, the ninth duke, had taken part in the First Crusade, but was best known for his poetry and his amorous exploits. He had packed two wives off to Fontevrault, an abbey patronized by his family, and had married his son to the daughter of his mistress, the vicomtesse of Chatellerault.

When Eleanor's father departed on his pilgrimage, he placed his daughters and his lands under the protection of Louis VI of France. When he failed to return, the logical outcome was a marriage between Eleanor and Louis's son and heir. Eleanor's right to the duchy was reinforced by the Crown, which in turn gained power in a large region of south-western France, where it had hitherto had no authority, with the presumption that, on the birth of a son, it would be incorporated permanently into the royal holdings. Soon after the marriage, Louis VI died and Eleanor became queen of France. Louis VII seems in the early years of his marriage to have been totally dominated by his young wife, who had not then learned to exercise power with responsibility. The result was an abortive campaign against the count of Toulouse, over whose territories the dukes of Aquitaine had long desired sovereignty, and a breach with the powerful house of Champagne during which 300 men, women and children were burned to death by royal troops in the cathedral at Vitry. France was placed under an interdict, but the settlement Louis made with the Church and his education in government by Abbot Suger led to a decline in Eleanor's influence. Nevertheless, when the king went on crusade in 1146, she insisted on accompanying him. Things military interested her far more than things domestic and she was very active during the preparations, recruiting many of her Poitevin vassals. It was not particularly unusual for wives to accompany their husbands on crusade, but it was rare for them to insist on taking all the trappings of courtly comfort with them as did Eleanor. This burdened the army with a huge baggage train and large numbers of ladies and female servants. While on crusade, Eleanor experienced danger and physical hardship and saw at first hand the Byzantine court and culture.

Her relations with Louis deteriorated still further when she opposed his military decisions and renewed her acquaintance with her youthful uncle, Raymond of Antioch, whose company she clearly preferred to that of the king. In the end, Louis insisted on her return home and for a few years there was domestic peace. Her mistakes had had a salutary maturing effect on Eleanor, but she no longer had any influence on her husband. The unsatisfactory nature of their marriage in personal terms was clear by this time, but it would have had little importance save for the fact that Eleanor had borne Louis two daughters but no son. In 1152 Louis had the marriage annulled. He took a calculated risk that since Eleanor had borne him no son, she would not produce one for any future husband, in which case Louis' elder daughter, Marie, would inherit Aquitaine on her mother's death. Eleanor acquiesced in the annulment, but it was to become quite clear that she knew what she was going to do with her freedom. If he had known, Louis might have been less willing to let her go. Immediately after their separation, she left Paris for her own city of Poitiers and almost immediately married Henry of Anjou, eleven years her junior and heir to the throne of England. Two years later she was queen of England. The couple were in many ways well matched, both supplied with limitless energy, intellectual curiosity and a strong physical attraction, but if Eleanor had hoped to dominate her young husband as she initially had his predecessor, she was mistaken. In many ways Henry's marriage was to mirror that of his parents. There, Geoffrey of Anjou had quickly subordinated his older, prestigious heiress of a wife, and although he never interfered in her English affairs Matilda had been forced to focus her love and ambition on her son Henry in a way that was to be echoed by Eleanor's devotion to Richard and Aquitaine.

The first decade of her second marriage was one of almost constant childbearing for Eleanor. She and Henry had eight children in all, only one of whom, the eldest, failed to reach full adulthood. Presumably to her intense satisfaction, five of them were boys. There was little settled home life for these children, for their parents' domains stretched from the Scottish border to the Pyrenees and Henry and Eleanor's court was even more peripatetic than most. It was during these child-bearing years that Eleanor was most formally involved in government, acting as regent in England if she did not accompany Henry to the continent, sometimes issuing writs in her own name, in the same form as Henry's own and often with the same witnesses. Essentially she was lending the authority of her name to the actions of her husband's ministers, and it would be a mistake to imagine that she wielded any real power of her own. The relatively even tenor of these years ended in the late 1160s and was largely due to the queen's advancing years. She had her last child, John, in 1167, at the age of forty-five. Henry, however, was in his prime, and may already have begun the series of liasons which culminated in his affair with Rosamund Clifford. Eleanor's jealousy was as much an indication of the former strength of her marriage as of Henry's love for Rosamund. She then began to vest her thwarted desire for power in her sons. In 1170 Richard, her second son, was installed as count of Poitou and future lord of Aquitaine. Henry was quite happy for his wife to take up residence in her duchy and leave him in peace. She set up a regency council for Richard, but even then the ultimate power lay with Henry if he chose to wield it. How far Eleanor was responsible for the rebellion of her eldest son, Henry, and his brothers in 1173 is not clear, but she had certainly been at work turning her sons against their father and her vassals against their overlord. It was Eleanor's revenge for years of subordination, culminating in the insulting rejection of her person in favour of Rosamund Clifford. Unsurprisingly, the rebellion failed and the queen paid the price of failure when she was captured. Henry was far too shrewd to follow Louis' example and divorce her, nor did he pack her off to a nunnery. She was sent back to England and though not physically confined, she was placed under constant supervision and lived the retired life of a queen dowager. She was permitted to come to court on formal occasions when it suited Henry and she recovered her liberty only by slow degrees before his death. In 1183 he permitted her to visit her extensive dower lands and it would seem she had regained control of her household by 1186, but during Henry's lifetime she was never free of restraints. Despite Henry's sense of betrayal and Eleanor's resentment, they obviously managed to establish some *modus vivendi*, and like many another warring couple, fought their battles through their children.

This long period of enforced inactivity, of fallowness, had an extraordinary effect on Eleanor when released by Henry's death in 1189. She launched into a period of high-powered political action which would have defeated most women half her age, let alone one of 67. She immediately set off on a ceremonial perambulation round the country with her court. Until Richard (whose elder brother had predeceased their father) reached England for his coronation, she was largely responsible for governing the country. Despite years of seclusion, her prestige was such that nobody questioned her right to do so. Although there is no clear evidence that she was responsible for Richard's marriage to Berengaria of Navarre, she almost certainly had a hand in it, and its diplomatic importance was to give Aquitaine a reliable ally on its southern borders. She escorted Berengaria to her crusading bridegroom and the couple were married in Cyprus. Eleanor's influence can also be seen in the marriage of her widowed daughter, Joanna, to Raymond VI, count of Toulouse, which finally settled the Aquitaine–Toulouse dispute in a manner preferable to the

Eleanor of Aquitaine, effigy in Fontevrault Abbey

military campaigns into which she had persuaded both her husbands. When news of Richard's capture broke, she exercised direct authority in England and it was largely due to her frenzied diplomatic efforts and the great sum she raised for his ransom that he was released at all. On his return to England Richard had a second coronation, with his mother, not his wife, at his side, and it was probably as a result of her pleading that he was as lenient to his treacherous brother John as he was. Only then did Eleanor retire, not to an English abbey, but to her family foundation of Fontevrault, where, in a final gesture of victory, she had interred her husband.

The death of Richard without an heir in 1199 brought her out of retirement, heartbroken as she undoubtedly was, in order to secure the throne of England for her only surviving son, John. She took over Richard's mercenaries and devastated the lands of those who supported the claim of her grandson, Arthur of Brittany, child of her third son, Geoffrey. She was well aware of John's failings, but regarded the throne as rightfully his. Next, she embarked on an extended tour of her Poitevan and Gascon lands to ensure their loyalty to herself before receiving John as her vassal for them. In 1198 her eldest child, Marie of Champagne, had died, closely followed by her two favourites, Richard and Joanna, leaving of her children only John and Eleanor, queen of Alphonso VIII of Castile, still living. In 1201 at the age of eighty Eleanor set off to cross the Pyrennees in winter to select one of her Castilian grandaughters as a bride for the son of Philip Augustus of France (the son her first husband Louis had finally begot). This was part of the terms of truce arranged between Philip and John, who had been warring for some time. As the chroniclers relate, she was responsible for choosing Blanche, rather than her elder sister, Urraca, a girl who proved to be made in Eleanor's own image, a noteworthy queen of France and mother of St Louis.

Even the last few years of Eleanor's life were not uneventful. In the war waged by her grandson, Arthur, against John, she found herself trapped by Arthur's forces at Mirebeau. Although John rushed immediately to her rescue, the incident led indirectly to Arthur's capture and eventual death at the hands of his uncle. Eleanor died at Fontevrault in March 1204. To the end she remained fascinated by the exercise of power, and her cultural interests, many and varied as they were, remained subordinate to her political intriguing. Her use of power was always personally motivated and not always wise, but by sheer force of personality she retained the ultimate loyalty of her volatile vassals in Poitou and Aquitaine for more than sixty years. After Richard's death, although John exercised some jurisdiction over her lands, Eleanor was the sovereign lady over her hereditary fiefs for the first time since her marriage to Louis. Her charters were not issued under any delegated power and did not require John's confirmation to make them effective. If she failed to exercise as much power as she felt she should during her marriages, there is little doubt that her influence was paramount during the reigns of her sons. Yet important though her children were to her, Eleanor had no scruples in using them as instruments in her power games. She virtually abandoned John when he was one year old, sending him to the monks at Fontevrault. He later spent some time in the household of his eldest brother, Henry, but his lonely and insecure childhood compared with that of his siblings, into whose family quarrels he was thrust as an adolescent, may go some way to explaining John's faults as a king.

Perhaps it is fitting to end a study of Eleanor with an opinion of her written by Richard of Devises, who described her as 'an incomparable woman; beautiful yet gracious, strong-willed yet kind, unassuming yet sagacious (which is a rare combination in a woman)'. He put his finger on what was probably the key to her character when he described her at seventy-five as 'even now unwearied of any task and provoking wonder at her stamina'.

The two letters addressed by Eleanor of Aquitaine to the Pope are undoubtedly the most literary of all the royal letters in this volume. They were certainly not composed by the queen herself, but by Peter of Blois, one of a number of highly talented men that her husband had gathered about him. A student of jurisprudence and theology, he served a number of royal and ecclesiastical masters, often as a secretary, and he boasted that he could dictate three letters simultaneously to scribes while writing a fourth himself. Peter was presumably responsible for the frequent biblical allusions and the purple prose, but the force of the emotions contained in the letters are all Eleanor's. The rage and despair she felt on behalf of her son and the reproaches she hurled at the head of the Pope leap from the page.

At the time Eleanor was writing, the reputation of the papal curia was very low. The conflict between Pope Alexander III and the Emperor Frederick Barbarossa for territorial power in Italy, in which Henry II and the French king had supported the Pope, had left the papacy heavily in debt and the subsequent corruption and avarice of the curia were such that on the death of Clement III in 1191, none of the cardinals was willing to accept election to the Holy See. In the end the eldest of them was persuaded to take office. When he became Pope, Celestine had been a cardinal for forty-seven years and was already eighty-five. He lived for another seven years. Incorruptable and a fine scholar, he was anxious to maintain peaceful relations with the Emperor Henry VI in order to be free to tackle corruption within the Church. Richard the Lionheart, returning overland from the Third Crusade, had been captured in Austria and handed over by its duke, Leopold, whom he had offended in the Holy Land, to his overlord, the emperor. Politically, Henry VI had two grievances against the Angevins: he was married to the Sicilian heiress while Richard supported her male rival, and in Germany one of his main opponents among the princes was Henry the Lion, duke of Bavaria, who was married to Richard's sister Matilda. Henry had every intention, therefore, of using the opportunity provided by Richard's capture to its uttermost. The ransom he demanded, 100,000 marks (£66,000), was the equivalent of twice England's gross annual income, and it had to be raised in a country that had already been drained to finance the crusade. Celestine was apparently not prepared to risk the uneasy peace between the papacy and the emperor on behalf of an English king, even if he was a crusader. Among the arguments Eleanor used in her first letter was the reminder of Richard's father's support for Pope Alexander III in his long battle with the emperor's father, Barbarossa, and England's financial generosity to the Holy See.

The second letter is far less restrained and objective. Eleanor's personal anguish is palpable and so is her contempt and rage at the Pope. She refers to all four of her sons, Henry, the Young King, and Geoffrey of Brittany, both dead, Richard a captive in chains and John ravaging his brother's kingdom, begging, demanding that the Pope honour the promises of aid he had made her when she visited Rome, warning that it was in the papacy's own best interests to stand up to the emperor rather than submit to his treatment of the Church in Germany and Sicily. In the end, it was Eleanor's own superhuman efforts to raise the ransom from Richard's kingdom and the king's agreement to the emperor's terms, rather than any intervention by the Pope, which led to the king's eventual release.

Eleanor, Queen of England, widow of Henry II, to Pope Celestine III, 1193

To the reverend Father and Lord Celestine, by the Grace of God, the supreme Pontiff, Eleanor, in God's anger, Queen of England, Duchess of Normandy, Countess of Anjou, begs him to show himself to be a father to a pitiable mother. I had decided to remain quiet in case a fullness of heart and a passionate grief might elicit some word against the chief of priests which was somewhat less than cautious, and I was therefore accused of insolence and arrogance. Certainly grief is not that different from insanity while it is inflamed with its own force. It does not recognise a master, is afraid of no ally, it has no regard for anyone, and it does not spare them – not even you.

So no-one should be surprised if the modesty of my words is sharpened by the strength of my grief – I am mourning for a loss that is not private; but my personal grief cannot be comforted – it is set deep in the heart of my spirit. The arrows of the Lord are truly directed against me, and their anger will drain my spirit. Races which have been torn apart, peoples which have been shattered, provinces which have been stripped, in general the whole western Church which is worn out with deep sorrow, they are all beseeching you in a spirit which has been ground down and humiliated, you whom God established above the races and kingdoms in the fullness of His power.

Please listen to the cry of the afflicted, for our troubles have multiplied beyond number; and you cannot conceal those troubles in as much as they are a mark of criminality and disgrace, since you are the Vicar of Christ Crucified, Peter's successor, the Priest of Christ, the Lord's Anointed one, even a God over Pharaohs. Father, may your face provide a judgement, may your eyes see impartially, the prayers of the people depend on your decision and on the mercy of your see; unless your hands seize justice more quickly, the complete tragedy of this evil event will rebound on to you. You are the Father of orphans, the judge of widows, the comforter of those who mourn and those who grieve, a city of refuge for everyone, and because of this, in a time of so much misery you are expected to provide the sole relief for everyone from the authority of your power.

In harsh times, the sons of Israel used to ask the advice of Moses, whose duties you now carry out, and they used to fall back on the Tabernacle of the Covenant in their moments of distress. Our king is in a difficult position and he is overwhelmed by troubles from every direction. Look at the state of his kingdom, or rather its sorry state, the evil of the time, the cruelty of the tyrant who does not stop making an unjust war against the king because of his greed; that tyrant who keeps him bound in prison-chains (after the king had been caught during a Holy Crusade, under the protection of God above and under the safeguard of the Roman Church) and he kills him with fear; for he despises God and His terrible judgements, he broods over his booty but there is no-one who can escape from His strength.

If the Church of Rome keeps its hands tightly clasped and keeps quiet about the great injuries to the Lord's Anointed, may God rise up and judge over our plea, may He look upon the face of His own anointed one. Where is the passion of Eli against Achab? The passion of John against Herod? The passion of Ambrose against Valentinian? The passion of Pope Alexander III, who solemnly and terribly excommunicated Frederick, father of this current prince, with the full authority of the Apostolic See, as we have heard and seen? In addition he has no due regard for the Apostolic keys, and he reckons the law of God merely as words.

All the more reason that you ought to sieze the sword of the spirit, which is the word of God, much more firmly. For it was written, 'He who rejects you, rejects me'. So if you do not want to see continuing injustice done either to you or to the Roman Church, you must not pretend the disgrace done to Peter or the harm done to the Lord's Anointed does not exist.

So may the word of the Lord not have been stuck in your throat, may the mortal fear in you as a man not destroy the spirit of freedom. It is easier to suffer at the hands of men than to forsake the law of God. The enemies of Christ Crucified trust in their own strength, they glory in the multitude of their own riches – their end is ruin, their glory will be in chaos.

Anything which is taken from what is needed by the Church and the poor is devoured by the insatiable appetite of avarice. But the time is nearly upon us when the hand of God will exact a timely vengeance upon them, and what Blessed Job claims to be true about the evil robber will happen: 'He swallows down riches and vomits them up again; God casts them out of his belly. He shall be punished for all that he did, and yet shall not be consumed.' For if they escape judgement during their human life, a more terrible divine judgement is hanging over them; their present joy is more like a passing moment, for in truth their eternal punishment will be fire and worms.

For is anyone who persecutes innocent men said to have escaped the avenging hand of God, which removes the lives of princes and punishes with power the powerful? To say nothing of the punishment of Hell, we often read of how the finger of God transfers kingdoms and empires as He decides; He establishes these powers just as He wishes and so He destroys them just as He wishes.

Please, I beg you, do not let a worldly eminence deter you. Moab is proud and his pride is greater than that man's strength; but on the other hand, the name of the Lord is the greatest strength.

Indeed, among the public it casts a shadow over the Church, and excites a rumour among the people (and it considerably damages your standing), the fact that in such a crisis, amid so many tears and with so many pleas coming from provinces, you have not sent those princes even one messenger from those around you. Often your cardinals, with great authority even, execute an embassy for relatively minor reasons to pagan regions. Yet for a cause so important, so distressing and affecting everyone, you still do not send even one sub-deacon, not even one acolyte; for nowadays papal legates are sent for a profit, not for a respect of Christ, nor for the honour of the Church, nor for the peace of kingdoms nor for the safety of a people. But in freeing a king, what profit or result could be more glorious for you than to exalt the honour of the sovereign Pontiff, to exalt you as the Aaron of Priests, as a Phinees?

You would not have injured the true worth of the Apostolic See too much if you had gone to Germany in person for the release of such a great prince. For the man whom one used to pay honour to so courteously in prosperous times one ought not to desert so casually in harsh times. Why do you not weigh in the scales the advantages of justice which Henry, of good repute and the father of King Richard, displayed to you, as we saw, at the critical point of your greatest suffering; and then on the other side, he exercised the tyranny of Frederick, which was to the advantage of you, the possessions of the Roman Church and of all those who were clinging faithfully to your side? For when the forenamed Frederick, author and accomplice of the great Schism, had sworn against Pope Alexander III, who, as you know, was rightly elected, and for the apostate of Octavian, and when the Church generally was in difficulties all over the world because of the confusion resulting from the Schism, the kings of England and France were approached by legates from each side; the king of France's opinion was racked with doubt, fluctuating as to which side he was on because of the different counsels he received, but King Henry was saddened at the tunic of Christ being torn for so long and so first agreed with Pope Alexander, then used great skill in bringing the king of France over to the Apostolic side; he then fortified that side with his own plans and strengthened it with support, so bringing the ship of Peter, shipwrecked from the quarrel, safely to shore.

We saw this at the castle of Ralph, where the royal generosity satisfied even the prayers of the Romans, for they themselves were publicly proclaiming a miracle, with the overflowing gifts of gold and silver. So it is a notable degrading of the glory of the Apostolic See, that any level of ingratitude could ever efface the memory of such benevolence. Whenever the ferment of schism can bubble again, may God prevent such a thing, then the memory of your present apathy and failure will be able to bring others to tears. For that old serpent, that coiling snake, may seek to impede the release of the king with remarkable devices, but we trust in the Lord that at the right time He will look upon the face of His Anointed and will give the empire to its own king.

Without doubt our anticipation has grown quite strong with an unfailing hope and a firm faith: for the prayer for him from the Church to God never ceases, but God who listens at the acknowledged time, who provides help on the day of salvation, will look upon the prayers of the humble and He will not despise them;

for the continual supplication of the just cause is very strong; the sun stood still in response to the prayers of Joshua and the moon was not moved opposite the valley of Achilon; since a just man's prayers obtain this, so may the sun of justice not withdraw from the heart of a sinner, and the mind of a man, though it may be inclined to failure, still it may be strengthened by the durability of its virtues. For it is not so much sin that is diminished by prayer, but the punishment of sin that is avoided by the profit of prayers.

So it is good for the king to wait in silence for the salvation of the Lord; for if he is now being cleansed in the furnace of affliction by God, who surrounds him with good and bad times in the healthiest of moderation, vexation will turn to glory and instead of double shame and disgrace on earth, he shall have double good times in heaven. Therefore blessed is the man who trusts in the Lord and the Lord will be his faith. Indeed, just as now the sorrows of the people and the tears of all hang over him, so he will be freed by prayers at the right time to the joy of the whole world, since his release has been rightly desired by peoples in general. O Lord, in your virtue will the king be exalted and the Roman Church, which must now take too much of the blame for delaying his release, will feel ashamed, and not without tears since it did not recognise how much difficulty so great a son as mine was in.

(Foedera, vol. 1 pp. 72–4, Latin.)

Eleanor, Queen of England, widow of Henry II, to Pope Celestine III, 1193

To the reverend Father and Lord Celestine, by the Grace of God, the supreme Pontiff, Eleanor, pitiable and hoping in vain to be pited, the Queen of England, Duchess of Normandy, Countess of Anjou, entreats him to show himself to be a Father of mercy to a pitiable mother

O holiest Pope, a cursed distance between us prevents me from speaking to you in person, but I must give vent to my grief a little and who shall assist me with my words? I am all anxiety, both within and without and as a result my words are full of suffering. There are fears which can be seen, but hidden are the disputes, and I cannot take one breath free from the persecution of my troubles and the grief caused by my afflictions, which beyond measure have found me out. I have completely wasted away with torment and with my flesh devoured, my bones have clung to my skin. My years have passed away full of groans and I wish they could pass away altogether. I wish that the blood of my body, already dead, the brain in my head and the marrow of my bones would dissove into tears, so much so that I completely melt away into sorrow. My insides have been torn out of me, I have lost the staff of my old age, the light of my eyes; if God assented to my prayers he would condemn my ill-fated eyes to perpetual blindness so that they no longer saw the woes of my people. Who may allow me to die for you, my son? Mother of mercy, look upon a mother so wretched, or else if your Son, an unexhausted source of mercy, requires from the son the sins of the mother, then let him exact complete vengeance on me, for I am the only one to offend, and let him punish me, for I am the irreverent one – do not let him smile over the punishment of an innocent person. Let the one who is striking me crush me, lift up his hand and kill me; let this be my consolation – that in burdening me with grief he does not spare me. I am pitiable, yet pitied by no-one; why have I, the Lady of two kingdoms, reached the disgrace of this abominable old age? I am the mother of two kings.

My insides have been torn out of me, my family has been carried off, it has rolled past me; the Young King and the earl of Brittany sleep in the dust – their mother is so ill-fated she is forced to live, so that without cure she is tortured with the memory of the dead. As some comfort, I still have two sons, who are alive today, but only to punish me, wretched and condemned. King Richard is detained in chains; his brother John is killing the people of the prisoner's kingdom with the sword, he is ravaging the land with fires. In every respect the Lord has become cruel to me, turning his heavy hand against me. His anger is so against me that even my sons fight against each other, if indeed it can be called a fight when one is imprisoned and crushed in chains while the other heaps grief upon grief by trying to usurp the former's kingdom for himself with his cruel tyranny.

Good Jesus! Who will grant me thy protection in hell and hide me until your fury passes away, until your arrows stop, the arrows which are in me, the arrows whose anger my whole spirit is drunk on? I long for death, I am weary of life. Though I am thus continually dying, I still want to die more completely; unwilling, I am compelled to live – my life is the food of death and is a means of torture. Blessed are those who do not know the capriciousness of this life, who do not know of the unpredictable events in our inconstant fate because of a blessed abortion! What do I do? Why do I yet live? Why do I, a wretched creature, delay? Why do I not go to see the man my soul loves, chained in beggary and iron? At such a time as this, how could a mother forget the son of her very womb? Affection appeases tigers, it even appeases the more fierce witches.

But doubt remains and I waver. If I go, I desert my son's kingdom, which is being plundered from every direction with formidable hostility, and in my absence it will have no common counsel, no relief. But if I stay, I will not see what I most want to see, the face of my son, and there will be no-one to concentrate on procuring the release of my son, but what I am more afraid of is that the most fastidious of young men will be tortured for some impossible sum of money and yet impatient of so much affliction will be easily tortured to death. O wicked, cruel, impious tyrant who is not afraid to lay his hands on the Lord's Anointed, nor has a royal anointing, nor a reverence for the holy life, nor a fear of God restrained you from such inhumanity.

In addition to this, the Prince of the Apostles still rules and reigns in the Apostolic See, and his judicial steadfastness is set up for the people; it rests with you, Father, to draw the sword of Peter against these criminals, for it was for this reason that Peter set the sword above peoples and kingdoms. The cross of Christ soars ahead of the eagles of Caesar, the sword of Peter is a higher authority than the sword of Constantine, the Apostolic See higher than an Imperial power. Is your power derived from God or from men? Did not the God of Gods speak to you through his apostle Peter, saying 'Whatever you have bound on earth will be bound also in heaven and whatever you have freed on earth will also be freed in heaven'? Why then have you, so negligent, so cruel, done nothing for so long about the release of my son or is it rather that you do not dare? Perhaps you will say that this power entrusted to you was over souls, not bodies: so be it, I will certainly be satisfied if you bind the souls of those who keep my son bound in prison. It is in your power to release my son, unless the fear of God yields to a human fear. So restore my son to me, man of God, if indeed you are a man of God and not a man of mere blood. If you are slow in releasing my son, then the Most High will require my son's blood from your hand. Alas, it is a sorry time when the chief shepherd turns into a mercenary, when he flies from the face of the wolf, when he abandons in the jaws of a bloodthirsty beast a lamb put in his care, or even the chosen ram, the leader of the Lord's flock. A good shepherd instructs and informs other shepherds not to run when they see a wolf approaching but rather to lay down their lives for their sheep. Please, I beg you, may you save your own soul while you apply yourself to procuring the release, not of your sheep, but I will say of your son, using numerous embassies, beneficial advice, thunderous threats, general injunctions and severe sentences? Though late, you should give your soul for him, the man for whom you have refused to say or write one word. We know from the testimony of the prophet, the Son of God came down from heaven to bring the chained out of the lake in which there was no water; what was fitting for God is surely fitting for God's servant. My son is tortured in chains, but you do not go down to him, you do not send anyone, you are not even moved by the sorrow which moved Joseph. Christ sees this and is silent, but in the final judgement retribution will be severe for those who are negligent in doing God's work.

Legates have now been promised to us three times, yet have not been sent; in fact they are servants rather than legates. If my son were in a prosperous position, they would hurry rather more quickly to his simple call, expecting plentiful rewards for their embassy from his splendid generosity and the public profit of his kingdom. But what profit could they consider more glorious than the freeing of a captive king and the restoring of peace to the people, of tranquillity to the religious and of joy to everyone? But now the sons of Ephraim, who aimed, who fired their bows, have turned round on the day of battle and in the time of stress; while the wolf comes upon its prey, the dogs are mute – either they cannot, or they will not, bark. Is this the promise you made me at the castle of Ralph, with the great authority of love and good faith? What benefit did you gain from giving my simple nature mere words, from mocking the prayers of the innocent with a hollow trust? So once King Achab was forbidden to form a friendship with Ben-hadad, and we have heard what disastrous effects their mutual love had. Divine providence blessed the wars of Judas, John, Simon and the Maccabaean brothers with felicitous auspices; but when an embassy was sent to secure the friendship of the Romans, they lost the help of God, and their corruptable friendship was more than once the cause of bitter regret. You alone force me to despair; after God, you have been my hope, the trust of our people. Cursed be he who trusts in man – so where is my refuge now? You are, my Lord, my God. The eyes of your maidservant are turned to you, O Lord, for you recognise my distress. You, the King of Kings, Lord of Lords, look upon your Christ's face, grant sovereignty to your Son, and save the son of your maidservant; do not bring on him the crimes of his father or the wickedness of his mother.

We know from a certified public report that after the death of the bishop of Liege whom the emperor is said to have killed with a death-blow from his sword, though wielded by a distant hand, he confined in prison-like misery the bishop of Ostia, four of his provincial bishops and even the Archbishops of Salerno and Treves; and the Apostolic authority ought in no way to deny that unlawfully and tyrannically he has also taken possession of Sicily, to the perpetual detriment of the Roman Church – for from the times of Constantine it has remained the patrimony of St Peter, and it was seized despite embassies, petitions and threats from the Apostolic see. The emperor's fury is not satisfied with all these gains, but his hand is still stretched out. Certainly he has done dreadful things, but most surely you can soon expect worse. For those who ought to be pillars of the Church are as light as reeds and every wind sways them. If only they would remember that the glory of the Lord was transferred from Israel because of the negligence of Eli, the priest ministering in Shiloh. That is not a parable applying only to the past, but to the present; for the Lord banished the Tabernacle from Shiloh, his own Tabernacle where he dwelt among men and he left their virtue to remain in captivity, their excellence in the hands of the enemy. The fact that the Church is being trampled upon is attributed to their timidity, as is also the fact that faith is being put to the test, liberty oppressed, trickery being fostered by compliance, wickedness by impunity. Where is the promise the Lord made to his Church: 'Thou shalt suck the milk of the Gentiles and shall suckle the breasts of kings; I shall make thee the pride of ages, a joy from generation to generation'? Once, the Church trod upon the necks of the proud and lofty with its own strength and the laws of emperors obeyed the sacred canons. But now things have changed – not only canons, but the makers of canons are restrained by base laws and profane customs. No-one dare murmur about the detestable crimes of the powerful, which are tolerated, and the canonical rule applies merely to the sins of the poor. So Anacharsis the philosopher had good reason to compare laws and canons with spiders' webs, which trap the weaker animals but let the stronger go.

The kings of the earth have set themselves and the rulers have all agreed to be against my son, the Lord's Anointed. One tortures him in chains, another destroys his lands with a cruel emnity, or to use a common phrase: 'one shears, another plunders, one holds the foot, another skins it'. The supreme Pontiff sees all this, yet keeps the sword of Peter sheathed, and thus gives the sinner added boldness, his silence being presumed to indicate consent. For the man who can rebuke, who ought to rebuke, but does not do so seems to consent, and the man who pretends to be patient will not be without a hidden alliance. The time of dissension is upon us, just as the Apostle predicted and the son of eternal damnation shall be revealed; dangerous times are at hand when the seamless tunic of Christ is torn, when the net of Peter is broken and the solid unity of the Catholic Church is dispersed. These are the initial stages of evil things – we perceive oppressive times, we fear worse. I am no prophetess, nor the daughter of a prophet, but my grief has made many suggestions about the troubles to come; yet it also steals the very words it suggests, for my writing is interrupted by my sobbing, my sadness saps the strength of my soul and it chokes my vocal chords with anxiety. Farewell.

(Foedera, vol. 1, pp. 74–6, Latin.)

BERENGARIA OF NAVARRE, WIFE OF RICHARD I

If Eleanor of Aquitaine may be regarded as one of the wonders of the medieval world, the same could hardly be said of her daughter-in-law, Berengaria of Navarre, in whom the chroniclers found little worthy of note save that she was sensible rather than beautiful. Berengaria was the daughter of Sancho VI, 'the Wise', of Navarre, whom Richard and his mother saw as a potentially strong ally on the southern borders of Aquitaine, who would guard Angevin interests while Richard embarked on crusade. Owing to her bridegroom's eagerness to travel east, Berengaria was brought to Sicily, from whence she continued on her journey under the chaperonage of Richard's sister, Joanna, widow of William II of Sicily. They were shipwrecked on Cyprus, where they were taken hostage by its ruler, Isaac Comnenus, an ally of Saladin. This brought Richard swiftly to their rescue and cost Isaac his island. Richard and Berengaria were married in the cathedral at Limassol and Berengaria crowned queen of England by the bishop of Evreux. Despite the romantic circumstances of her marriage on the Third Crusade, it was clearly not a success in personal terms. In practical terms, however, Richard I gained all he could have hoped from it, a large dowry and an active ally on the southern flank of Aquitaine. The circumstances of the Crusade meant that the couple could see little of each other in their early married life, for the queen was left behind in Acre. While Richard chose to travel back overland the ladies embarked by ship and travelled to Rome, where they learned of the king's capture. They stayed for six months as the guests of the Pope. On his release, Richard evinced little desire for her company, despite his need for an heir.

Berengaria is the only medieval queen of England never to have set foot in that country. This is probably a reflection of the Poitevan Richard's lack of interest in his kingdom rather than an illustration of his cool and casual relationship with his queen. Nor did Berengaria ever hold any English lands. She was first dowered with all Richard's possessions south of the Garonne during the lifetime of his mother and on Eleanor's death she was to receive all the latter's dower lands in England, Normandy and Poitou. On his return from captivity in 1196 Richard settled on his wife the county of Bigorre and the city of Le Mans together with the royal revenues arising from the Cornish tin mines, valued at 2,000 marks p.a. On John's marriage, Berengaria compounded with him for her dower rights in England for an annuity of 2,000 marks p.a. John, not surprisingly, neglected payment, and she was forced to appeal to the Pope, who in 1207 awarded her half the personal goods of her husband, but it is fairly safe to say she received little of what was due to her. Following John's loss of Normandy, Berengaria had to petition the victorious Philip Augustus for her dower rights there. The French king, in contrast to his English counterpart, was both just and generous and settled on her the county of Maine. It was here, in Le Mans, that the queen chose to spend her long widowhood. She founded the Abbey of l'Espau and lived there in retirement. It was for her abbey that she required her dower monies rather than for herself. John died owing her money and in the early years of Henry III's reign, the sum owing had mounted to £4,040. This time when Berengaria appealed to the Pope, it was arranged that the Templars in England should become agents and guarantors for its payment. From then on the situation improved, although she still had to write reminders for it.

Berengaria's childlessness was the greatest curse that could befall a medieval queen, especially, as in Richard's case, the king had a bastard to prove his fertility, and this barrenness was to have an incalculable effect on the course of English history. It is quite possible that Richard considered an annulment. The marriage of his sister Joanna to the count of Toulouse had removed the strategic importance of the Navarre alliance, and even if the king was temperamentally unsuited to marriage, he realized the importance of an heir of his body. Whatever his future plans, his unexpected death at Chalus, when he called not for his wife but for his mother, brought them to nought, leaving Berengaria to spend more than thirty years at l'Espau as queen-dowager.

Compared with the high emotion and drama of the letters of her mother-in-law, Berengaria's letters are models of simplicity and directness. But then they concern

Detail of an effigy of Berengaria of Navarre, Le Mans Cathedral

matters of money rather than life or death. By the time the first one was written, she was owed more than £4,000 in lieu of dower by the English Crown. It was addressed to Peter des Roches, a Poitevin who had made his career in England and was rewarded with the rich see of Winchester by King John, whose loyal servant he remained. On John's death he was made guardian of the person of the boy king, Henry III. On the death of the regent, William Marshal, earl of Pembroke, des Roches and the Justiciar, Hubert de Burgh, governed the country between them. In her letter, Berengaria explicitly states that the bishop was one of those responsible for the composition of her dower rights in England for the sum of 1,000 marks a year. She had made this agreement in person with her brother-in-law, John, at Chinon in 1201 and a copy was sent to the Pope for confirmation. The Pope remained her protector when poverty forced her to go and live with her sister, Blanche, countess of Champagne. John's loss of Normandy to the French Crown, while it threatened Berengaria's dower lands there, ultimately worked to her advantage, since Philip Augustus granted her the county of Maine in lieu. A new agreement with John in 1213 doubled the queen's annual sum to be paid from England in recognition of the sums by then owing to her, but John's promises were rarely worth the paper they were written on. Matters were finally resolved in 1220 when the queen's English dower reverted to 1,000 marks a year and she received in addition the revenues of the tin mines of Devon and Cornwall in lieu of the arrears she was owed. This time the Order of Templars were to become agents and guarantors of payment. Thereafter Berengaria received her payments regularly, and Brother Walter and Master Simon, to whom she refers in her letter to King Henry, were the men she delegated to receive payment. Both were Cistercian monks. Berengaria and other members of her family were particularly attached to the Order, and the abbey that she founded at l'Espau belonged to it.

Queen Berengaria, widow of Richard I, to Peter, Bishop of Winchester, 1220

To her venerable father in Christ and most cordial friend Peter, by God's grace bishop of Winchester, Berengaria, by the same grace formerly the humble queen of England, wishes health and every good thing.

We send to you our well-beloved Friar Walter, of the Cistercian order, the bearer of these presents, beseeching you humbly and devotedly, with all the humility that we can, that, in reference as well to this present feast of All Saints as to other terms now past, you will cause us to be satisfied about the money due to us according to the composition of our dower, which, by your mediation, we made with our brother John, of happy memory, formerly king of England. Fare you well.

(PRO SC 1/1/23, Latin. Wood, vol. i, letter ix.)

Queen Berengaria, widow of Richard I, to Henry III, 26 October 1225

To her lord and dearest nephew Henry, by God's grace illustrious king of England, lord of Ireland, duke of Normandy and Aquitaine and count of Anjou, Berengaria, by the same grace formerly the humble queen of England, wishes health and prosperous success to his utmost desires.

We requested you by our letters patent, sent to you by Brother Walter de Persona, our chaplain of the Cistercian order, that you would send to us by the said Brother Walter and Master Simon, our clerks, 1000 marks sterling, which you owe us at this feast of All Saints, according to the composition of our dower solemnly drawn out between us and you. But since the said Master Simon, being detained by sickness, cannot come over to you, we send in his stead our servant Martin, the bearer of these presents, earnestly requesting you to send us the thousand marks by the said Brother Walter, and by this Martin, or by one of them, if by any chance impediment both cannot come to you. In testimony of which we send you our present letters patent. Given at Mans, the Sunday next before the Feast of the Apostles Simon and Jude, in the month of October, the year of our Lord 1225.

(PRO SC 1/2/156, Latin. Wood. vol. i, letter x.)

ISABELLA OF ANGOULÊME, WIFE OF JOHN

As a boy, a number of marriages were proposed for John, but in 1176 he was betrothed to an English heiress, Isabella, daughter of William, earl of Gloucester, and granddaughter of Earl Robert, who had so loyally supported his half-sister, the Empress Matilda. John and Isabella were married in 1189, and although she had two sisters, they appear to have resigned their rights to the earldom to Isabella. This was another marriage which failed. The couple had no children and she appears to have played little part in John's life, public or private. Immediately he became king he divorced her on the grounds of consanguinity. They seem to have parted without rancour and he continued to send her presents of cloth and wine. John chose his queen himself. She bore the same name as his first wife and was the daughter and heiress of Aymer, count of Angoulême, one of Aquitaine's most powerful vassals. Isabella had been betrothed as a child to the son of Hugh de Lusignan, leader of a powerful Poitevan family with whom her father was in dispute over the county of La Marche, and had been brought up by her future husband's family. John, conscious as the Angevin kings always were, of the need for a strong southern ally, was negotiating for a possible Portuguese marriage, when, on his first tour of Aquitaine, he saw Isabella and married her forthwith. In political terms it made sense in that he gained control of Angoulême, while the Lusignans could be compensated with La Marche. In addition, a marriage alliance between two such powerful families would not have been in the best interests of the Crown. None the less, rumour had it that John married Isabella because he wanted her whatever the consequences. Support is given to the rumour by the fact that he married her straight away. A betrothal would have had the same political effect and given him time to judge local reaction. According to one chronicler, John was later to tell his wife that their marriage cost him all his continental possessions. It was in fact only a minor and indirect cause.

At the beginning of their married life John was clearly infatuated with his fifteen-year-old bride, twenty years his junior, and the chroniclers later ascribed the loss of Normandy to the king's habit of spending the morning in bed with his wife when he had more important things to attend to. While the loss of Normandy can safely be ascribed to other factors, it does not necessarily invalidate the picture of John and his queen. When the romance began to turn sour is not clear, but it may have been due, at least in part, to Isabella's failure to produce an heir. It was seven years before her first child, the future Henry III, was born, in October 1207. For five years after the death of Arthur in 1202, John was the only surviving male Angevin, and he was not getting any younger. However worrying for individual monarchs, it was not to prove unusual in young queens for the birth of their first child to be delayed, but then be followed rapidly by other children. This suggests that whatever the legal age of marriage, the menarche was later in the Middle Ages than today. Isabella went on to bear John a second son and three daughters.

It is perhaps hardly surprising that, given his family history, John was unable to sustain a happy married life. His several known bastards may have been born before his second marriage, but he was flagrantly unfaithful to his queen. He had a reputation for lechery, pursuing the wives and daughters of his nobles; certainly the sister of the earl of Warenne had a child by him. How accurate then is Matthew Paris's description of the queen as an incestuous and depraved woman, so notoriously guilty of adultery that the king gave orders for her lovers to be seized and throttled on her bed? It is hardly necessary to believe Paris's tale to accept that Isabella was generally regarded as an adulteress. It is hardly likely that such a story would be in circulation, even about an unpopular queen, without some behaviour on Isabella's part to give it credence. It seems that in 1212 the queen had been under a form of imprisonment at Gloucester. A writ was issued to Theoderic de Tyes 'to go to Gloucester with our lady queen and there keep her in the chamber where the lady Joanna (born 1210) had been nursed, til he heard further from the king'. Since Isabella did not, unlike her mother-in-law, dabble in politics, the confinement was presumably for some personal fault. The royal couple seem to have been reconciled the following year, when Isabella inherited Angoulême on the

Isabella of Angoulême, effigy in Fontevrault Abbey

death of her father. They visited her county in 1213, betrothing the infant Joanna to Hugh de Lusignan, son of the queen's former betrothed. When Prince Louis of France invaded England, the queen and the royal children were in the comparative safety of Gloucester, and when the news of the king's death reached them, the queen and William Marshal, earl of Pembroke, had young Henry, then aged nine, crowned in Gloucester Cathedral within a few days. His brother Richard was prudently sent to Ireland for safety.

The queen-mother was still young, but was given no role in the minority government of her son. Despite many precedents John had never named her regent during his absences abroad and Pembroke clearly intended to follow the late king's example. Isabella was obviously unpopular in England and any remarriage there would be fraught with political difficulties. Misliking the look of the future, she abandoned her children and went back to Angoulême. In 1220, still beautiful and only in her early thirties, she surprised everyone by marrying Hugh count of La Marche, son of her former betrothed and affianced to her own daughter. Although she had no intention of returning to England, Isabella wanted the income from her dower lands. The Council, angry that the queen had acted without their knowledge or consent, withheld it, but she held the trump card in the person of her small daughter. The Council wanted the princess Joanna returned to England as a bride for Alexander of Scotland to seal a peace treaty. No money, no princess. The Council capitulated. Henry III was to have difficulties with his mother and stepfather over many years. He was always generous to them but their behaviour was governed solely by greed and self-interest and they cheerfully transferred their loyalties to Louis IX when it suited them to do so. Isabella's letters to her son reveal her as greedy, arrogant and selfish, traits which her English children seem largely to have escaped, but which reveal themselves in many of her nine children by de Lusignan who, like their mother, regarded Henry as a meal ticket. While it is clear that Isabella was an unpleasant woman, it is difficult to authenticate many of the crimes attributed to her in France, including an attempt to poison Louis IX, but they indicated that public opinion was as hostile to her in France as in England. She finally found it expedient to retire to Fontevrault, where she died in 1246, the fifth Angevin to be buried there.

Queen Isabella was widowed in 1216 and very soon decided that her future lay in her own county of Angoulême rather than in the retired life of an English queen dowager. The Angevin heartlands of Normandy, Anjou and Maine had been won from her husband by Philip Augustus of France. The truce John had negotiated with France ran out in 1220 and was renewed for a further four years, but this period of grace was not spent in strengthening the defences of Poitou and Aquitaine. The feudal lords were untrustworthy and the communes, though preferring English to French rule, were reluctant to incur expense on defence; the Seneschal of Aquitaine was usually penniless and in debt. The defence of Poitou depended on the Lusignan family, whose loyalty could never be taken for granted. The marriage that John had arranged between his daughter Joanna and the son of Geoffrey de Lusignan, count of La Marche, was part of a long-term strategy to save Poitou and win back the lost provinces.

When she arrived back in Angoulême, Isabella realized how dangerous the situation really was. An early letter she wrote to her son soon after she returned to Angoulême has a note of genuine desperation in it and was aimed not so much at the young king but at his council. Without help from England she felt even Angoulême itself might be lost. She refers to lands that John had bequeathed her and later describes these as being the castles of Exeter, Rockingham and Niort, near Poitiers; the first two of these were in fact dower lands, and John's will makes no mention of any of them or the sum of 3,500 marks which his wife claimed he had bequeathed her. The details of the defences of Angoulême and the money required for them she left for the two members of her household, who had brought the letter, to explain in person. In the second letter, written to the Legate Pandulph, some of the problems which beset her are illustrated. In 1214 John had submitted to the papacy and ended a six-year interdict in England. In doing so he accepted the Pope's overlordship of the country and the appointment of a legate as his representative there. Pandulph was the second legate to come to England and he took up his position at the end of 1218. He was given the bishopric of Norwich and his position on the regency Council was very powerful. In this instance, the queen was seeking his intervention on her behalf with the Council which had acted against her interests in a dispute with a local Poitevin landowner, Bartholomew de Podio, and ordered the two leading men of the area, the Seneschal of Poitou, Sir Geoffrey de Neville, and Hugh de Lusignan, betrothed to her daughter, to support Podio also. All the locals regarded their long-term interests as lying with the French rather than the fast-crumbling Angevin empire. Eventually, so did Isabella.

To protect and defend her own county became her priority. If her son's kingdom could not or would not help then she was willing to consider abandoning the English connection. Her decision to remarry was announced in a letter to her son a year later. She set aside her daughter's betrothal and married Hugh de Lusignan herself. He had recently inherited the county of La Marche and whether or not he was really contemplating a French marriage in preference to the one arranged with the ten-year-old English princess Joanna, that is the excuse Isabella gave. She made much of her sacrifice for the sake of her son and his remaining French possessions, but in truth it suited her very well. The attitude she and her new husband were to take with her eldest son is set out clearly from the start. Since the queen had not sought the consent of the king and his council for her remarriage, she could be legally deprived of her dower. On the other hand, she held the trump card in the person of her young daughter and her price for returning Joanna to England is very clearly spelt out in the letter. Needless to say, her terms were eventually accepted.

Isabella, Queen of England, to her son, Henry III, c. 1218/19

To her dearest son, Henry, by the grace of God, the illustrious king of England, lord of Ireland, duke of Normandy and Aquitaine, count of Anjou, I Isabella, by the same grace of God, his humble mother, queen of England, always pray for your safety and good fortune.

Your Grace knows how often we have begged you that you should give us help and advice in our affairs, but so far you have done nothing. Therefore we attentively ask you again to despatch your advice quickly to us, but do not just gratify us with words. You can see that without your help and advice, we cannot rule over or defend our land. And if the truces made with the king of France were to be broken, this part of the country has much to fear. Even if we had nothing to fear from the king himself, we do indeed have such neighbours who are as much to be feared as the said king of France. So without delay you must formulate such a plan which will benefit this part of the country which is yours and ours; it is necessary that you do this to ensure that neither you nor we should lose our land through your failure to give any advice or help. We even beg you to act on our behalf, that we can have for the time being some part of those lands which our husband, your father, bequeathed to us. You know truly how much we owe him, but even if our husband had bequeathed nothing to us, you ought by right to give us aid from your resources, so that we can defend our land, on this your honour and advantage depend. Wherefore we are sending over to you Sir Geoffrey de Bodeville and Sir Waleran, entrusting to them many matters which cannot be set down in writing to you, and you can trust them in what they say to you on our behalf concerning the benefit to you and us.

(PRO SC 1/2/5, Latin. Shirley, vol. i, pp. 22–3.)

Isabella, Queen of England, to Pandulph, bishop-elect of Norwich, c. June 1219

Dearest father and lord Pandulph, by the grace of God, bishop-elect of Norwich, chamberlain of our lord the Pope and legate of the apostolic see, I Isabella, by the same grace, queen of England, lady of Ireland, duchess of Normandy and Aquitaine, and countess of Anjou, greetings.

You will know that we have offered to restore to Bartholomew de Podio, at the entreaty of our son, the king of England, and of his Council, in entirety all his land, his possessions and the rents he received before we came hither, with the exceptions of our castles, and also all his hostages, save for his two sons, whom we desire to hold in fair and fitting custody until we are without fear that he will seek to do us wrong, as he once sought to wrong the count of Augi and the other barons of the land to our despite. If he refused this offer of ours, we offered him the sure judgement of our court, but he totally rejected all this. We are very surprised that our son's Council should have instructed Sir Hugh de Lusignan and Sir Geoffrey de Neville, seneschal of Poitou, to support the said Bartholomew against us. Granted that the king our son, or his Council, does not order that we be attacked, nevertheless we know many who will trouble us on Bartholomew's behalf, and our son's Council should be aware lest it issues any instructions as a consequence of which we are driven away from our son's Council and affairs. It will be very serious if we are to be removed from our son's Council, You should know that we have been reliably informed that the aforesaid Bartholomew came into the presence of the king of France and made it known to him that our land was part of his fief; he asked that the king order us to reinstate him in his lands. I certainly think he does not regard our son the king of England very highly, in as much as Bartholomew himself, running hither and thither, is working to do harm to the king and his people. You should know that Sir Hugh de Lusignan and the seneschal are more eager to carry out this order which is against us, than they would be if ordered to help us. For if indeed they have been so ordered, until now they have done very little. So we ask you to have orders given, by a letter from the king our son, to Sir Hugh de Lusignan and the seneschal of Poitou to help us and to take counsel for our land and the land of our lord the king; please write back to us what your will is.

(PRO SC 1/3/181, Latin. Shirley, vol. i, pp. 32–4.)

Isabella, Queen of England, Countess of March and Angoulême, to her son, Henry III, 1220

To her dearest son, Henry, by the grace of God, king of England, lord of Ireland, duke of Normandy and Aquitaine, count of Anjou, Isabella, by the same grace queen of England, lady of Ireland, duchess of Normandy and Aquitaine, countess of Anjou and Angoulême, sends health and her maternal benediction

We hereby signify to you that when the Counts of March and Eu departed this life, the lord Hugh de Lusignan remained alone and without heirs in Poitou, and his friends would not permit that our daughter should be united to him in marriage, because her age is so tender, but counselled him to take a wife from whom he might speedily hope for an heir; and it was proposed that he should take a wife in France, which if he had done, all your land in Poitou and Gascony would be lost. We, therefore, seeing the great peril that might accrue if that marriage should take place, when our counsellors could give us no advice, ourselves married the said Hugh, count of March; and God knows that we did this rather for your benefit than our own. Wherefore we entreat you, as our dear son, that this thing may be pleasing to you, seeing it conduces greatly to the profit of you and yours; and we earnestly pray you that you will restore to him his lawful right, that is, Niort, the castles of Exeter and Rockingham, and 3500 marks, which your father, our former husband, bequeathed to us; and so, if it please you, deal with him, who is so powerful, that he may not remain against you, since he can serve you well – for he is well-disposed to serve you faithfully with all his power; and we are certain and undertake that he shall serve you well if you restore to him his rights, and, therefore, we advise that you take opportune counsel on these matters; and when it shall please you, you may send for our daughter, your sister, by a trusty messenger and your letters patent, and we will send her to you.

(PRO SC 1/3/182, Latin. Wood, vol. i, letter viii.)

ELEANOR OF PROVENCE, WIFE OF HENRY III

Like her mother-in-law, Isabella of Angoulême, Eleanor of Provence was not a popular queen consort, deservedly so, for she was often unwise. Unlike Isabella, however, she was a devoted and loving wife and mother, and her personal qualities form a considerable counterpoise to her public acts. Eleanor's marriage was another whose diplomatic end was the forging of an alliance in France to protect the southern part of the Angevin empire. Henry III, who had been king since he was nine, did not marry until he was twenty-nine, twice the age of his bride, who was the daughter of Raymond Berengar, count of Provence. She had four sisters, the eldest of whom, Margaret, was already queen to Louis IX. Berengar was renowned for his poverty as much as for his poetry and the beauty of his daughters. Although Henry asked for a dowry of 20,000 marks, he was willing to reduce the sum to as little as 3,000 marks, and it is quite possible that Henry took Eleanor dowerless. Yet the coronation provided for her was magnificent in the extreme. Henry and Eleanor were both lavish spenders, on their persons, their artistic patronage, their family and their charities. The coronation was an augury of things to come. In other ways, too, the couple seem to have been well-matched. They were both deeply pious, cultured and by no means unintelligent, but equally they both seem to have lacked a sense of the true responsibility of kingship, seeing England in terms of the money it could and should supply them with, and diplomacy purely in terms of their extended family. As a couple they were devoted, their life together a complete contrast to the debauchery of Henry's parents. The queen's ascendency over her husband was established early in the marriage and he never ceased to put her interests first. In return she provided a loving family life that had been so conspicuously missing from Henry's own childhood.

One of the causes of Eleanor's unpopularity in England was her family, in particular the brothers of her mother, Beatrice of Savoy, who saw the marriage of their niece to a wealthy king as providing great opportunities for their own advancement. Nor were they disappointed. Peter of Savoy received from Henry the honour (though not, as is sometimes stated, the earldom) of Richmond and land in London, where he proceeded to build the palace of 'Savoy'. The queen later purchased the palace for her younger son, Edmund of Lancaster. Boniface of Savoy was appointed to the see of Canterbury after Eleanor had written to the Pope, urging her uncle's case; together with their brother, William, bishop-elect of Provence, of whom Henry became deeply fond, the Savoyards became the king's chief counsellors. They were able men but their attitudes and outlook were not necessarily those of the English, and no wise king would have permitted them the powers they exercised in England. Their influence was further strengthened by the marriage of the queen's younger sister, Sanchia, to Henry's brother, Richard, earl of

Cornwall. Henry III's folly was underlined by the lack of welcome the brothers had received at the French court of their eldest niece. The problem was compounded by the welcome that the king extended to his Lusignan half-brothers when they were old enough to make their way to England. Henry's pockets were less capacious than they had been, but his brother William was made earl of Pembroke, and Aymer bishop of Winchester. The younger boys, Geoffrey and Guy did less well. So strong was English reaction to this misguided policy that no foreign queen was ever again permitted to retain fellow-countrymen of rank in her household or introduce her relatives to England. The issue of the queen's relatives was to remain dormant in English politics until the time of the first English queen consort.

The second cause of Eleanor's unpopularity sprang from her financial problems. She is the first queen for whom some study of her finances is possible. In the course of her marriage, from 1236 until she became a widow in 1272, she moved from a modest establishment and a financial role totally subordinate to her husband to an effective control over her extensive resources. One reason for the change was undoubtedly the very happy marriage she enjoyed, another was Henry III's belief in her abilities. Although she was assigned dower lands on her marriage, she did not receive income from them, let alone administer them; receipts continued to be paid to the king along with the rest of the issues of the royal demesne. Eleanor's income came from wardships, farms of shires and towns, issues from vacant bishoprics and similar sources. Gradually the system changed so that more and more came from wardships, where she was free to exploit the lands while she held them, and to make from them what she could over and above the sum for which they were assessed. Likewise, queen's gold, which at the beginning of her marriage was simply paid to the king who spent it on her behalf, gradually passed into the direct control of the queen and her officials. In 1268 her financial situation improved when her uncle, Peter of Savoy, bequeathed to her the honour of Richmond. She then exchanged it with the king for lands worth 800 marks p.a. so that the honour might be restored, with its earldom, to the duke of Brittany, husband of her daughter, Beatrice. The lands thus granted she was permitted to administer herself. Eleanor's expenditure always exceeded her income and she leaned heavily on the king for supplements. In 1272 she petitioned for, and received, wardships worth £1,000 p.a. to support her household when she was not with the king. She was often reduced to borrowing from foreign merchants and by the time Henry died her debts amounted to the spectacular sum of £20,000. To be fair to Eleanor, however, it must be emphasized that most of the debt was incurred from the high cost of maintaining her household in France between 1263 and 1265 and her continuous diplomatic activity on her husband's behalf. It was to repay her debts that she was permitted to retain her property for some years after she took the veil at Amesbury.

Henry III and Eleanor of Provence, boss in the north porch of Bridlington priory
(photo: Fred H. Crossley and Maurice H. Ridgway)

Eleanor's need for money led her into a number of practices unbecoming in a queen consort, however admirable in a businessman. The tolls of Queenhithe, one of the quays of London, had, as the name suggests, long formed part of a queen's income; Eleanor used her influence to ensure that almost all the vessels with valuable cargoes were unloaded there in preference to any of the other London quays. In 1253, when Henry appointed her regent on his departure for Gascony, she took advantage of her position to press the city for a considerable sum she claimed in queen's gold on large fines extorted from the citizens by the king, and for non-payment committed the two sheriffs to the Marshalsea. Queen's gold should have been levied only on voluntary fines. Such extortions on country estates might pass unnoticed by most of the country, but if committed in London ensured the maximum publicity. London took its revenge in 1263. An outbreak of mob violence so frightened the queen that she decided to leave the Tower, where she and the king were staying, and travel to Windsor by water and join her son Edward. Her barge was recognized and pelted with filth, the queen was insulted and forced to take refuge in the bishop of London's palace at St Paul's. Henry thereafter prudently removed her and their younger children to France before the outbreak of civil war. It is, however, the first and only time in our period when a queen was attacked by a mob of her husband's subjects, and her husband and son ensured that London paid dearly for it in the years that followed. Nor was it the end of the strained relationship between Eleanor and the capital. Shortly before his death, Henry granted his wife the custody of London Bridge for six years. Before the term expired, the citizens were forced to petition Edward I for relief because his mother was taking all the tolls and failing to keep the newly built bridge in an adequate state of repair.

An account of Eleanor's wardrobe expenses covering about eight years in the late 1250s and early 1260s gives some idea of how the queen's income was spent. The largest proportion, some £6,816, went on the running of her household. We do not know its exact size, but it probably numbered about 100 persons, all to be fed, clothed, waged and transported. Clothing her ladies cost the queen £180 11s 11d, and she spent £145 4s 4d on jewels, emeralds, pearls, sapphires and garnets for her own use. Unfortunately the category covering Eleanor's own clothes also includes the purchase of horses, saddlery and wax, but it totalled £1,691 12s 1d. The queen's official charity in offerings and alms came to £151 18s, but far the most interesting item of all was the huge sum of £4,017 10s 3d given by the queen in 'secret gifts and private alms'. Eleanor, like her husband, was extremely devout, but the period covered by the accounts was that of the baronial opposition to her husband that amounted almost to civil war, and it is highly likely that most of this money went to Henry's wavering political supporters at home and possible allies abroad.

Not all Eleanor's difficulties were the result of her extravagance. At the outset of the political troubles which were to develop into the Barons' War, she pawned her jewels to the Knights Templar to raise money for her husband. Her son Edward recovered them by the simple expedient of marching into the Temple and taking them, together with £10,000 to pay his troops. The queen then took her jewels to France where she pawned them again, this time to her sister, the queen of France. Eleanor and her younger children spent two years in France where, after the defeat of her husband at Lewes, she pledged her jewels and her credit to raise an army and equip a fleet to come to his aid. While her fleet remained wind-bound off the coast of France, Edward defeated his uncle, Simon de Montfort, earl of Leicester, at Evesham, and the queen was free to return home again. Neither Henry nor Eleanor were vindictive and no further blood was shed, but she brought with her the papal legate, Cardinal Ottobone, who solemnly excommunicated all the followers of the late earl of Leicester. This caused a London source, never favourable to the queen, to comment that she returned with the legate and made a great cursing.

Whatever Eleanor's faults as queen, her conduct as wife and mother was of the highest order. She bore Henry nine children, but only four survived to adulthood. Her daughters, Margaret, queen of Scotland, and Beatrice, duchess of Brittany, visited their parents as often as possible, just as Henry and Eleanor visited her own sister in France. Indeed, both Margaret and Beatrice died on visits to London, the queen of Scotland soon after her father's death and the duchess when she and the duke attended her brother Edward's coronation. Edward I was deeply attached to his mother and was considerably influenced by her. Her second son, Edmund, earl of Lancaster, was always a loyal supporter of his elder brother, never a political intriguer, and the solidarity of the family unit must in part be attributed to Eleanor.

On the death of King Henry in 1272 Eleanor began to contemplate retiring to the religious life. A number of earlier queens, notably Eleanor of Aquitaine and Berengaria of Navarre took up residence in a favoured abbey when they became widows, and early in the 1280s Eleanor went to live at Amesbury, a cell of the great Plantagenet abbey of Fontevrault. Unlike her predecessors, however, she wished to go one stage further and take the veil. She professed as a nun in 1284, and at her insistence, so too did two of her granddaughters, Edward's sixth daughter, Mary, and Eleanor of Brittany. The reason for the delay in entering Amesbury was that the queen needed papal dispensation from the vow of poverty. The income from her dower was required to pay off her debts, many dating from the period when she was raising forces for her husband in France and not the result of personal extravagance. Eleanor died at Amesbury in 1291, in the same year that saw the death of her son's queen, Eleanor of Castile.

The letter Queen Eleanor wrote to her husband in the spring of 1244 shows a markedly different attitude to her uncle, Boniface of Savoy, from that only a few years before. Boniface and his elder brother, Thomas, count of Savoy had arrived in England in 1241 and the subsequent death of Edmund Rich, Archbishop of Canterbury, furnished the king with an opportunity of providing for one of his wife's indigent relatives by conferring on him the primacy of England. The chronicler, Matthew Paris, claims that Eleanor wrote to the Pope herself urging the appointment for no other reason than Boniface's relationship to her. The candidate's unsuitability for high ecclesiastical office does not seem to have occurred to his pious proposers. The Pope accepted the proposal and Boniface held the primacy for nearly thirty years. The matter of the bishopric of Chichester arose on the death of the former bishop, Ralph Nevill, in February 1244. The Chapter had attempted to secure royal favour by electing the Archdeacon of Lewes, Robert Passelaw, a worldly and not very able courtier. Boniface and his suffragans had refused to accept him and had appointed the more suitable Richard Wich instead. In any dispute between the wishes of her lord the king and her uncle, Eleanor makes it quite clear where her loyalties lay. In this case Boniface was in the right and, in spite of royal pressure, he maintained his position and Wich remained bishop.

The tone of Eleanor's letter to Henry is a clear expression of the very loving nature of their marriage. Following it is a letter Eleanor wrote to her adored elder son Edward after he became king and it is included here simply to illustrate the informal and curiously modern chattiness of Eleanor's letter-writing style. The state of the air seems to have been a matter of constant concern to Eleanor; it is possible that she suffered from some form of bronchial complaint. In a later letter to Edward, describing herself as a humble novice, she says she has learned that he planned to take his son Edward north with him. 'We have doubts about his going', she writes, because when she goes north 'We cannot escape from being ill, from the bad air' and she recommends her grandson should 'have a place in the southern parts where there is good and temperate air and should not think of sojourning in the northern parts'.

Eleanor, Queen of England, to Henry III, between April 1244 and January 1245

Most excellent, most reverend King Henry, by the grace of God, the illustrious king of England, lord of Ireland, duke of Normandy and Aquitaine and count of Angoulême, his own consort, the most humble and devoted Eleanor, by the same grace of God, queen of England, greetings and obedient duty with all reverence. We inform your lordship that by the grace of God we and our children are safe and well, which we lovingly hope you are also with all our heart and soul. We also inform your royal majesty that a day past, the Archbishop of Canterbury elect sent his messengers to us with a letter. Through them he informed us that he had learned by the reports of some people, that we were angry with him because of what he had done in the matter of the diocese of Chichester; he begged that we would not be upset over this matter nor be turned against him. We in turn informed him through messengers carrying a letter from us that it was not surprising if we were turned against him, since he offended you in this matter, and he could in no way have our good wishes while he incurred your wrath. Having heard and learned this, he came to us in person, signifying to us that in the aforementioned and all other matters he would fulfil your wishes to the best of his powers. We advised him that if he wanted to assuage our indignation, then he would fulfil your wishes. For while you and he remained in discord, there was no way we would forego our own anger and indignation.

Therefore we beseech your most excellent lordship, with all possible affection, that you will deign to inform us often, if you so wish, of your state (pray God it be well and happy) and of what pleases your will. May your excellency prosper forever in the name of the Lord.

(Shirley, vol. i, p. 22–3, Latin.)

Eleanor, Queen-Dowager of England, to her son Edward I, 3 October (?1274–5)

Eleanor by the grace of God, queen of England, to our very dear son, Edward, by the same grace king of England, greeting and a mother's blessing. Know, dear sire, that we are most desirous to have good news of your health and how things have been with you since you left us. We are letting you know that we are in good health, thanks be to God. We have left Gillingham sooner than we expected, because of the noisomeness of the air, and the thick clouds of smoke which rise in the evenings and have come to Marlborough, arriving on the Friday after Michaelmas. Thanks be to God we are in good health, and we greatly desire to know the same of you. As well as this, we beg you will remember that we asked you at Wilton, that you will send us Sir John de Lovetoft and Sir Walter de Helyon, to have their advice about certain business that concerns us, and we beg you will send them to us as you promised. Command us at your will and pleasure, if it pleases you.
Greetings and we commend you to God. Given at Marlborough, the third day of October.

(PRO SC1/16/157, French.)

The next communication from Eleanor to Henry shown here is not in fact a letter but a more formal request relating to her dower. It was made in October 1272, just before Henry's death. Although Eleanor had been assigned dower lands at the time of her marriage, she had no right of income from them until she became a widow. Her household was financed by a combination of *ad hoc* payments and wardships granted her, and at this time, just before she was widowed, it was agreed that she should have wardships to the value of £1,000, the equivalent in value to her English dower lands and the full sum necessary to support her household. The petition is followed by a list of those holding wardships for her as trustees. It is dominated by ecclesiastics, and includes the bishops of Worcester and Lichfield, and the Chancellor, William de Merton, Archdeacon of Bath and elevated to the bishopric of Rochester two years later.

Eleanor, Queen of England, to Henry III, October 1272

The lady queen requests that whereas the king recently granted her custody of the lands and tenements lately held of him in chief by John de Grey with everything pertaining to that custody, worth three hundred pounds a year, in part sustenance of the upkeep of her household, he may grant to her in addition the custody of the lands and tenements which formerly belonged to the Percy family worth three hundred pounds yearly if it attains that sum per year etc. and the custody of the lands and tenements of Hugh the Fleming and other wards which are in his hand or which may happen to fall to the lord king up to the sum of four hundred pounds. In such a way the queen may have in total one thousand pounds worth of land towards the full upkeep of her household. The king is bound to provide clothing at will for the same. Should the abovesaid custodies not amount to the aforesaid sum of one thousand pounds, then the king will make it up from other sources. But if anything is left over and above that amount, then that will fall to the king.

(PRO SC1/16/207, Latin.)

When Henry went to Gascony in August 1253, he named his queen as co-regent with his brother, Richard, earl of Cornwall. The province had been under the authority of Henry's brother-in-law, Simon de Montfort, earl of Leicester, whose abilities had finally restored the authority of the English crown, but whose shabby treatment by the king had led to his resignation. Henry was left to carry on without him. His regents in England were given the unenviable task of raising yet more money. The need was presented as more urgent by the threat from Castile, whose king, Alphonso X, was planning to invade Gascony to make good his claim to it based on his descent from Eleanor, daughter of Henry II. In fact, Henry had already concluded a peace with Castile by arranging a marriage between his son Edward and Alphonso's half-sister, Eleanor. The response from the various sections of English society is graphically set out in the regents' letter. Rumours of the treaty had begun to surface, and the magnates were only prepared to offer their aid if there really was a Castilian invasion, and it was their personal service they offered rather than money. Other representatives of the laity were prepared to help only if the royal officers in the shires were ordered to maintain the provisions of Magna Carta. The earl marshal referred to was Walter, grandson of William Marshal, earl of Pembroke, while John de Balliol, married to a niece of William the Lion of Scotland, had just become the father of the man Edward I was to have crowned king of Scots.

Eleanor, Queen-Regent of England, and Richard, Earl of Cornwall, to Henry III,
13 February 1254

To their most excellent lord, the lord Henry, by God's grace, the illustrious king of England, lord of Ireland, duke of Normandy and Aquitaine, and count of Anjou, his most devoted consort Eleanor, by the same grace, queen of England, and his devoted and faithful Richard earl of Cornwall, send health with all reverence and honour.

Be it known to your revered lordship that the lords the earl marshall and John de Balliol, being hindered at sea by a contrary wind during twelve days, came to us in England on the Wednesday after the Purification of Blessed Mary last past [4 February].

We had been treating with your prelates and the magnates of your kingdom of England before the advent of the said Earl and John, on the quinzaines of St Hilary last past [27 January] about your subsidy, and after the arrival of the said earl and John, with certain of the aforesaid prelates and magnates, the archbishops and bishops answered us that if the King of Castile should come against you in Gascony each of them would assist you from his own property, so that you would be under perpetual obligations to them; but with regard to granting you an aid from their clergy, they could do nothing without the assent of the said clergy; nor do they believe that their clergy can be induced to give you any help, unless the tenth of clerical goods granted to you for the first year of the crusade, which should begin in the present year, might be relaxed at once by your letters patent, and the collection of the said tenth for the said crusade, for the two following years, might be put in respite up to the term of two years before your passage to the Holy Land; and they will give diligence and treat with the clergy submitted to them, to induce them to assist you according to that form with a tenth of their benefices, in case the King of Castile should attack you in Gascony; but at the departure of the bearer of these presents no subsidy had as yet been granted by the aforesaid clergy. Moreover, as we have elsewhere signified to you, if the King of Castile should come against you in Gascony, all the earls and barons of your kingdom, who are able to cross the sea, will come to you in Gascony, with all their power; but from the other laymen who do not sail over to you we do not think that we can obtain any help for your use, unless you write to your lieutenants in England firmly to maintain your great charters of liberties, and to let this be distinctly perceived by your letters to each sheriff of your kingdom, and publically proclaimed through each county of the said kingdom; since, by this means, they would be more strongly animated cheerfully to grant you aid; for many persons complain that the aforesaid charters are not kept by your sheriffs and other bailiffs as they ought to be kept. Be it known, therefore, to your lordship, that we shall hold a conference with the aforesaid clergy and laity at

Westminster, in the quinzaines of Passover next, about the aforesaid aid, and we supplicate your lordship that you will write us your good pleasure concerning these affairs with the utmost possible haste. For you will find us prepared and devoted, according to our power, to solicit the aforesaid aid for your use, and to do and procure all other things . . . which can contribute to your convenience and the increase of your honour. Given at Windsor, the 13th of February, in the thirty-eighth year of your reign.

(PRO SC 1/3/82, Latin. Wood, vol. i, letter xii.)

Despite the affection between the four sisters of Provence, there were still some areas of dispute between them and their respective husbands, chiefly over their inheritance in Provence itself. For some years after the death of their father the county was governed by Charles of Anjou, younger brother of Louis IX and husband of the third sister, Beatrice. It is therefore hardly surprising that the two 'English' sisters, Eleanor and Sanchia (who married Henry's younger brother, Richard, earl of Cornwall) attempted to keep a close watch over their interests. A number of Eleanor's letters are concerned with her Provençal affairs, asking various influential persons to bring pressure to bear on her behalf. The first is to the chancellor, who was to visit the French court and plead her case over the revenues of the county of Agenais with her brother-in-law, the king of France. Agenais had been held by Henry and Eleanor's son-in-law, John of Brittany, and when Henry restored him to the earldom of Richmond, he surrendered 1,200 marks p.a. for Agenais, which sum Henry granted to his wife for life.

The second is to her son, couched in the affectionate, chatty tone that characterizes all her letters to him, but nevertheless dealing with matters of importance both to her and to Edward as her heir. By the time of Henry III's death, both Beatrice and Sanchia were dead and Charles of Anjou had become king of Sicily. Until 1250 Sicily had been ruled by the Emperor Frederick II of Germany, who had married Henry III's sister, Isabella, and who was an implacable opponent of the papacy. On his death, rule passed to his illegitimate son Manfred. Henry III, urged on by his wife, accepted the offer of the throne of Sicily for his second son, Edmund, from the Pope and demanded large sums of money from the English barons and clergy to finance the adventure. Needless to say, it failed to achieve its purpose and and left Henry heavily in debt. The throne eventually went to Charles of Anjou, who had successfully governed Provence. The king of Germany in 1279 was Rudolph of Hapsburg, and while the marriage referred to did not in fact take place, Edward I did indeed write to him, asking him to facilitate the business of his mother in Provence, assuring him that her concerns were as dear to him as his own.

Eleanor, Queen-Dowager of England, to the Chancellor, William de Merton, 17 May (1273)

Eleanor by the grace of God, queen of England, Lady of Ireland, Duchess of Aquitaine, to her discreet and well-beloved servant in Christ Sir William de Merton chancellor to the king, greetings.

Out of the great love and affection which you bear chiefly towards the king and to a lesser extent towards us, we beg you to act on our behalf at the court of the illustrious king of France at this coming Pentecost regarding matters of law and fact concerning our land in the Agenais. We do not have to hand the documents concerning the said business, and so we depend upon you to pursue the matter on our behalf as carefully and prudently as possible. Relying on your love for us, we ask you to bring to light those malicious errors against our eldest son and ourselves in the said petition concerning the land. Lest, we being unwary and unskilled in these matters, the force of law should run against us. Certain letters of our lord the King have ordained that we should receive from the King of France a certain sum of money formerly collected by our beloved son John Duke of Brittany in exchange for a piece of land in Richmond under the King's seal patent. We ask you without delay to sort out this matter freeing the honour of our lord the King and ourselves on receipt of these presents. For which we will evermore be in your debt.

Given at Pevensey on 17 May.

(PRO SC 1/7/98, Latin.)

Eleanor, Queen-Dowager of England, to her son, Edward I, c. 1279

Eleanor, by God's grace queen of England, to our dear son Edward, by the same grace king of England, health and our blessing.

Know, sweet son, that we have understood that a marriage is in agitation between the son of the King of Sicily and the daughter of the King of Germany; and, if this alliance is made, we may well be disturbed in the right that we have to the fourth part of Provence, which thing would be great damage to us, and this damage would be both ours and yours. Wherefore we pray and require you, that you will specially write to the aforesaid king, that since Provence is held from the empire, and his dignity demands that he should have right done to us about it, he will regard the right that we have, and cause us to hold it. Of this thing we especially require you, and we commend you to God.

(PRO SC 1/16/180, French. Wood, vol. i, letter xvii.)

Eleanor, Queen-Dowager of England, to her son, Edward I, 8 July 1282

Eleanor, by the grace of God, queen of England, to our dear son the king, health and our blessing.

We have sent your prayer to the king of France, that he may lend his aid in purchasing our share of the land of Provence. We have done the letter for you which you sent to us, and we pray you to hear it read, and if it please you, have it sealed; and if not, that you would be pleased to command it to be amended, and sent forthwith to your aunt, my lady of France. We also entreat you that you would send to mestre Bonet, your clerk, that he would show and advance this request in the court of France as much as he can. We commend you to God.

Given at Waltham, 8th day of July 1282.

(*Foedera, vol. II, p. 207, translated, Strickland, vol. 1, p. 28.*)

In 1282, Eleanor wrote to her son on behalf of her son-in-law, John, duke of Brittany, who wanted permission for Sir Nicholas de Stapleton to act on his behalf in England. The king was campaigning in Wales, and Brittany's seneschal could not spare the time to go to the king in person. John of Brittany had married Eleanor's second daughter, Beatrice, in 1260, and she bore him six children. She died in London in March 1275 a few days after the coronation of her brother which she and her husband had been attending. Eleanor and King Edward remained in close and affectionate contact with the duke, as this letter witnesses. The earldom of Richmond had been held by the dukes of Brittany for generations and Henry III also granted his son-in-law the honour and rape of Hastings, so John certainly needed an administrator for his English lands. He mortgaged some of the Richmond lands for 2,000 marks so that he could go on crusade with his brother-in-law, Prince Edward, in 1269.

Eleanor, Queen-Dowager of England, to her son, Edward I, 8 October 1282

Eleanor by the grace of God, Queen of England, to the king our son, greetings and our blessing.

John of Brittany, our son, is in foreign parts and has commended his needs to us as his mother and to you as his lord. We are writing to you now because our knight Jean de Maure, his seneschal in England, is in haste to go to Dover to get news of his lord.

We pray and request your permission for our knight Sir Nicholas de Stapleton to attend to his needs in this country and ask that you order him by your letter that he attend to it, for he would not do it without your explicit command.

We ask this so that with your letters he will be able to act as attorney in all matters, just as you granted to Sire Dreu. And please excuse Sir Jean de Maure for not having taken his leave of you at his departure; he could not do this as he was in haste. We commend you to God.

(Foedera, vol. ii, p. 221, French.)

Eleanor was a kind and warm-hearted person, and the two following letters show her writing on behalf of others. She took the veil at Amesbury in 1284; it was a cell of the great Plantagenet abbey of Fontevrault, whose abbess was not above using her most powerful votaress to implore influence in high places to protect the abbey's possessions. The second letter is written solely in response to a plea from a mother, that Eleanor, herself one of the best of mothers, could not resist.

Eleanor, Queen-Dowager of England, to her son, Edward I, between 1286 and 1291

To the most noble prince and our dearest son, Edward, by God's grace king of England, lord of Ireland and duke of Guienne, Eleanor, humble nun of the order of Fontevrault of the convent of Amesbury, health and our blessing. Sweetest son, our abbess of Fontevrault has prayed us that we would entreat the King of Sicily to guard and preserve the franchises of her house, which some people wish to damage. And, because we know well that he will do much more for your prayer than for ours, for you have better deserved it, we pray you, good son, that for love of us you will request and especially require this thing from him; and that he would command that the things which the abbess holds in his lordship may be in his protection and guard, and that neither she nor hers may be molested or grieved. Good son, if it please you, command that the billet be hastily delivered. We wish you health in the sweet Jesus, to whom we commend you.

(PRO SC 1/16/156, French. Wood, vol. i, letter xx.)

Eleanor, Queen-Dowager of England, to her son, Edward I, between 1286 and 1291

To the most noble prince and her very dear son, Edward, by God's grace king of England, lord of Ireland and duke of Aquitaine, Eleanor, humble nun of the order of Fontevrault, of the convent of Amesbury, wishes health and her blessing.

Sweetest son, we know well how great is the desire that a mother has to see her child when she has been long away from him, and that dame Margaret de Nevile, companion of Master John Giffard, has not seen for a long time past her child, who is in the keeping of dame Margaret de Weyland, and has a great desire to see him. We pray you, sweetest son, that you will command and pray the aforesaid Margaret de Weyland, that she will suffer that the mother may have the solace of her child for some time, after her desire. Dearest son, we commend you to God. Given at Amesbury, the 4th day of March.

(PRO SC 1/16/151, French. Wood, vol. i, letter xxi.)

The Plantagenet Queens

ELEANOR OF CASTILE, FIRST WIFE OF EDWARD I

Eleanor, daughter of Ferdinand III of Castile and his second wife, Joanna, countess of Ponthieu, was married to the future Edward I as the result of a peace treaty between Henry III and her half-brother, Alphonso X of Castile. The couple were married at Burgos in 1254, the prince being fifteen and Eleanor a year or so younger. Eleanor was the last royal bride chosen with a view to protecting English interests in southern France. Her dowry, however, was the county of Ponthieu in northern France which in 1279 she inherited from her mother. Eleanor of Castile was like her mother-in-law only in name. Whereas Eleanor of Provence was extravagant and her view of affairs totally family-orientated, the younger Eleanor possessed financial acumen, showed comparatively little concern over her numerous offspring and had wide-ranging interests. Although not of Eleanor of Aquitaine's stature, some of the earlier queen's steel seems to have descended to her great, great granddaughter. Eleanor and Edward married young and their union was clearly a very happy one. The queen's vigour, her love of travel and new experiences made her an ideal wife for Edward. Their relationship was cemented during their early, childless years, but even later, despite almost constant child-bearing, Eleanor went everywhere with the king, even to the Holy Land (their daughter Joan was born in Acre), and the only time they were parted for any period was during the months when Edward was a prisoner of Simon de Montfort. The exact number of their children is a matter of some dispute, but it was at least thirteen and may have been as high as sixteen. Their three eldest sons, John, Henry and Alphonso, were each in turn heir to the throne and died at the ages of five, seven and ten respectively, the first two while their parents were on crusade. Only their youngest son, the last of their children, Edward of Carnarvon, survived to adulthood, as did five of their daughters.

At the time of his son's marriage, Henry III settled on him the Angevin possessions in southern France and Edward and Eleanor took up residence there, where they remained until 1260, when the political situation brought Edward back to England. As merely the wife of the Lord Edward, who did not bear her first son until 1266, Eleanor lived quietly and in obscurity until the defeat of the baronial opposition to her father-in-law. In 1269 the prince decided to take the cross and accompany his uncle, Louis IX, to the Holy Land. The king of France died in Tunis but Edward continued to Syria where he had some success campaigning. While at Acre, Edward was the victim of an attempted assassination, and an apochryphal story tells of Eleanor courageously sucking poison from the wound, but a more likely version of events is the one that describes an hysterical princess being carried forcibly from the room by Edward's close friend, John de Vesci, so that her husband could be operated on. He took a long time to recover, and always attributed his final recovery to his wife's devoted nursing. On their return journey they learned in Sicily of the deaths of their two sons and of King Henry, but it was over a year before they returned to England, travelling as they did via Rome and Paris, where for the first time an English king did homage to the French king for his Gascon possessions.

A large number of Eleanor of Provence's personal letters have survived, giving a vivid insight into the essentially kind nature of that queen, but there is comparatively little of a similar nature to throw light on her daughter-in-law's thoughts and emotions. As a person, Eleanor remains remote, best known for the Crosses erected in her memory by a grieving husband. Described by one contemporary chronicler as 'a pious, modest and merciful lady, a lover of all English people and a support for the whole realm', recent research has painted a less appealing picture of the queen in her capacity as landowner (see pp. 10–11). Eleanor's official correspondents included bishops and earls and suggest that she played some role in public affairs. That her influence on the king was considerable cannot be in doubt, but the marriage of their minds means that there were few overt signs of it. Despite all her apparent ability and strength of character, Eleanor would never have been able to dominate Edward as her mother-in-law had dominated Henry III. Edward was far less willing to allow a female even titular control of affairs. Eleanor never acted as regent for her husband, partly at least because she always travelled abroad with him, but when he made his will at Acre, he did not leave the guardianship of his lands and his children to his wife, but to his friend and brother-in-law, John of Brittany. Henry III, in contrast, appointed his queen regent of England in the only will he made. Since his heir was abroad at the time of his death, this was not an empty role.

This attitude extended itself to domestic affairs. At the time of her marriage, Eleanor of Castile's dower was set at £1,000 in the event of her husband's death and she had her own wardrobe, but it was subordinate to her husband's, whose clerks moved freely from his wardrobe to that of his wife and back again. As the wife of the Lord Edward, Eleanor's household was comparatively small, consisting only of a steward, a keeper of the wardrobe, a knight and several ladies, together with the usual servants. A roll of robes for her household, dating from 1285–6, when she was queen, excludes her officials and the ladies but is comprehensive for the servants, all of whom are named. They include two cooks, a butler, chamberlain, saucer, tailor, huntsman and coachman and twenty-three valets who were divided between the five household departments, the wardrobe, the chamber, the robes, the pantry and butlery and the kitchen. There was also a messenger and two keepers of hounds. In many ways the most striking feature of the list is the large number of men responsible for the transportation of the household: eight carters and twenty-four sumptermen. The itinerant nature of court life meant a positive army of carts, sumpter horses and riding horses had to be fed, cared for, repaired and maintained. Although Eleanor spent periods at Windsor, Caernarfon and her own favourite castles of Leeds and Guildford, for much of the time the queen's household was regularly on the move alongside that of the king. From the presence of hawks and hounds in her own household, it is clear that Eleanor was a keen huntswoman, but she was equally fond of music and books, particularly the French romances of her day. She employed two clerks to copy books for her and a painter to illuminate them. She also commissioned a translation of Vegetius' work on the art of war for her husband. Not all her reading was light because in 1290 she corresponded with an Oxford scholar about one of her books, and Geoffrey de Aspall, keeper of her wardrobe, was a noted scholar of Aristotle. When Edward was presented with a chessboard and men of jasper and crystal, he gave it to his wife. Since we know that Edward played chess, presumably Eleanor did also. Her brother Alphonso wrote an important chess manual. The queen's purchase of a set of writing tablets for her eldest daughter is a strong indication that, rare as it was in laywomen, she herself could write and saw that her daughters were taught also. Her concern for her daughters extended to objecting strongly that her daughter Eleanor was too young to marry at thirteen (the age at which the queen herself was married), an argument which she won. She also protested at her mother-in-law's desire to have her daughter, Mary, sent to Amesbury at the age of six.

It was not until about ten years after her marriage that Eleanor was granted any lands. In 1275 she was guaranteed dower lands of £4,500, half of which were in Gascony. The income from these were obviously less secure than that from English lands and there is clear evidence that Eleanor had already embarked on a campaign to acquire further lands in England, a campaign in which her husband was an approving partner. In both the aquisition of these new lands and their subsequent administration the queen forfeited the good opinion of her husband's subjects. One favoured means was through debts owed to Jews. Any fines paid by Jews in queen's gold were often settled by selling on the debts owed them by Christians to the queen herself. Eleanor was then free to foreclose on lands pledged to secure the original loan or hold them in reversion, with the original owner retaining only a life interest. If the debts were paid off, the queen used the money to purchase lands. Her behaviour led the Archbishop of Canterbury, John Pecham, to write a strong letter of correction, telling her that her use of Jewish debts to acquire land amounted to usury and mortal sin. The queen's reaction to the letter is unrecorded. Lands she

Detail of a gilt-bronze effigy of Eleanor of Castile in Westminster Abbey by William Torel, *c.* 1291

purchased or sought to acquire were always close to those allocated her in dower. In supporting and facilitating his wife's land dealings, the king was able to supplement her income without diminishing the Crown's estates. During Eleanor's lifetime there were complaints about the behaviour of her officials, and even when known to her, little was done to correct it. It was only on her deathbed that she asked for any wrongs committed in her name to be sought out and corrected.

Although so little is known about Eleanor personally, she clearly had the character necessary to make Edward happy, echoing the deep attachment of his parents to each other. Her importance to the king is illustrated by the deterioration of his character after her death in 1291. With his youngest son apparently surviving when his brothers had died (young Edward was fifteen), Edward saw no need to remarry and had no wish to replace Eleanor. He remained a widower for eight years and it was only diplomatic considerations which made him change his state. In 1294 war broke out with France, after Philip IV confiscated Gascony, and continued until 1297. The war was extremely costly for both countries and Edward sought allies in the duke of Brabant and the German king, both of whom were paid substantial subsidies for little return. English forces held on bravely in Gascony but an invasion of France from the north planned by Edward for 1297 failed to become reality and, with his financial resources exhausted, Edward was forced to negotiate a peace. The outward and visible signs of the peace were to be two royal marriages: the sixty-year-old king to Philip's sister, Margaret, and his heir, Edward, to Philip's only daughter, Isabella.

The first of Eleanor of Castile's letters, written well before she became queen, and when she can have had very little control over the properties herself, shows how very detailed her knowledge and interests were. John of London was one of her own officers and John de Kirkeby was at the time keeper of the rolls of Chancery and thus responsible for the records of all lands in the Crown's possession, either permanently or temporarily. He was one of Edward I's most trusted financial officials and became treasurer of England in 1284 and bishop of Ely two years after that. The bishop of Bath and Wells, Walter Giffard, was Chancellor at the time Eleanor was writing. The fear that she expresses this early in her marriage that she might be thought covetous is quite startling, for the contemporary rhyme which accuses her of just that (quoted on p. 10), is somewhat later in date. None the less, although Eleanor held the manor of Barwick for just three weeks, in that time her officials managed to collect the Michaelmas rents for a whole quarter. Knowing that she must give up Barwick, she showed a detailed knowledge of nearby properties that might suit her instead. The letter she wrote to Kirkeby himself, nearly twenty years later, shows that her interest in lands and rights had certainly not lessened, though the habit of leaving the details of any important business to be explained by the clerk or other official who carried the letter means that the finer points of her proposed purchase of Roger Clifford's Irish lands are not given.

Eleanor of Castile to John of London (c. 1265)

Eleanor, consort of lord Edward, to her loyal and faithful Sir John of London, health and good love.

Know that our lord the king gave us the other day the manor of Berewic with its appurtenances, at the solicitation of Sir Roger de Leyburn, and because it is appurtenant to the guardianship of Cantilupe, my lord has given it to another, so that nothing of it is remitted to us, but there is another manor close by in the county of Somerset, which is at the town of Heselbere, which belonged to Sir William the Marshal, who is dead and held it of the king in chief. Wherefore we would desire that you should ask of Sir John de Kyrkbi if the guardianship of that manor is granted, and if it is not, then that you should pray Sir Roger de Leyburn and the Bishop of Bath on our behalf that they should procure from our lord the king that he grant us the manor until the coming of age of the heir of Sir William. And, if it is given, there is another manor in the county of Dorset which is called Gerente, which belonged to Sir William de Keenes, who is dead, and he held it in chief of the king, wherefore we would that if we cannot have the other, you should pray them on our behalf that these should apply to the king to allow us this one; the manor of Heselbere is worth less. And if neither, pray Sir Roger in this way. Tell him that the manor of Berewic that the king gave us at his suggestion has been taken from us, for this will tend to make us seem less covetous; and say the same to the bishop of Bath. And if the letters which you have concerning it can profit nothing for this affair, give them to the bearer of this letter, for he will carry them to Walter of Kent, our clerk. Be careful to dispatch this affair, for it will be to our profit, and so suitably procure the affair that they shall not set it down to covetousness. Farewell.

(French. Shirley, vol. ii, letter dcxlvii.)

Eleanor, Queen of England, to Sir John de Kirkeby, 16 February (1283)

Eleanor by the grace of God, Queen of England, lady of Ireland and Duchess of Aquitaine, to her beloved clerk, Sir J. de Kirkeby, greetings.

This concerns lands and tenements held by Sir Roger de Clifford in Ireland to be repaired by him for King H. himself. The bearer of these presents R. De Coyton, our beloved clerk, has been sent to deal with this business. He [Clifford] asks that our aforesaid clerk may give you a fuller explanation as to how best to deal with this business. Dated at Rhuddlan on 16 February under our privy seal.

(PRO SC 1/10/50, Latin.)

The friendly and affectionate tone of the following letter from the queen to the chancellor is explained by the fact that Robert Burnell had been her husband's chancellor before he succeeded to the throne and was therefore an old and trusted advisor, who had a considerable influence over King Edward. Burnell was at this time archdeacon of York and held the office of Chancellor of England until his death in 1292. In this instance Eleanor was writing on behalf of a servant of Constance of Bearn, widow of Richard, earl of Cornwall's son, Henry. Henry had been murdered by the sons of Simon de Montfort in Italy on his return journey from the Holy Land. Constance's father, Gaston de Bearn was one of Henry III's more troublesome Gascon subjects, and on being widowed Constance had returned to her own country. She still, however, had dower lands in England.

Eleanor, Queen of England, to Robert Burnell, Chancellor, between 1274 and 1279

Eleanor, by God's grace queen of England, lady of Ireland, and duchess of Aquitaine, to lord Robert Burnell, sends loving greeting.
We require and affectionately entreat you to give counsel and assistance in this affair, that the transgression injuriously committed against the bearer of these presents, the servant of the lady Constance our cousin, which Master John Clarell will show you, may be reasonably redressed. For the confidence which we have in your benevolence is the cause why we so often direct to you our prayers on behalf of our friends. And do you for love of us give such diligence in this affair, that we may henceforth be bound to you by special favour. Given at Guildford, 14th day of October.

(PRO SC 1/22/29, Latin. Wood, vol. i, letter xv.)

The following letter to the sheriff of Northumberland was written on behalf of the queen's cousin, Isabel de Beaumont (daughter of Eleanor's paternal aunt, Berengaria of Castile), who had married John, Lord Vesci, one of the king's dearest friends and companion in arms. John had died in February 1289 and had been succeeded by his brother, William. The manor of Sprouston was in Roxburghshire and it was simply a matter of convenience that Sir Richard Knout, one of the king's most northerly officials, was involved. It turned out, however, to be far from convenient for the unfortunate sheriff. Armed with a safe-conduct he arrived in Scotland to carry out Queen Eleanor's request only to be arrested and imprisoned by the constable of Roxburgh. By the time he was eventually released he claimed damages of £10,000 for being prevented from carrying out his duties as sheriff and £2,000 for the disgrace of imprisonment.

Eleanor, Queen of England, to Sir Richard Knout, 1289

Eleanor, by the grace of God, queen of England, lady of Ireland and duchess of Aquitaine, to her dear friend in God, Richard Knout, sheriff of Northumberland, greetings and good love.

Whereas our dear friend in God, Sir William de Vesci, wishes to endow our dear cousin, the lady Isabel, late the wife of lord John de Vesci, with his manor of Sprouston in Scotland, and we have heard that the law and custom of that country is such that she should have the moiety under the name of dower; we therefore pray you that, out of love towards us, you would yourself go thither, along with the bailiff of our cousin aforesaid, and would survey the things above mentioned; and what she shall have, the third part or the half, according to the usages of the country. We require you faithfully to take the trouble, to the utmost of your power and skill, to see that she has her full share therein, so that she be no loser in anything from want of advice or help of friends. And should it so happen that you yourself, in consequence of some reasonable cause or hindrance, cannot go thither to prosecute the business aforesaid, we pray you to send thither some one on your part along with the bailiff aforesaid, who can sufficiently know and advance the affair in the best and most profitable manner possible for the aforesaid lady, according to the law and usages of the country, as we have stated already. And herein do so much, out of love to us and for our request, that the aforesaid lady may congratulate herself upon the assistance and advice which you employ therein. We are already especially beholden to you, and hereafter we shall be inclined to do whatever may be pleasing to you.

We commit you, sir, to God's keeping. Given at Westminster, the 30th of December, under our privy seal.

(PRO SC 1/30/50, French. Stevenson, vol. i, p. 115.)

MARGARET OF FRANCE, SECOND WIFE OF EDWARD I

Margaret was the first daughter of the French royal house to become queen of England. Although the future Richard I had been betrothed for years to a French princess, the marriage had never taken place; nor had any English princess ever become queen of France. English kings hitherto had defined their relations with their fellow monarchs in terms of securing allies in southern France against them, the better to protect their Gascon territories.

Margaret was married to Edward I in 1299 at Canterbury; she was twenty and the king sixty. The new queen seems to have been a pious, good and gentle woman, and no doubt proved a comfort to Edward's old age, but she has been largely ignored by historians. Her impact upon her contemporaries was somewhat greater, for she seems frequently to have used the queen's prerogative to intercede with the king on behalf of his subjects. Chief of these was her stepson, the prince of Wales, who was not on good terms with his father. Prince Edward referred to her as 'our dear mother' and addressed her as 'very dear lady', and there seems little doubt that for him she did indeed fill the long empty role of mother. She promoted a reconciliation between him and the king, though she could not, if indeed she tried, persuade her husband to allow Piers Gaveston to rejoin his son's household. She rescued the city of Winchester from the king's wrath after it allowed a hostage to escape, and among countless other kindnesses she prevailed upon the king to order the treasurer to remit the debt of her good friend, Margaret, widow of Robert Howard. The goldsmith Godfrey de Coigners, who had committed the heinous crime of making the crown for the coronation of Edward's enemy, Robert the Bruce, as king of Scots, was pardoned solely at the intercession of 'our dearest consort'. Margaret herself was never, in fact, crowned, since very soon after her wedding the king was forced to leave London for Scotland, but Edward had two crowns made for her, one a gold circlet, costing £22 10s and the other a jewelled state crown for which the goldsmith, Thomas de Frowick, charged over £440. She spent the first months of her marriage in residence at the Tower, but in later years she accompanied her husband north in much the same way that Eleanor had, and was with him when he died at Burgh-on-Sands. She bore the king two healthy sons, Thomas of Brotherton, later earl of Norfolk and ancestor of the house of Howard, and Edmund of Woodstock, later earl of Kent, whose daughter, Joan, was to marry the Black Prince. A daughter, named Eleanor, after Edward's first queen, died as a small child.

A little is known of the queen's personal tastes and habits: she seems to have been fond of music and employed a number of minstrels, chief of whom was Guy of the Psaltery, who was paid the generous salary of 28s p.a. and had the use of three horses when the queen's court was travelling. She was also very fond of hunting and the story goes that while staying at Cawood in Yorkshire, while the king was in the north, she occupied her time hunting in Wharfedale even while in an advanced state of pregnancy. The inevitable happened and the queen's eldest son, Thomas, was born in the village of Brotherton, the nearest place in which she was able to find refuge.

The treaty of Montreuil agreed that Margaret's marriage portion should be the equivalent of £15,000, a sum bequeathed her by her father Philip III, and Edward settled on her a dower of £4,500. Despite the fact that the crown's resources were drained through war, he later increased this to £5,000. Both the two previous queens had been dowered to roughly this amount and indeed it was to become the accepted size of the queen's dower throughout the fourteenth century. The country had been without a queen for eight years and all the traditional dower lands were thus available. These lands, which included the towns of Marlborough, Cambridge,

Detail of the statue of Margaret of France, Lincoln Cathedral

Southampton, Gloucester, Worcester and Oxford, several manors and the New Forest, were all specified at the time of Margaret's marriage in a way that was quite unusual, since most young queens had to wait until the death of a queen-dowager. Marlborough, which was to become her favourite residence, had belonged to her husband's mother, so too, had Gloucester, and indeed most had been held by Eleanor of Provence, while a few, like Leeds, had been in the possession of Eleanor of Castile. In 1317, when civil war seemed imminent, Margaret surrendered to her stepson the strategically important castles of Berkhamsted, Odiham, Gloucester and Leeds. As in the case of her predecessor, Margaret's financial affairs were kept largely under the control of her husband, and many persons formerly in Eleanor's service passed into that of Margaret's.

Although widowed in her twenties, Margaret made no attempt to remarry, but retired to her dower castle of Marlborough, where she died in 1317 at the early age of thirty-six. Her will left her two sons as joint heirs to her goods and chattels, and co-executors. The king empowered his half-brothers to collect all monies owing to her and to pay all her debts, but the troubles of his reign meant that not all her obligations were discharged, and in 1335 Thomas of Brotherton had to petition Parliament for the king to order the payment of her outstanding debts.

Comparatively few letters of Queen Margaret have survived, and none of them have before been printed, a reflection perhaps of the general lack of interest in her; but, equally, none of them shed any real light on her personality. The first two included here relate to a case of trespass in one of the queen's parks, Camel in Somerset. The two men accused, Sir Alexander Cheverel and Roger Parker, were with the king in Scotland, but their case was ordered to be heard before a commission of oyer and terminer led by Aymer de Valence, Sir Hugh Despenser and Sir Henry Spigurnel. Aymer de Valence, later created earl of Pembroke, was the son of Henry III's half-brother, William de Valence, and was a friend and companion in arms of his cousin, Edward I, while Hugh Despenser was to become a favourite of the future king, Edward II. At Aymer's request the queen wrote to the chancellor, asking that there be a postponement so that the absence of the accused would not be held against them. In 1303 William Greenfield, dean of Chichester, had held the office of chancellor for a year; he was elevated to the archbishopric of York in 1304. A little later Margaret was able to write again to the chancellor informing him that one of the two, Roger Parker, had paid his fine for the trespass and no further action should be taken against him; the wardrobe to which she refers was the main financial department of her household. Both the queen's letters were written from Tynemouth, Northumberland, where she stayed in safety while the king was in Scotland.

Margaret, Queen of England, to William Greenfield, Chancellor, 16 September 1303 or 1304

Margaret, by the grace of God, Queen of England, Lady of Ireland and Duchess of Aquitaine, to our dear clerk, Master William de Grenefield, Chancellor of our very dear lord the King, greeting and good love.

Because we have granted, at the request of our dear cousin, Sir Aymer de Valence, that the exigence [writ] which is running upon Sir Alexander Cheverel and Roger Parker (who remain in the service of our said lord the king in Scotland) in the county of Somerset by the order delivered to the sheriff of the same place by our said cousin, Sir Hugh le Despenser and Sir Henry le Spigurnel, justices assigned to hear and determine the trespass which was committed against our said lord the king and against ourself in our park of Camel, should be adjourned until the feast of St Hilary next coming [i.e. January], we command and request you that you hereupon make the said Sir Alexander and Roger have our lord the king's writ to the aforesaid sheriff in due manner, so that they in the meantime do not incur damage or danger by it for this reason. Our Lord protect you.

Given at Teignmouth, the 16th day of September.

(PRO SC 1/28/86, French.)

Margaret, Queen of England, to William Greenfield, Chancellor, 10 October 1303 or 1304

Margaret, by the grace of God, queen of England, Lady of Ireland and Duchess of Aquitaine, to our dear clerk, William de Grenefield, Chancellor of our very dear lord the King, greeting and good love.

Because Roger le Parker, who has recently done right concerning the trespass committed in our park of Camel, has paid to us into our Wardrobe his fine which he made for us, for this reason we request and command you that you hereupon cause him to have writs of our said lord the King to the sheriff of Somerset, that he should suffer him to be quit of all manner of exigences and other demands that he made against him by reason of the before mentioned trespass. Our Lord protect you.

Given at Teignmouth, the 10th day of October.

(PRO SC 1/28/87, French.)

Both the next two letters relate to Margaret's financial affairs and the collection of money due to her. The first, rather incoherent in its style, was addressed to the chancellor, William Hamilton, dean of York, and relates to what seems rather a small sum, 30 or 40 marks, with which to trouble the king's senior official. The second, to the archbishop, concerned a rather more serious matter. Hailes, the Cistercian abbey founded by Richard, earl of Cornwall, was in Gloucestershire, where the queen held land. The abbey farmed the royal manor of Lechlade for £100 p.a. and Edward I had granted £50 of that to his wife. Edward II, ignoring his stepmother's claims, had granted the whole sum to Piers Gaveston. On Piers' death, Edward was prepared to honour his father's grant and issued a mandate to the abbot to pay it. Why the abbot was still withholding the due rent is obscure, but the queen very properly referred the matter to a Church court, while reminding the archbishop that her stepson the king had commended her affairs to his concern. Walter Reynolds, bishop of Worcester, had just been rewarded with the primacy after a long period in royal service, first as keeper of the wardrobe to Edward II as Prince of Wales, then as the new king's treasurer and finally as chancellor from 1310 until late in 1314.

Margaret, Queen of England, to the Chancellor, William Hamilton, 7 April 1306

Margaret by the grace of God, Queen of England, Lady of Ireland and Duchess of Aquitaine to our beloved clerk, William de Hemelton chancellor of our lord the king greetings and our true love. In view of the fact that we are due to receive from our clerks the sum of 30 or 40 marks (of which we would have quick delivery) as an advance from the Holy Church, we beg and pray you, as quickly as possible lest any ill befall us, as it is in the gift of the king, that you make this known but do nothing in the matter until we know of it, for love of us. May the Lord keep you. Given at Wolvesey on 7 April.

(PRO SC 1/25/201, French.)

Margaret, Queen-Dowager of England, to Walter Reynolds,
Archbishop of Canterbury, 29 April 1314

To our very honoured father in God, Walter, by the grace of God Archbishop of Canterbury, primate of all England, Margaret by the same grace Queen of England, greetings in our Lord.
Recently our very dear lord and sovereign king especially commended us and our concerns to you at St Albans in our hearing. You have always acted well and faithfully towards us in all our affairs for which we thank you from the bottom of our heart and are truly grateful. Since we have been unable to obtain from the Abbot of

Hailes fifty pounds which he owes us as annual rent for a farm which he holds of us, which rent he has recently withheld in defiance of the terms of our charter; and even though we may distrain the said Abbot by our bailiffs for our rent, we prefer to seek assistance in your court; we are therefore sending word to you, and asking you to issue a writ from your chancery on this matter so that we may obtain our rent annually according to the terms of the said charter, and also the arrears due from unpaid rent in the past. May the Lord keep you. Given at Risborough on 29 April.

(PRO SC 1/35/131, French.)

ISABELLA OF FRANCE, WIFE OF EDWARD II

Soon after Queen Margaret was widowed, she travelled to Boulogne with her stepson, Edward II, to receive his bride, her own niece Isabella, daughter of Philip IV of France. The new queen had the rare good fortune in a princess in having near relations of her own at the English court to help and advise her. Not only was the queen-dowager her aunt, but she had two English half-uncles in Thomas and Henry of Lancaster, whose father, Edward I's younger brother Edmund, had married the widowed Blanche of Navarre, Isabella's maternal grandmother. Despite this promising situation at the beginning of her marriage, no other English queen has been so execrated as Isabella, whom Englishmen nicknamed the 'she-wolf of France'. She is the only queen to have committed both the most heinous crimes with which a queen could be charged: involvement in politics and adultery. Of the other queens in our period, only Isabella of Angoulême and Katherine Howard can reasonably be supposed adulteresses, while Eleanor of Aquitaine, Margaret of Anjou, Elizabeth Woodville and Anne Boleyn played political roles. Isabella's adultery led to her lover's three-year government of the kingdom. She was queen and dowager for fifty years, but her place on the centre of the stage occupies only one decade, the 1320s. Until that time, Isabella fulfilled her role in a perfectly satisfactory manner. She was twelve at the time of her marriage to the 23-year-old Edward, and they shared a joint coronation. As befitted the only daughter of the king of France, she brought with her a magnificent wardrobe of gowns and jewels. The treaty that had negotiated her betrothal as a small child had specified for her a dower of the same size as that of her aunt, but since Margaret still held her lands and the Crown was suffering the economic effects of years of war, there was no immediate act of endowment. The queen's financial position was finally resolved by the appropriation of the revenues of Ponthieu and Montreuil (the inheritance of the king's mother) for her benefit. It was five years before the birth of her first child, the future Edward III, but this lapse of time was by no means uncommon in a young queen.

A surviving account book for Isabella's early married life, covering the financial year 1311–12, illustrates the workings of the queen's household. The king's wardrobe was responsible for her household finances. The senior officers were her steward, Eubolo de Montibus, her controller, Hugh de Leominster, her wardrobe keeper, William de Bondon, and her cofferer, John de Fleet. All four had seen previous service in the household of the king, his father or younger brothers and thus provided an experienced staff for the new queen. The position of steward was usually held by an experienced knight or landowner, those of the other three offices by clerics who could expect ecclesiastical promotion to become canons and deans if not bishops. Outside the immediate household was the receiver, who gathered in the queen's revenue, her stewards of lands and then her bailiffs, castellans, keepers of forests and manors. Among Isabella's more personal attendants were five ladies of high birth, including Eleanor de Clare, niece of Edward II, and wife of Hugh Despenser; Isabella de Vesci, born a Beaumont (and related both to the king and the queen); and the latter's sister-in-law, Alice, countess of Buchan in her own right. These ladies received no wages or fees but drew allowances for winter and summer robes. Great ladies had their own duties and responsibilities to perform and had only a certain amount of time they could devote to the queen and therefore operated a shift system for their attendance on her. There were also eight damsels, not necessarily young as the name suggests, but of lesser birth and often married to male members of the household. They included Theophania de St Pierre, the queen's nurse. Isabella had two household knights, Sir John de Sully and Sir William de Sully, who drew livery allowances of 16 marks p.a. each and received fees of a further 8 marks p.a. There were ten senior clerks, including those named previously, together with a physician, a chaplain and an almoner, twelve other clerks and servants including her butler, pantler, cook, sergeant-at-arms, writing clerk and usher, twenty-eight squires and other upper servants, a total of at least seventy. Lower servants such as grooms, sumptermen, carters, messengers, laundresses and boys brought the total of the household to about 180 people.

The household accounts shed very little light on the taste or personality of the queen. She had a fool called Michael, a number of hawks and eight greyhounds, and on Christmas Eve she lost 100 shillings playing dice with the king. They do, however, emphasize again the peripatetic nature of the queen's household. The sum of 3s 8d was spent mending the axle of the queen's chariot, a type of covered wagon in which the queen and her ladies travelled when not on horseback, five members of the household were given 40s each to replace sumpter horses that had died, and her sergeant-at-arms, Peter de Monte Ozeri, was given 10s 2d to pay various guides for leading the queen and her chariots on the 'right and best roads' during her travels. On the occasion of the birth of the queen's second son, John, at Eltham, in August 1316, her steward was given £100 for bringing the news first to the delighted king. Isabella herself sent her valet, Goodwin Hawtyne, with letters to Bishop John Salmon of Norwich and Edward's cousin, Thomas, earl of Lancaster, asking them to be sponsors at her son's christening. Her clerk of the chapel received one piece of cloth of gold and one piece of Turkey cloth for arraying the font and her tailor, Stephen Taloise, was given five pieces of white velvet for making a robe for the queen's churching after the birth. In 1318, after the birth of their eldest daughter, Eleanor, King Edward gave his wife £333 for her churching feast.

It is clear that in the early years of her marriage, Isabella played an insignificant role in her husband's life. The death of Gaveston and the birth of an heir, however, seem to have changed for a time at least Edward's attitude to his wife. Isabella acted as mediator between Edward and his disaffected peers, who seem to have pitied the queen, neglected for a favourite they all detested. In the next few years she bore two more children, John and Eleanor, but by 1318 what little influence she had gained over the king was eclipsed by the rise of another favourite, Hugh Despenser, while a second blow was the death of Queen Margaret, whose affection for both king and queen had helped to sustain their relationship.

There are several stories illustrative of Edward's care for Gaveston at the expense of his wife, for instance his bestowal on the favourite of gifts of plate and jewels made him by his wife, but however much Isabella may have disliked Gaveston, there was little she could do about him. Edward's devotion to the Gascon was deep and went back to his emotionally neglected childhood, while Isabella was herself little more than a child and was unlikely to have the emotional maturity to cope with the situation. The Despensers, father and son, were another matter. They were not as beloved of the king, but as English barons with the support of some of their peers and a desire for political power as well as personal aggrandisement, they were formidable opponents.

Isabella's role in the events from 1322 to 1326 is now very difficult to disentangle. Agnes Strickland condemns her utterly, in true Victorian manner, placing the beginning of her liaison with the Marcher lord, Roger Mortimer of Wigmore, soon after the birth of her last daughter, Joan of the Tower, in 1321, and believes that her hostility to the Despensers sprang from a desire to destroy them because they were Mortimer's enemies and that her subsequent ill-treatment by the king was a result of the king's displeasure at the liaison. In fact, the reverse sequence of events seems far more plausible. Isabella had her own reasons for opposing the Despensers. They had usurped her own growing influence with her husband and they also dared to restrict her own revenues from the exchequer. In 1324 when war broke out with her brother, Charles IV of France, she was treated not as queen of England but as a virtual enemy of the state. Her lands were sequestered and her servants dismissed, some of them to imprisonment. She was allowed only 8 marks a day for her household and 1,000 marks for other expenses (approximately £37 per week). The English had little

Isabella of France, from a stone carving in Bristol Cathedral

enthusiasm for a war, having just been forced into a humiliating peace with Scotland, and no money to pay for it; the constable of Bordeaux had difficulty feeding his troops, let alone paying them. Edward had no alternative but to negotiate, but he dared not go to France himself and leave the Despensers unprotected from their enemies. There was one obvious intermediary and that was his wife. In this ironic situation, Edward finally bowed to circumstance, effected a superficial reconciliation with Isabella and sent her to France. Part of the terms she agreed with her brother were that Edward would do homage for Aquitaine, but since he would not leave England, he was finally persuaded to let Prince Edward go in his place. With the heir to the throne in her hands, Isabella held a trump card. She refused to allow her son to return until the Despensers were removed from power and exiled.

At this point Isabella had the support of her brother and a group of English exiles in France and the sympathy of many important men in England, a number of whom, sent to France as emissaries, chose to remain there. They included the king's half-brother, Edmund, earl of Kent. The queen was certainly regarded as more sinned against than sinning, even in the withholding of the prince. However, her subsequent affair with one of the exiles, Roger Mortimer, caused a major scandal and forfeited almost all the goodwill she had had. It was not a casual liaison which might perhaps have been forgiven her in the circumstances, but on her side at least, a passionate affair of the heart which lasted until her lover's death. The couple were constantly together, but what was worse, Prince Edward was associated with his mother's behaviour. Several piteous letters from the king survive, begging his son to come home and condemning his wife for allowing their son to 'consort with our said enemy [Mortimer], making him your counsellor and you openly to herd and associate with him in the sight of all the world'. There is no reason to believe that the scandal forced Isabella to leave France. On her brother's death, her cousin Philip of Valois continued, as Philip VI, to support her and to promote the marriage she was negotiating for Prince Edward with a daughter of the count of Hainault, who was Philip's niece. In return Isabella resigned her own claim and that of her son to the French throne. Philippa of Hainault's dowry financed the invasion of England and its military leader was her uncle, John of Hainault. The aim of the invasion was ostensibly to remove the Despensers from power, but it led inevitably on to the deposition of Isabella's husband in favour of her son, and Edward II's murder. It is impossible now to tell whether Isabella connived at the murder or was ignorant until after the event. Her remorse for her part in it, whatever it was, was shown years later when she chose to be buried wearing her wedding dress and with Edward's heart in her coffin.

For the first three years of Edward III's reign, England was ruled by the queen-dowager and her paramour. Who wielded the ultimate power is open to question; everything was done in the name of the queen-dowager and her son, but contemporaries believed it to be Mortimer, and there seems little reason to doubt this judgement. In 1330 Edmund, earl of Kent, the youngest brother of Edward II and Isabella's own cousin, was executed for treason. Six months later, the young king, by then eighteen and the father of a promising prince, engineered a coup which brought him control of the government. Mortimer was executed and Isabella sent to confinement at Castle Rising in Norfolk. King Edward's position with regard to his mother was a difficult one. Her relationship with Mortimer was deeply mortifying to him, and his horror at his father's murder can only be guessed at. There could be no question of a public trial, and in order to avoid exposing her shameful behaviour, all her actions were attributed to Mortimer's influence. His arraignment states 'The said Roger falsely and maliciously sowed discord between the father of our lord the king and the queen his consort, making her believe that if she came near her husband he would poignard her or murder her in some other manner. Wherefore by this cause, and by other subtleties, the said queen remained absent from her said lord, to the great dishonour of the king and of the said queen his mother, and great damage, perhaps, of the whole nation hereafter, which God avert.'

In 1327, when she and Mortimer gained power, Isabella's dower was increased to 20,000 marks and she was subsequently granted lands or rights in every English county save the four northernmost ones, and more in Wales besides. While this has often been used to illustrate Isabella's greed it was more likely to have been a means of providing patronage for a regime which had no constitutional basis. On her disgrace in 1330, Isabella was stripped of all her lands, but gradually her position improved and by 1337 she was in possession of revenues equivalent to those originally assigned her in dower. She remained at Castle Rising, living in the affluent retirement of a queen-dowager, hunting, reading, entertaining and occasionally receiving visits from her son. In her old age she donned the habit of the Poor Clares, and dying in 1358 was buried in the Franciscan church at Newgate founded by her aunt, Queen Margaret.

Although the early letter from Isabella to Edward cannot be dated with any certainty, it is tempting to place it in the year 1313, after both the death of Gaveston and the birth of their heir, Edward. Isabella, still only seventeen after five years of marriage, addressed her husband in a tone of affectionate respect. Ponthieu, a county at the mouth of the Somme in northern France, was King Edward's inheritance from his mother and was used to dower the young queen during the lifetime of the dowager-queen Margaret. To his father's fury, Edward had once asked for it to be bestowed on Gaveston. Isabella's brother, Philip V of France, forcibly annexed it in 1320, but returned possession to his brother-in-law soon afterwards when Edward did homage for all his French lands.

Isabella, Queen of England, to Edward II, 11 August (1310–13)

My very dear and dread lord, I commend myself to you as humbly as I can. My dear lord, you have heard how our seneschal and our controller of Ponthieu have come from Ponthieu concerning our affairs; the letters they had to bring can remain in the state they are at present until the parliament – except one which concerns your inheritance in Ponthieu and the Count of Dreux, which should be acted upon immediately in order to keep and maintain your inheritance. I beg you, my gentle lord, that by this message it may please you to request your chancellor by letter that he summon those of your council to him and take steps speedily in this matter according to what he and your said council see what is best to do for your honour and profit. For if action is not speedily taken, this will do you great harm and be of much benefit to the said count your enemy, as I have truly heard by my council. May the Holy Spirit keep you, my very dear and dread lord. Given at Chertsey 11 August.

(PRO SC 1/35/29, French.)

The challenge mounted by the queen to the corrupt rule of the Despensers, father and son, took both them and her husband by surprise. When war had broken out with France in 1324 the queen seemed to be the most suitable person to negotiate a peace with Charles IV, the third of her brothers to succeed their father. Charles had already been the recipient of complaints from Isabella that she was held in no higher consideration than a servant in the palace of her husband and it is an indication of the lack of importance that Edward placed on his queen that he foresaw no danger in sending her to France. When, as part of the peace terms which she helped to negotiate, Prince Edward was sent to do homage for Aquitaine on behalf of his father, he was escorted to Paris by Bishop Stapleton of Exeter. Once homage had been paid, however, Isabella refused either to return home or let her son go until the Despensers were removed. Stapleton, who as treasurer was deeply implicated in the government, thought it prudent to remove himself to the safety of England, whence this letter from the queen pursued him. Although she had begun to gather some of the English political exiles about her, Isabella made no criticism of the king, but reminded the bishop that it was the king's order that he supply her with funds to support her stay in Paris. Among the exiles was Roger Mortimer of Wigmore, a long-time rival of the Despensers in the Welsh Marches, who had escaped from the Tower in 1326 just before his execution was due. Without Mortimer by her side, it is possible that Isabella would not have contemplated mounting the armed expedition from Hainault that supplanted her husband with her son. On their arrival support for Edward and his favourites melted away but one of the key factors in her success was the support she received from London. This unfortunately expressed itself in the lynching of Bishop Stapleton, who was dragged from his horse and beheaded with a butcher's knife.

Isabella, Queen of England, to Walter Stapleton, Bishop of Exeter, 8 December (1325)

We have understood what you have told us by your letters and your excuses for leaving us in the way you did. Know that since our very dear lord, the King of England sent you with Edward our son into the regions of France, and we promised faithfully to keep you from harm and to take good and safe care of you, and our said lord the King commanded you to make a money loan for the expenses of our household, but as we understand it, you have done nothing. And we forbade you to leave without our permission, and you gave us to understand that you had orders by letter from our very dear lord the King to leave, but you have never been able to show his letters to this effect, as it appears to us and we are certain of it. In spite of our very dear lord and brother [Kent] and ourselves, in disobedience and despite our prohibition and to the great dishonour of our said lord of England and ourselves, and to the advantage of Hugh Despenser, you left us in an ill-intentioned way, so that we can see clearly that you are in league with the said Hugh and more obedient towards him than towards us. We would therefore have you know that we do not consider you in any way excusable, though this is what it is our duty to do. Given at Paris on 8 December.

(PRO SC 1/49/188, French.)

The next of Queen Isabella's letters is not a personal one, but was issued in conjunction with her son and brother-in-law, Edmund, earl of Kent, as an open justification of their return to England and action against the Despensers. Nowhere is there any hint of blame against the king. Among the lords who joined them on their arrival in England from Hainault were Kent's brother, Thomas, earl of Norfolk, and Henry, earl of Leicester, the king's first cousin. The other person, singled out for opprobrium was Edward's chancellor, Robert Baldock, who was an ally of the Despensers.

Open letter from Isabella, Queen of England, Edward, Prince of Wales, and Edmund, Earl of Kent, 15 October 1326

We, Isabella, by the grace of God, Queen of England, Lady of Ireland, Countess of Ponthieu; and we, Edward, elder son of the Lord King of England, Duke of Guyenne, Earl of Chester, Count of Ponthieu and Mount Royal; and we, Edmund, son of the noble King of England, Earl of Kent; to all those to whom these letters may come, greetings.

Whereas it is well known that the state of the Holy Church and the Kingdom of England is in many respects much tarnished and degraded by the bad advice and conspiracy of Hugh le Despenser; whereas, through pride and greed to have power and dominion over all other people, he has usurped royal power against law and justice and his true allegiance, and through the bad advice of Robert de Baldock and others of his supporters, he has acted in such a way that the Holy Church is robbed of its goods against God and Right and in many other ways insulted and dishonoured, and the Crown of England brought low in many respects, through the disinheritance of our lord the king and of his heirs; the magnates of the kingdom, through the envy and wicked cruelty of the said Hugh have been delivered to a shameful death, many of them blamelessly and without cause; others have been disinherited, imprisoned, banished or exiled; widows and orphans have been unlawfully deprived of their rights, and the people of this land much hurt by many taxes and held to ransom by frequent unjust demands for money and by divers other oppressions without any mercy, by virtue of which misdeeds the said Hugh shows himself to be a clear tyrant and enemy of God and the Holy Church, of our very dear lord the king and the whole kingdom.

And we, and several others, who are with us and of our company, who have long been kept far from the goodwill of our said lord the king through the false suggestions and evil dealings of the aforesaid Hugh and Robert and their supporters, are come to this land to raise up the state of Holy Church and of the kingdom, and of the people of this land against the said misdeeds and grievous oppressions, and to safeguard and maintain, so far as we can, the honour and profit of the Holy Church, and of our said lord the king, and the whole kingdom as is stated above. For this reason we ask and pray you, for the common good of all and each of you individually that you come to our help well and loyally whenever the time and place are right and by whatever means lie within your power so that the above matters may be speedily put right. For be assured that we all and all those who are in our company intend to do nothing that does not redound to the honour and profit of the Holy Church and the whole kingdom, as you will see in the course of time if it please God. Given at Wallingford on 15 October in the 20th year of the reign of our very dear lord the king.

(Foedera vol. iv, p. 236, French.)

One of Isabella's actions when she assumed control of the government was to make provision for her new daughter-in-law, Philippa of Hainault. Queen Philippa was granted 1,000 marks p.a. for her chamber expenses, but she was not granted any dower lands until after 1330. (The document has an interesting misprint, for it actually specifies 10,000 marks (X m), but since this is half as large again as the dower of any fourteenth-century queen it is clearly wrong.) John Stratford had been Edward II's treasurer, and became chancellor to Edward III. He was translated from the bishopric of Winchester to the archbishopric of Canterbury in 1333.

Isabella, Queen-Dowager of England, to John de Stratford, Bishop of Winchester, 19 May (1327–30)

Greetings and true love. We pray you from the depths of our heart to make immediately available to our very dear daughter the Queen those letters patent under the Great Seal in which the King our son assigned her 10,000 marks [*sic*] for her chamber to be received from the exchequer of our said son, and which, as you know, his father agreed to. And in addition to this, please also cause writs of liberate issued for 500 marks for the term of Easter last past, and for the remaining 500 marks for Michaelmas next coming, for the whole year, and have these delivered to Sir William de Colby his clerk for the love of us. May the Lord keep you. Given at our manor of Eltham on 19 May.

(PRO SC 1/41/48, French.)

The original of the following letter has neither superscription nor indication of the sender; there can be little doubt that it was sent by Isabella in the period 1327–30 and the most likely recipient is John de Bohun, earl of Hereford, the constable of England. He was her husband's nephew rather than the queen-dowager's, being the son of Edward I's daughter Elizabeth, widowed countess of Holland and Zeeland and her second husband, Humphrey de Bohun, earl of Hereford. There were three occasions in this period when Edward III requested his cousin's presence: in May 1327 when he was gathering the magnates to discuss the moving of an army towards the Scottish borders and again the following September on the death of Edward II, and once more on the approach of a Scottish army in October 1327. Isabella's letter was almost certainly written on the occasion of her husband's death, when the regime she and her lover, Mortimer, were controlling in the name of her son needed all the support it could get, particularly from magnates of the blood royal. Bohun's apparent reluctance to come may have indicated disapproval but may also have been a result of ill-health. Three years later the constableship was granted to his brother on account of the earl's infirmity.

Isabella, Queen-Dowager of England, to her nephew, ? the Earl of Hereford, c. 1328

Most dear and beloved nephew,

We have well understood what you have sent us word by your letters; and, as to our estate, we give you to know that we are even in great trouble of heart, but, considering the condition we are in, we were in good health of body at the setting forth of these letters, which our Lord ever grant to you. Dearest nephew, we pray you that you will leave off all excuses, and come to the king our son in the best manner you can, and as he commands you more fully by his letters. For you know well, dearest nephew, if you come not, considering the necessity that now exists, it will be greatly talked of, and will be a great dishonour to you. Wherefore make an effort to come at this time as hastily as you can, and you know well, dearest nephew, we shall ever be ready to counsel you as well as we can in all things that shall be to your honour and profit. Most dear and beloved nephew, our Lord have you in his keeping. Given at Nottingham, the 10th day of October.

(PRO DL 34/22, French. Wood, vol. i, letter xxiii.)

In 1330, when Edward III successfully staged a coup against Roger Mortimer and personally took over the government of his kingdom, he was faced with the acute dilemma of what to do about his mother. The royal family's face was saved by attributing all her actions to Mortimer's influence, but in her disgrace she was stripped of all her lands and banished to Castle Rising. During the three years she and Mortimer had been in control, her dower had been greatly increased and large grants of lands had been made to her, but in 1330 she became totally dependent on the goodwill of her son. Her punishment was of a limited duration. In 1332 her dower was restored to two-thirds of its original amount, and by 1337 it was back at £4,500, the sum settled on her at her marriage. This letter raises queries about two of the properties he had just assigned her in 1332. One, the manor of Bistlesham in Berkshire, the queen claimed, was in fact held by the countess of Lincoln and her companion, Sir Ebles Lestraunge. Alice de Lacy, countess of Lincoln and Salisbury in her own right, was the widow of Thomas, earl of Lancaster, executed by his cousin King Edward II in 1322; Lestraunge was her second husband, and he and the countess were quite willing to give up the manor provided they were properly compensated for it. The second, the fee farm of the town of Derby, was already charged with an annuity to Edward Chandos for nearly the full amount and Isabella requested other lands to make up the deficiency.

Isabella, Queen-Dowager of England, to her son Edward III, January 1332

To her very dear sovereign lord, the king, Madam Queen Isabel his mother prays that it may please him to give and grant [her] the knights' fees, advowsons of churches and chapels, wards, marriages, escheats and all the other gifts and franchises in the lands and fee farms which he gave her recently for her sustenance for the rest of her life to the value of 3000 pounds per annum, such as she had in the lands which she made over into the hands of her very dear suzerain on the first day of December in the fourth year of his reign.

That is, the manor of Bristelsham is to be given to my said lady as one of her dwellings amongst the three others which were given to her recently as is stated above; which manor Ebles Lestraunge holds by the king's charter for life, according to what he says. The countess of Lincoln, his companion, will willingly give up the said manor to my said lady the queen provided he has the value of the said manor in land elsewhere from my said lord the king. We pray that it may please our said lord the king to act in such a way towards Ebles that he has the said manor delivered up to my said lady seeing that it is granted to her amongst other lands to the value of £41 17s 2½d per annum.

Item: his said mother prays that, since he has granted her amongst other said lands the farm of the town of Derby to the value of £46 10s, for which farm he had made a promise by charter to Edward de Chandos for £40 per annum for life, and since you command that the said Edward according to the aforesaid grant, may it please you to grant your said mother other lands to the value of the abovesaid farm of Derby.

(PRO SC 1/38/77, French.)

PHILIPPA OF HAINAULT, WIFE OF EDWARD III

It would be difficult to imagine two women more dissimilar than Isabella of France and her daughter-in-law, Philippa of Hainault. There are indications that during his stay at the court of Hainault with his mother, the fifteen-year-old Prince Edward showed more interest in the count's second daughter, Philippa, than in her sisters, and talked to her more frequently. They were close in age and the political necessity of a marriage with Hainault was tempered by allowing the prince some slight choice between the count's daughters. Froissart's comment about their conversations may carry the key to their subsequently happy marriage, namely they were good friends as well as husband and wife. The couple were married at York in January 1328, since the prince was with an army in the north. The birth of an heir eighteen months later, much earlier than a young queen often bore her first child (Philippa was sixteen) may have provided the psychological boost the young king needed to seize power. Edward III and Queen Philippa remained close and deeply attached, although the king was not totally faithful to her, particularly during the last few years of her life when she was suffering from dropsy. She was an important moderating influence on him and Edward relied on her advice and encouragement. Her strong sense of the responsibilities of kingship, so lacking in the previous reign, was one of the major factors in the success of Edward's search for national unity after 1330.

For the first time since the reign of Henry II, the king had a large family of sons growing up. Philippa bore him twelve children, three of whom died in infancy, and one, Joan, who died of the plague at Bordeaux on her way to marry the heir of Castile. Their five sons remained on remarkably good terms with each other and, more importantly, with their father, in stark contrast to the family of Henry II and Eleanor of Aquitaine. For this, much of the credit must go to their mother. The queen remained very close to her own mother, Jeanne of Valois, sister of Philip VI, and the births of their second two sons, Lionel in Antwerp and John in Ghent, reflect both the king's political connections in the Low Countries and the queen's desire to be there with him. She did not bring a host of relations to England with her, nor a large train of Hainaulters, but men of talent from her country received a warm welcome at the English court and she was served loyally by Hainaulters like Sir Walter de Mauny and Jean Froissart, while Geoffrey Chaucer married one of her ladies, Philippa de Roet.

A personal description of Philippa by Bishop Stapleton of Exeter makes it clear that although pleasant-looking, she was by no means beautiful. She was deeply religious and brought up her children in that spirit. Generous, warm-hearted and physically hardy, she accompanied Edward on most of his campaigns, but unlike Eleanor of Castile, she did not neglect her children in doing so. The story that she breast-fed her eldest child, the Black Prince, though not in fact contemporary, is certainly in character. Philippa's greatest fault, perhaps her only one, was her extravagance. New hangings for her bed before her confinement in 1335, together with robes for her churching thereafter totalled a staggering £700. At her marriage, the by then conventional dower of £4,500 was assigned her. Since the queen-dowager, Isabella, held a vastly inflated dower at the time of Philippa's marriage, there was little left to bestow on the new young queen. She was granted 1,000 marks p.a. for her chamber expenses in 1329, which was at her personal disposal and did not have to be accounted for at the exchequer from whence it was paid. The king made her special gifts and grants whenever he chose and paid the expenses of her household. After 1330 Philippa was gradually granted dower lands to the value of £4,000 p.a. Some of these lands had familiar names: Nayland, Havering, Cookham and Bray, Bristol, Rockingham, Devizes, Marlborough, Southampton and Gillingham had all been held by one or more former queens, but Knaresborough and Pontefract were new and so was the castle of Kingsborough on the Isle of Sheppey, where the king demolished the old building and began a new palace for his queen, which he named for her, Queenborough. She was assigned a further £2,000 worth of lands in 1359, after Isabella's death, to help support her growing family, but even that was not enough to rescue the queen from her financial difficulties and in 1363 Edward resumed responsibility for his wife's household. As every other queen had done, Philippa collected queen's gold, but it was an incalculable and unreliable source of income, for instance in the Michelmas term of 1337 she received £112 but in the Easter term of 1339 only £16.

Philippa may not have been able to deal successfully with her own finances, but she was responsible for a major advance in the economic affairs of her new country when she established a cloth manufacturing colony of her fellow-countrymen at Norwich in 1335. England until that date had been a wool-exporting country but the financial benefits of manufacturing cloth had been in the hands of the Flemings who bought English wool. She paid regular visits to Norwich, usually when her husband visited his mother at Castle Rising. Contemporary chroniclers were unanimous in the praise of the queen, bestowing on her the epithet 'good', before applied only to Matilda of Scotland. Despite her strong French connections, Philippa undoubtedly benefited from the fact that she came from the Low Countries, associated in English minds with trade and not war. There is no reason to disbelieve the story of her pleading with the king for the lives of the Calais burghers he had condemned to death, or her similar action on behalf of carpenters who erected a faulty scaffolding which collapsed under her and her ladies while they were watching a tournament held in honour of the birth of her eldest son, and from which she luckily escaped without injury. The devotion of the king and the obviously close and affectionate life of the royal family were rightly regarded as her achievements. The king and queen were surprisingly lenient with their children. Their eldest daughter, Isabella, for whom a number of foreign husbands were proposed, was finally betrothed to the heir of one of the great Gascon nobles, the Sire d'Albret. At the last minute she refused to sail for Gascony and her parents permitted her to break off the match. Furthermore she was then allowed to remain at the English court enjoying an income and estates the equivalent of those of an English magnate until she chose to wed (at the age of thirty-three) a French hostage, Enguerrand de Coucy, whom her father created earl of Bedford. Isabella was

An effigy of Philippa of Hainault in Westminster Abbey by Henniquin de Liege, 1367

undoubtedly her father's favourite. He once described her as 'our very dear eldest daughter whom we have loved with a special affection'. Her two younger sisters, Mary and Margaret both married boys with whom they had grown up in the royal household, John IV, duke of Brittany and John Hastings, earl of Pembroke. The marriages of Edward's four younger sons were all designed to provide them with appropriate endowments without weakening the crown by alienating royal estates. The marriage of his heir was another matter and is discussed later.

Philippa, who died in August 1369, was ill with dropsy for about two years before her death. Edward's notorious liaison with Alice Perrers seems to have begun about 1364 and she was officially given a place at court in the queen's household in 1366. It was only after the queen's death and the king's subsequent deterioration in physical and mental health that Alice's role became significant. When Philippa died at Windsor all her children save Thomas of Woodstock, her youngest son, were abroad. Her devoted secretary and countryman, the great chronicler Froissart, described her deathbed. Holding the king's hand she asked him for three promises: that all her engagements with merchants be honoured, that her legacies to the church and to her servants be paid and that Edward should be buried at her side. Weeping, the king gave his word. Froissart committed to paper his view of his mistress, that she was 'wise, gladsome, humble, devout, free-handed and courteous and in her time she was richly adorned with all noble virtues, and well beloved of God and men'. It was a verdict with which all his contemporaries seem to have agreed.

Despite the length of time Philippa of Hainault was queen, relatively few letters of hers have survived, and none of any real personal nature. Yet those that do, reveal the just and kindly nature of the queen and it cannot be accidental that almost all are written on behalf of others. The first letter included here was written only a few months after her marriage and was a plea to expedite the delivery of a man from prison, though who John Baillief was and what his crime was is now lost.

Philippa, Queen of England, to Henry de Clife, 1 April 1328

Philippa, by the grace of God, Queen of England, Lady of Ireland and Duchess of Aquitaine, to our dear clerk, Master Henry de Clife, greeting.
We especially request you in the business concerning the deliverence of John de Baillief, who is in prison at Newgate, as to which the letters of our most dear lord, the king, are coming to you by the [keeper] of his Great Seal, you will please make your writ and speedily issue it for love of us, and the favour you request [I will grant] in reason.
Given at Eltham, the first day of April.

(PRO SC 1/36/107, French.)

The recipient of the next two letters, written in the late 1340s, was the then chancellor, John Offord, who was also dean of the diocese of Lincoln. In 1349 he was elevated to the primacy but died a few months later. His background was in civil law and he held a university degree. He was clearly able and was appointed without the usual administrative experience in royal service. The tone of the letters is warm, and it may be that the queen cherished a particular regard for Offord. In the first she sought to obtain a benefice for one of her chaplains, whose service both to herself and her second son, Lionel, duke of Clarence, she praises; since Lionel was born in 1338, the chaplain, de Orreville, was almost certainly his tutor. The earldom of Richmond, temporarily out of the hands of the dukes of Brittany, had been given to Philippa's infant son, John, later duke of Lancaster and the queen had been granted the wardship. This included rights of advowson (the choice of incumbents for benefices). Her application to Offord, therefore, despite its suppliant nature, was little more than a formality.

The second letter to Offord also relates to a wardship. Philippa was requesting the chancellor to protect her interests in the wardship of John de Sinclair. Granting wardships to a queen was a recognized way of providing her with temporary lands which she could exploit during the ward's minority. The ward was usually brought up in the queen's care, and since there were likely to be several of them, they provided companionship or service for the royal children, depending on their status.

Philippa, Queen of England, to John Offord, Chancellor, 28 April 1348

Philippa, by the grace of God Queen of England, lady of Ireland and Duchess of Aquitaine, to our dear and wellbeloved Master John Offord, Dean of Lincoln, Chancellor of our very dear lord the king, greetings and dear friendship.
Whereas the vicarage of the church of Swaffham Market is now vacant, as is said, and in that the parson of the same church is an alien, we understand that you, by reason of your office, are at this time making the gift of its aforesaid vicarage. Since we are patroness of this church by reason of the earldom of Richmond being in our hands, we greatly desire that someone of ours may have the said vicarage before others. We therefore request you that you will please present our dear chaplain, Sir Gerrard de Orreville, by regard to charity and for our love and for our very dear son Lionel for a long time past, we greatly desire his honour and advancement in this behalf.
Very dear Sir, may God always have you in his worthy protection.
Written at Windsor, the 28th day of April.

(PRO SC 1/40/31, French.)

Philippa, Queen of England, to John Offord, Chancellor, 1 May 1346–8

Philippa by the grace of God, Queen of England, Lady of Ireland and Duchess of Aquitaine, to the praiseworthy, wise man, our most dear and wellbeloved Master John Offord, Dean of Lincoln, Chancellor of our very dear lord the King, greeting and our good love.

Because, Sir, you give us to understand that certain people have made, or will make in time, a request to you for things which may turn to the prejudice and disinheritance of our dear and wellbeloved John de Seyntcler, who is under age and in our hands, being so by the grant of our said lord, we request you as dearly as we can that you will not, for any request or suggestion, suffer any writ to issue from the Chancery which shall be in disinheritance of the said John, or to the damage and prejudice of his lands and tenements while he is under age, for our love.

May God be your protector. Written at Guildford, the first day of May.

(PRO SC 1/40/31, French.)

When John Offord died, he was succeeded as chancellor by John Thoresby, bishop of Worcester, who subsequently became archbishop of York. Preferment to the great offices of the English Church was the recognized reward for royal service. In the 1450s Philippa wrote twice to Thoresby seeking remedies for injustices suffered by her tenants. In the first she asked for a commission of enquiry into the overtaxation of her tenants at Havering atte Bower, Essex. Taxes were usually paid on moveable property and were granted in Parliament as a sixth or a tenth, or a third or a sixth of the value, with the higher rate paid by the towns and the royal demesne. The clergy were usually taxed separately. In the second letter she wanted the removal of a coroner who had been misusing his office.

Philippa, Queen of England, to John Thoresby, Chancellor, 22 May c. 1350

Most reverend father in God, and our very wellbeloved. Because William de Northtoft and William atte Hurst, who were formerly assigned by commission of Esmon de Northtoft, chief collector of the triennial tithe [tenth] granted to our very dear lord, the King, in the county of Essex, have raised in our manor of Havering atte Bower more than they should have done by 40 shillings, and they are still demanding maliciously and outrageously against reason, beyond what is lawful, £7 from our poor tenants there, to the great harm and impoverishment of their estates, as you will be more plainly informed by our dear clerk, Sir Thomas de Brayton. I therefore request you, most reverend father in God, that to chasten and punish according to law and reason the aforesaid William and William for their misprision in this behalf, and to make great profit to our said lord, you will be pleased to cause a commission to be issued to Sir John de Leukenore and Sir John de Goldyngham, knights and to Thomas Tyrell, esquire, and to [any] two of them, to sit and enquire by the oath of the good and loyal people of the said manor, and of the lawful parties, neither nearly related nor open to suspicion, whether it is so as is said above, or not, and that they are to have by the said commission power to impose such punishment as the law shall require and adjudge in such case, for our love. Very reverend father in God, may our almighty Lord have you always in his worthy protection.

Written at Colchester, the 22nd day of May.

(PRO SC 1/42/102, French.)

Philippa, Queen of England, to John de Thoresby, Chancellor, 16 December 1350–5

Very reverend father in God and our wellbeloved, since John Alscy, one of the coroners of our very dear lord the King in the county of Bedford, has behaved himself underhandedly and maliciously towards us and our tenants in the said county and other of our household servants and is not worthy of so high an office, we pray you earnestly to remove and eject the said coroner from that office and there appoint another worthy person in his place for love of us, and for this reason we will be ready to grant your request on another occasion. May you be commended to God, dearly beloved lord.

Written at Windsor on 16 December.

(PRO SC 1/41/85, French.)

In the next of Philippa's letters she was again seeking to ameliorate the hardship suffered by various of her husband's subjects, for in it she instructs her attorney not to execute writs against those indebted to the queen, probably for the payment of queen's gold, until she and her council have ascertained their ability to pay.

Philippa, Queen of England, to Sir John de Edington, her Attorney, 14 May 1354

Philippa, by the grace of God queen of England, lady of Ireland, and duchess of Aquitaine, to our dear clerk Sir John de Edington, our attorney in the exchequer of our very dear lord the king, sends greeting.

We command you, that you cause all the writs which have been filed from the search lately made by Sir Richard de Cressevill to be postponed until the octaves of

Easter next ensuing; to the end that, in the meantime, we and our council may be able to be advised which of the said writs are to be put in execution for our profit, and which of them are to cease to the relief of our people, to save our conscience. And we will that this letter be your warrant therefore.

Given under our privy seal, at Westminster, the 14th day of May, in the year of the reign or our very dear lord the king of England the twenty-eighth.

(PRO E 13/79, Wood, vol. i, letter xxiv.)

   The last letter is a request for one of her valets to be discharged for a debt incurred on her behalf.

Philippa, Queen of England, to John Sheppey, bishop of Rochester, Treasurer, 22 February 1357–60

Reverend father in God, and our very wellbeloved.

Because the reverend father in God, our very dear godfather, the bishop of Winchester, in the time that he was Treasurer before you, kindly and of his free will because of us, lent to our dear servant Richard de Heigham, who at that time was involved with our works as appertained to his office, £10 to pay for the work of certain workmen in London, which £10 the said Richard requested by writ of the Exchequer. Whereupon we signified to you the other day by our dear clerk and yours, Sir Roger de Chestrefield, whom we had entrusted to discharge the said Richard and to charge it to our account and in our name, as it is right that you should do so for his reimbursement. Therefore we beg you very dearly to do so as you know our wishes in the matter. Please make an acquittance to the said Richard of the aforesaid £10, and cause it to be charged to our own account in such a way that the said Richard may not hereafter be distrained or aggrieved because of this, by any writ or averment, for our love, as we are bound to him. And may the Holy Spirit have you in His protection.

Written at Westminster, the 22nd day of February.

(PRO SC 1/42/100, French.)

JOAN OF KENT, WIFE OF EDWARD, PRINCE OF WALES

It might naturally be supposed that a match would have been made for the Black Prince with a suitable foreign princess. Yet Edward entered his twenties unwed and then fell in love with his cousin Joan of Kent, daughter of Edward I's youngest son. After the death of her father, Joan had been made a ward of Queen Philippa and had been brought up at Woodstock with her royal cousins and other wards in the charge of the earl and countess of Salisbury. Two years older than the prince, Joan by that time had had a somewhat chequered matrimonial career. At twelve she had apparently unwisely entered into a secret marriage with Thomas Holland, who then departed on crusade to Prussia. In his absence she was then given in marriage to William Montague, son of the earl of Salisbury, and did not have the courage to confess to the existence of her first husband. When Holland returned to England he then sought a position with Montague, becoming steward of William and Joan's household. This situation existed for several years until Holland petitioned the Pope for the annulment of Joan's marriage to Montague. Two years later the papal court decided in favour of Holland, and Joan became his acknowledged wife and bore him several children. It was on his death in 1361 that Joan married the Black Prince. Described by contemporaries as 'the Fair Maid of Kent', she was reputedly one of the most beautiful women in England. The king and queen were unhappy about such a bride for their heir, but like wise parents they allowed the prince to make his own choice.

After their marriage, the couple departed for the prince's duchy of Aquitaine, where their two sons were born, the short-lived Edward at Angoulême and Richard at Bordeaux. As countess of Kent in her own right, Joan was not in need of the size of dower that might have been assigned to a foreign bride, but she was allocated £1,000 p.a. for her expenses, increased to 2,000 marks p.a. in 1363. In England, she and the prince lived chiefly at Kennington, the prince's London palace, or at Berkhamsted. On the prince's death, Joan was granted dower amounting to £2,500 from the lands he had held. With her Kent lands as well, she was as well-provided for as most queens-dowager. On the accession of her nine-year-old son Richard in 1377 on the death of his grandfather, Joan achieved the position and influence of a queen-mother. Since she was as good and kind as she was beautiful, this influence was considerable and almost entirely for the good. She was deservedly popular among her fellow countrymen. No letters by Princess Joan have been traced, but to have omitted her from this survey would have been to overlook her considerable influence as the king's mother. It was only the premature death of the Black Prince before his father which prevented Joan from becoming the first English queen since the Conquest.

ANNE OF BOHEMIA, FIRST WIFE OF RICHARD II

Anne of Bohemia never attained her mother-in-law's popularity, but after Joan's death in 1385, took her place in the king's heart. Anne was the eldest daughter of Charles of Luxemburg, king of Bohemia and Holy Roman Emperor. The social prestige of the match was high, but Anne brought no dowry and, indeed, her brother (for Charles IV was by that date dead) had to be offered a £15,000 loan. Although Anne had been brought up in Prague, her family had close links with northern France and it would probably be wrong to think of her solely in a German or Bohemian context. She was the niece of the duke of Brabant and distantly related to Queen Philippa. The marriage was negotiated by Richard's tutor, Sir Simon Burley, to whom the king was much attached. Anne travelled from Prague in the company of the duke and duchess of Saxony (her aunt) and a large number of Bohemians and stayed *en route* in Brabant with her uncle. Although London staged its customary spectacular entertainment to welcome the bride, it could hardly be said that the xenophobic English were overjoyed to receive a penniless bride accompanied by a train of outlandish Bohemians. Anne's coronation followed swiftly upon her wedding and it was then that she begged the king to issue a general pardon to those previously involved in the Great Revolt. Thereafter the new queen's reputation as a mediator and thus her popularity began to grow, but there is much to support the view that this first instance was a result of prompting by the Princess of Wales. Joan, far more conversant with the issues involved, and kind and generous by nature, had found a way of establishing her new daughter-in-law in the good graces of her husband's subjects.

Anne's dower was set at the customary sum of £4,500, and since Richard's mother did not hold any of the traditional dower lands, the queen received a large grant of lands soon after her marriage, which contained many of the now familar names, such as Bristol, Leeds, Langley, Gillingham and Havering. A few months later she was granted the castles of Conway, Nottingham and Devizes for life, and then manors worth £800 p.a. formerly held by Richard's late aunt, Isabella, countess of Bedford, to make up deficiencies in the sums her dower should have brought her but did not. Two years later, in return for the surrender of various fees and grants from customs, the queen received the great honour of Richmond, which, with the additional grant of Geddington in Northants, was worth £1,000 p.a. Richmond had long been held by the dukes of Brittany, closely related to the royal family, but the current duke, John IV, married to the king's Holland half-sister, had forfeited it by allying with the French against the English (he was restored after Anne's death). Later, in 1384, Anne was also given the royal manor of Woodstock.

We know very little of Anne's household or life-style. Bohemia was one of the leading countries of central Europe and was also open to influence from Byzantium,

A wooden head, part of the funeral effigy of Anne of Bohemia, in Westminster Abbey Undercroft Museum

and since England was at the time going through a period of great artistic flowering, it would be surprising if Bohemian influence did not make itself felt to some degree, but no overt evidence of it can be traced to the queen or her immediate household. Several of the Bohemians who accompanied her to England remained in her household, but two of them caused dissension within the ranks of the English peers. During a campaign against the Scots, archers of Lord Stafford, attempting to protect a knight of the queen's, called by Froissart simply Sir Meles, inadvertently killed a squire of Sir John Holland, the king's half-brother, who in a rage slew Stafford himself. The dying Princess of Wales begged for the life of her son, who was sent into exile. The second Bohemian was politically more dangerous, despite her sex. Agnes Launcecrona became the mistress of the king's close friend, Robert de Vere, earl of Oxford. This was in itself unimportant, but Robert wanted to marry the lady and that meant obtaining an annulment of his existing marriage. The queen made a major error in pressing the Pope to sanction such an annulment, for Robert's countess was no less a person than Philippa de Coucy, daughter of Isabella, countess of Bedford and thus a granddaughter of Edward III and the king's cousin. In fact the annulment was first of all granted in 1387 and then rescinded two years later, so the royal dukes, the king's uncles, were offended for nothing. After Robert's death it was Philippa who received benefit as his widow and not the unfortunate Agnes. This was Queen Anne's only error, and her more usual role in politics was that of mediator.

The royal couple's lack of children, while dynastically unsatisfactory, probably had little effect on the closeness of their relationship. Richard is said never to have forgiven his political opponents for their humiliation of the queen when she begged on her knees for the life of Sir Simon Burley, whom the king loved and who had arranged her marriage, but was spurned by Thomas of Woodstock, duke of Gloucester and his fellow appellants. When Anne died in 1394 at their favourite palace of Shene, apparently of plague, Richard's grief knew no bounds and he had a wing of the palace razed to the ground and never visited it again.

Only two of Anne of Bohemia's letters appear to have survived and therefore both are included here. The intrinsic interest of the first is slight, but the second is of slightly greater importance. The office of escheator was a county one and, like the shrievalty, was, in theory, an annual appointment, as the queen pertinently points out. The task of the office was to safeguard royal interests where land was held directly of the Crown, for if the holder died without heirs, then the property lapsed to the Crown. Offices of this type were eagerly sought after by the gentry in each county. Since Roger Toup had the ear of the queen, he got his post; it was confirmed on 23 December. Michael de la Pole, the chancellor, was the son of a rich wool merchant from Hull, whose loans to the Crown in the reign of the king's grandfather, Edward III, had enabled him to climb to the ranks of the landed

Crown made for Anne of Bohemia in 1350

gentry. Michael was summoned to parliament as a baron, fought with the king's father and had been one of those sent to Bohemia to treat for the king's marriage. Two years after the date of this letter he was created earl of Suffolk.

Anne, Queen of England, to Thomas More, her Treasurer, 5 February 1394

Anne, by the grace of God, Queen of England and of France, and Lady of Ireland, to our dear clerk, Thomas More, our treasurer, greeting. We command you to cause to be paid to John Pevensey, clerk of our closet, all that is in arrear on our account of his wages from the feast of Easter last past until the day of the making hereof; and this letter shall be the warrant thereof to you.

Given under our signet at the manor of Langley, the fifth day of February in the seventeenth year of the reign of our most redoubted lord the King.

(PRO SC 1/51/21, French.)

Anne, Queen of England, to the Chancellor and the Treasurer, 12 December 1383

Anne, by the grace of God, Queen of England and of France and lady of Ireland, to our dearly beloved Michael de la Pole, Chancellor of England and Hugh de Segrave, Treasurer, greetings.

We understand from many reports that William Skipworth the younger has held the office of escheator in Lincolnshire for the past three years, and according to the statutes of England he should already have been removed from that office. By these letters we bestow on you the honour, seeking that in respect of the postponement, you should wish to constitute our beloved Roger Toup to the office in place of the said William, knowing that in doing so you are following the law of the kingdom laid down for this great office. Farewell. Given at Shene on 12 December.

(PRO SC 1/56/116, French)

ISABELLA OF VALOIS, SECOND WIFE OF RICHARD II

Grief at the death of a beloved first wife could not prevent a king without an heir from seeking a new bride, but the age of Isabella of Valois, who became queen of England at the tender age of seven, was surely something of a relief to the king. He nevertheless became very fond of the child, who adored him, and with only twenty years between them all might have turned out very well if he had lived. The marriage was a cornerstone of Richard's peace policy. The French king, Charles VI, was very eager for the match with his daughter, and Isabella brought with her £50,000 as the first instalment of her dowry. The expense of Richard's trip to France to fetch her and the style by which he maintained the prestige of the English monarchy is said to have exceeded £200,000. The customary dower of £4,500 was settled on the little queen, but her age meant that her household was smaller and more dependent on the king's than that of an adult queen. Isabella brought with her from France her 'gouvernante', Isabel de Coucy, daughter of the duke of Lorraine and second wife of Enguerrand de Coucy, son-in-law of Edward III. To complete the family connection, Lady de Coucy's stepdaughter, Philippa, wife of Robert de Vere, was also appointed to the queen's household. Both ladies were only in their twenties, and age and dignity was added to the household in the person of Joan, widowed countess of Hereford. There were other French in Isabella's household; one of them, probably a clerk, is plausibly suggested as the author of a major narrative source for the last three years of Richard's reign, *Traison et Mort de Richard II*. In 1339, before he left for Ireland to quell the revolt that had broken out on the death of his viceroy, his cousin and heir presumptive, Roger Mortimer, the king dismissed Lady de Coucy for her extravagance and replaced her with the widowed Lady Mortimer, his niece, Eleanor Holland.

On Henry IV's usurpation, the presence in England of his cousin's child-widow placed the new king in a difficult position. Isabella was ill with grief for two weeks and then her household was moved discreetly from Windsor to Wallingford, then to Leeds and finally to Sonning. There the earl of Kent informed her of the rebellion in favour of restoring her husband, and there she learned of the rebellion's failure and the subsequent death of Richard. From Sonning the queen was removed to Havering, where she remained for the rest of her sojourn in England. There is no doubt that, for Henry, the most satisfactory solution would have been to marry Isabella to his own son and heir, the future Henry V. The French were opposed to such an alliance with a usurper, while the former queen herself refused to countenance such a match. The cost of maintaining her and her household was about £3,000 p.a. and in the circumstances Henry was not reluctant to arrange for her return to her father. The difficulty was the return of her large dowry. In May 1400 a French envoy arrived, bringing her letters from her parents, her uncle, the duke of Orleans, and the duke of Burgundy, all of which were first read by the earl of Worcester, Henry's lieutenant during the king's absence in Wales. According to the envoy, Jean de Hengest, however, he contrived to talk to Isabella privately and tell her that her father would do his utmost to get her back, but that she must never agree to any fresh marriage arrangements. On receiving her assurance that she would not do so even under threat of death, he was able to negotiate with the king and his council for her return. The English wished to consider the claim for the return of the 200,000 franc dowry in the light of the counter-claim for the ransom of King John, Isabella's great-grandfather, captured by the Black Prince at the battle of Poitiers. Before he returned to France, de Hengest was allowed to visit the former queen again, though only in front of witnesses, when she wept and clung to him, imploring her father to take her away at once from where she was. It was nearly another year before Isabella finally returned to France, with her jewels and other possessions, and it cost Henry £4,000 to send her back in a manner that was fitting. The little queen's sad story is concluded by her marriage in 1406 to her cousin Charles, son of the duke of Orleans, and her death at the birth of her daughter, Jeanne, in 1410. No letters written on her behalf as queen of England are known to have survived.

The Lancastrian and Yorkist Queens

JOAN OF NAVARRE, WIFE OF HENRY IV

When Henry IV came to the throne in 1399 he was a widower. He had married in 1380 at the age of fifteen, Mary, daughter and co-heiress of the last Bohun earl of Hereford. Mary was ten at the time, and two years later she bore her first son, who died, but before her own death in childbirth in 1394, she produced for Henry four sons and two daughters who lived. In 1396 a marriage was proposed between the widowed earl of Derby, as Henry then was, and a daughter of the king of Navarre, supplementary to the negotiations for Richard II's marriage with Isabella of Valois, but it came to naught. Henry did not need a queen to bear him sons, for the succession seemed more than assured, but he did need a wife to give him comfort and share the loneliness of a king's life. A foreign alliance gave credibility to a usurper, but there are good reasons for believing Henry selected his second wife for himself. In 1399 Joan of Navarre was the widow of Duke John IV of Brittany. The duke had been very much older than his third wife and had been married earlier to Henry's aunt Mary, daughter of Edward III and then to Joan Holland, daughter of Joan, Princess of Wales. Joan of Navarre, however, was the mother of his children and regent for her ten-year-old son, John V. Henry had certainly visited Brittany before he became king, and from the beginning of his reign had maintained close connections with the duchy. In April 1402 the couple were married by proxy and Joan became the first widow to be queen since 1066. There were no children of the marriage, but none were needed. The new queen had perforce to leave her young sons in Brittany, but she brought her daughters to England. She seems to have succeeded in establishing a good relationship with her stepchildren; years later, when her stepson Henry V was king, grants were made, not to the queen, but to the 'king's mother, the queen'.

Despite its personal success, the marriage of Henry and Joan was never popular in England, largely because of the Breton connection. Despite the close ties between the English and Breton royal families, rivalries betwen English and Breton seamen were strong and the ever present problem of piracy kept Anglo-Breton relations at a low ebb. Any chance that Henry might have been able to control Breton affairs through his young stepson was firmly eliminated when Joan was required to surrender her regency to her uncle, the duke of Burgundy, and her son, Duke John, then passed into the French control of his father-in-law, Charles VI. The cool reception given to the news of the marriage was compounded when Joan arrived with a large train of attendants. A committee of lords in the parliament of 1404 requested that 'all French persons, Bretons, Lombards, Italians and Navarrese be removed out of the palace'. Exceptions in the first instance were made only for the queen's two daughters, Blanche and Marguerite, one lady, Marie de Parency, and two gentlemen and their wives. Since neither the king nor queen made any objection, the lords relented and allowed her to keep a further dozen, including a cook, a nurse, two knights, two esquires and a damsel. While it was only reasonable that her daughters should have been brought up with a number of their fellow countrymen in their household, Joan undoubtedly courted unpopularity by the excessive numbers she brought to the country. Additional anger was felt when she solicited the king to grant her Breton prisoners taken at Dartmouth by Sir John Cornwall, and then released them without ransom. It took some time for Joan to reverse this initial poor impression.

When she married Henry, Joan brought no dowry from her father, Charles II of Navarre, but she did have a large sum of money bequeathed her by her late

An effigy of Joan of Navarre from the tomb of Henry IV, Canterbury Cathedral

husband and the income from her Breton dower lands, the county of Nantes, the administration of which she had to surrender. For neither two sources of income was she answerable to the king of England. Despite this unprecedented situation, Henry settled on his new wife an extraordinarily large English dower. As we have seen, for 200 years or more, the recognized dower for a queen was £4,500 p.a. It may often have proved an inadequate sum to support the queen during her husband's lifetime, and was often increased by additional grants when necessary, particularly if she had young children, but it provided a dowager with a very comfortable income. Henry chose to dower Joan to the sum of 10,000 marks (more than £6,500). It is not appropriate to discuss the financial problems of Henry IV's reign here, but they were exacerbated by granting the queen a dower he could not afford and which was to become a burden on the country for the rest of her husband's reign and much of his son's. As was customary, Joan was paid by exchequer grant until she received lands to the equivalent value. Almost immediately she was granted the castles of Bristol, Nottingham and Leeds, and the manors of Geddington, Langley, Woodstock, Ludgershall, Gillingham and Rockingham, all familiar as having long been queens' possessions. A little later she received Hertford castle and the manor of Havering. On the death of Henry's stepmother, Katherine Swynford, duchess of Lancaster, her annuity of £1,000, charged upon duchy lands, was transferred to the queen. Various grants of a smaller nature were made at various times, but by June 1404 Joan's dower was already £3,500 in arrears, which had to be paid off from money raised as part of a clergy tax of a tenth on their moveable possessions, despite the threat of an invasion from France. In May 1408 Joan received another substantial grant, which included a number of manors formerly held by Queen Anne, among them Devizes and Odiham. It was not until she had been married six years that Joan received some sort of endowment for all her dower and even then it was not all secured in the most satisfactory way, on land, fee farms and customs. Henry had been forced to rely on temporary expedients and the problems of his wife's dower were to be raised again in an extraordinary way during his son's reign.

As well as her dower payments from the duchy, the queen also received occasional deliveries of delicacies from her old home at Vannes. In England, her favourite residences seem to have been Cirencester, Sonning and Devizes, the latter also favoured by a number of earlier queens. At Westminster the new tower at the great gate of the palace served as her business premises. Here her treasurer, John Chandeler, later bishop of Salisbury, conducted her affairs and stored his records. Although some of her personal attendants were Breton, there was no question of her officials being anything other than English, like her receiver-general, William Denys, her chancellor, John Tubbay, who was murdered in 1414 (though not apparently in connection with the queen's affairs), and who was replaced by John Mapleton, and Henry Luttrell, her steward.

The marriage of Henry IV and Joan of Navarre, though lacking the passionate attachment of some earlier royal unions, seems to have been happy enough. The queen spent a considerable amount of her time in the king's company, always a sign that a couple were content, and Henry proved to be a loyal and generous husband. Joan's influence over him, though not immoderate, was exercised in the traditional queenly ways. She made constant attempts to promote better feeling between the English and the Bretons, whose relations were bedevilled by the question of piracy, and once in 1407, at her special request, a short truce was arranged with France. She also used her influence on Henry to secure preferment for scholars at Oxford and Cambridge. The countess of Oxford had her property restored at the instance of the queen after she had sued for pardon in 1404, and in 1405 Joan was instrumental in obtaining pardons for the abbots of Colchester and Byleigh. This type of intercession on the part of a queen was time-hallowed, if not obligatory, and most queens practised it; the best known example is probably Queen Philippa begging on her knees for the lives of the burghers of Calais, but while a queen could hope to soften her husband's heart, she could not necessarily hope to have the same effect on others, as Queen Anne found when she pleaded for the life of Simon Burley only to be told brutally by the earl of Arundel that she would do better to save her prayers for herself and her husband.

On Henry's death in 1413 Joan showed no desire to rejoin her family in Brittany. Her relations with her stepchildren were affectionate and since Henry V did not marry until 1420, for much of his reign she remained the only queen of England, participating on state occasions in that role. On his departure for France in 1414, Henry graciously licenced her to reside with her retinue in any of his castles of Windsor, Wallingford, Berkhampsted and Hertford during his absence. During these years her Breton family caused her considerable grief. Her daughter Marguerite died in 1407 and her youngest son Jules on a visit to England in 1412. Although Henry V disliked her son John V of Brittany, at her request he was persuaded to sign a truce with him whereby they each agreed to keep out of the other's way and refrain from all acts of war against each other. Despite this, the queen's son Arthur fought for the French at Agincourt and was seriously wounded and taken prisoner. The duke of Alençon, husband of her eldest daughter, was killed and so was her brother, Charles of Navarre, the Constable of France. As queen of England, Joan was expected to suppress her tears and rejoice with the rest. This somewhat ambivalent position goes some way towards explaining the major event of her widowhood.

In September 1419 on the orders of her stepson, John, duke of Bedford, the regent, and the council, Joan was was arrested at her manor of Havering and all her possessions were sequestered. The reason given by the council was that her confessor, John Randolph, had accused her of witchcraft in attempting the death and destruction of the king. The charge obviously required some response from the council and though

Joan was never formally charged, she suffered an initial imprisonment at Pevensey, in the custody of Sir John Pelham, before being sent to live in comfortable confinement at her own castle of Leeds until Henry V on his deathbed commanded her release. It is reasonably safe to say that the charges against her were unfounded and were not even taken too seriously in court circles; she had, after all, nothing to gain from Henry's death. The real reason behind them was the need for the war-impoverished crown to resume her lands and for three years it had an additional income of nearly 10,000 marks p.a. Before her arrest the king had tried desperately hard to borrow as much money from her as he could and it may be that her resistance made the charge of witchcraft seem a godsend to Henry. He was himself about to marry and needed the wherewithal to support his new wife. Nor was the queen left penniless for she still had the income from her Breton dower. After her release no stigma seems to have been attached to her, but she had difficulty in regaining her dower because much of it had been regranted; however, she received other grants in compensation. After Henry V's death her life was that of a typical queen-dowager; his son, Henry VI seems to have been fond of her and regarded her as a grandmother. She died in 1437 and was buried beside her husband at Canterbury.

Queen Joan's first husband, John, duke of Brittany, had been brought up by Edward III who had been appointed his guardian by his father. His first wife was Edward's daughter Mary, who died less than a year after their marriage. He then married Joan, daughter of Thomas Holland, earl of Kent and his wife Joan, afterwards Princess of Wales. Joan of Navarre was his third wife and the mother of his four sons. The close ties of Brittany with England had meant that for a long time he was on very bad terms with the French and indeed in 1378 his duchy was formally confiscated. It was restored after a reconciliation with the French king in 1381. This in turn led to an estrangement with Richard II, who judged his English earldom of Richmond forfeit. It was these lands that the Duchess Joan was referring to in her letter. The earldom was, in fact, restored in May 1398 following a visit to England by the duke and duchess. It is clear that the English and Breton royal families knew each other well and Joan's letter is familiar, even fulsome. Duke John died in November 1399, only a few weeks after the deposition of Richard II.

Joan of Navarre, Duchess of Brittany, to Richard II, 15 March (1398)

My most dear and redoubted lord,

I desire every day to be certified of your good estate, which our Lord grant that it may ever be as good as your heart desires, and as I should wish it for myself. If it would please you to let me know of it, you would give me great rejoicings in my heart, for every time that I hear good news of you I am most perfectly glad at heart.

And if to know tidings from this side would give you pleasure, when this was written my lord, I, and our children were together in good health of our persons, thanks to our Lord, who, by his grace ever grant you the same. I pray you, my dearest and most redoubted lord, that it would ever please you to have the affairs of my said lord well recommended, as well in reference to the deliverance of his lands as other things, which lands in your hands are the cause why he sends his people promptly towards you. So may it please you hereupon to provide him with your gracious remedy, in such manner that he may enjoy his said lands peacefully; even as he and I have our perfect surety and trust in you more than in any other. And let me know your good pleasure, and I will accomplish it willingly and with a good heart to my power.

My dearest and most redoubted lord, I pray the Holy Spirit that he will have you in his holy keeping.

Written at Vannes, the 15th day of March.

(Cotton. MS. Julius B. VI, fol. 25, French. Wood, vol. i, letter xxvii.)

Henry of Bolingbroke was as well known to the duke and duchess of Brittany as Richard II. Duchess Joan calls him 'cousin', a term used loosely to any relative, but in fact he was the nephew of her husband's first wife. It was quite likely that when he went into exile in 1398 that he visited the Breton court. The following letter was written only a few months after Duke John died and before there was any suggestion of marriage between his widow and the new English king, but its affectionate tone indicates how much personal preference was involved when the marriage was proposed. Henry's willingness to aid the duchess's namesake in her affairs may not have been entirely altruistic.

Joan of Navarre, Duchess of Brittany, to Henry IV, 15 February 1400

My very dear and most honourable lord and cousin,

Since I am desirous to hear of your good estate, which our Lord grant that it may ever be as good as your noble heart knows best how to desire, and, indeed, as I would wish it for myself, I pray you, my most dear and honoured cousin, that it would please you very often to let me know the certainty of it, for the very great joy and gladness of my heart; for every time that I can hear good news of you, it rejoices my heart very greatly. And if of your courtesy you would hear the same from across here, thanks to you, at the writing of these presents, I and my children were together in health of our persons, thanks to God, who grant you the same, as Joanna of Bavalen, who is going over to you, can tell you more fully, whom please it you to have recommended in the business on which she is going over. And if anything that I can do over here will give you pleasure, I pray you to let me know it, and I will accomplish it with a very good heart, according to my power.

My dearest and most honoured lord and cousin, I pray the Holy Spirit to have you in his holy keeping.

Written at Vannes, the 15th day of February.

(Cotton. MS. Julius B. VI, fol. 25, French. Wood, vol. i, letter xxviii.)

The following letter was written only a fortnight after the great victory of Agincourt, and it was addressed to Joan's third stepson, John, who had been left in England as regent for his brother the king. Queen Joan seems to have had a very good relationship with her stepchildren, having had to leave her own sons behind in Brittany, and her affection for John is clearly expressed, even in a letter which is essentially a business one concerning a fee due to her own attorney-general. Family feeling, however, did not prevent the queen's 'dearest and best-beloved son' from ordering her arrest and imprisonment when reasons of state dictated it.

This letter is the first of a queen of England which bears a signature; neither of Joan's earlier ones do, but they were more formal, written from one court to another. There is, however, no reason to suppose that Joan was the first queen to know how to write; a signature was not regarded as necessary on a letter which bore a seal.

Joan, Queen of England, to her stepson, John, Duke of Bedford, 10 November 1415

High and puissant prince, our dearest and best-beloved son,

We thank you entirely, because we know well that you desire to know of our good estate. So be it known unto you, dearest son, that at the making of these presents we were in good condition of our person, God be thanked, who ever grant you the same; and be good enough to certify us by all messengers of your health, of which we are equally desirous to know, for our consolation and joy, always when we can know good news of you.

Our dearest and best-beloved son, the very singular desire that we have for the accomplishment of the matter contained in the supplication herein enclosed, touching the fee of our dear and good friend John Faringdon, our attorney-general, on account of his own commendable desserts, causes us at present to write to you, praying you, with most entire heart, that, having understood the tenor of the said supplication, you will therein grant him your good and gracious service for love of us, that, according to the effect and purpose of this, he may be paid his said fee; that thus is our hearty prayer may take full effect in accomplishment of our desire in this matter, according to the entire confidence we have in you.

And if there be anything on our part that we can do to your pleasure, be pleased to signify it, and we will accomplish it with very good heart, according to our power. Our Lord give you in honour and perfect health a very good life, and as long as you desire. Written at our manor of Langley, the 10th day of November.

(Cotton. MS. Vespasian F. III, art. 5, fol. 5, French. Wood, vol. i, letter xxxv.)

KATHERINE OF VALOIS, WIFE OF HENRY V

The negotiations which preceded the marriage of Henry V and Katherine of Valois, youngest sister of Queen Isabella, must rank among the most protracted in the annals of English royal marriages. What had begun in 1408 as a match proposed as part of the general peace negotiations, ended at the Treaty of Troyes in 1420 with Henry finally taking Katherine as his wife, assuming the regency of France during the remainder of her father's lifetime and the throne after his death. Henry had met Katherine briefly in 1419 and had clearly been charmed by what he saw (thus giving rise to one of Shakespeare's most delightful love scenes as he depicts the meeting).

Contemporary chroniclers on both sides of the Channel tell of their love at first sight and even making allowances for their conventional romanticism, there was probably at least an element of truth in the story. Little is known of Katherine's feelings, but the king's actions at least suggest that his infatuation was short-lived. Katherine had beauty to recommend her but neither the intelligence nor personality to captivate for long a man of Henry V's qualities. The couple were married at Troyes Cathedral in June 1420 and in the following February Henry brought his queen to England on what was to be his last visit. Katherine made her state entry into London and was crowned the following day by Archbishop Chichele of Canterbury. Before Henry was required to return to France, they were sure of Katherine's pregnancy, and she remained behind to bear what all hoped would be a son to inherit the combined thrones of England and France. The future Henry VI was born at Windsor in December 1421 and early in the new year Katherine returned to France. She was staying with her parents at Senlis at the time of Henry's death. He made no attempt to send for her and few of his dying thoughts, so concerned for his son, were spared for his wife. She accompanied his body back to London, a widow at twenty-one.

Whatever problems Katherine faced in 1422, they did not include poverty. Her dower had been set at 40,000 crowns (or 10,000 marks), the same as that granted to Queen Joan. Since she had in effect brought her husband the throne of France, it was agreed that she should bring no cash dowry. Having seen at first hand the problems caused by his stepmother's dower, and since, of course, Joan was still very much alive in 1420, though technically deprived of her lands, there were none of the traditional dower lands available for Katherine. Initially, at least, Katherine's household was supported by the income from Joan's confiscated lands. Her four damsels each received 'ten livres apiece out of the funds of Queen Joan', and her confessor, Master John Boyars received twenty livres. Henry decided to endow her mainly from his personal Lancastrian lands and settled on her what was essentially the Bohun inheritance of his own mother, together with the major duchy of Lancaster honours of Leicester, Knaresborough, Hertford and Melbourne. Hertford was to become the queen's most favoured residence, while Joan spent most of her time at Havering and Langley. For the rest of Katherine's life, that is, until 1437, no records survive of the administration of this part of the duchy. Although she was free to appoint her own officials, she wisely, presumably on the advice of her husband and lacking any interest on her own part, chose duchy officers for her own officials. For instance her steward, John Leventhorpe, was also receiver-general for the duchy and her chancellor, John Wodehouse, fufilled the same office for the duchy. One surviving valor of her lands, taken in 1432, shows that after all charges were met, the total left in Katherine's hands for her own use was £4,360 9s 7d, nearly 6,540 marks, considerably less than the sum specified for her dower in the Treaty of Troyes, but similar to the sum received by queens before Joan. The treaty had also specified that although France paid no dowry it would provide her with an annuity of 20,000 crowns in the event of her widowhood. This was secured on lands after 1422 and the queen had her own French officials. However, the income from these lands was clearly dependent on continuing English success in France. When dealing with her French officials, Katherine described herself as Queen of England, daughter of Charles, King of France and mother of Henry, King of England and France.

During the first eight years of his reign, while Henry VI was still a small child, Queen Katherine spent much of her time with her son, but by the time of his return from his French coronation in 1430, new preoccupations had claimed her. The position of a youthful queen-dowager was never an easy one. Since the Conquest there had been five of them; Adela of Louvain, Berengaria of Navarre and Katherine's own sister, Isabella, had no children, and were thus free to remarry if they chose. Margaret of France was not the mother of her husband's heir and only

Isabella of Angoulême's situation was analagous to Katherine's. Yet she had her own inheritance in southern France to which to return and it was there she chose to remarry. There was little point in Katherine returning to France, of which her son was titular king and where her brother, Charles VII, was fighting a guerilla war against the English occupation, but the question of her possible remarriage in England raised all sorts of political questions. Chief of these was the possibility of a stepfather gaining undue influence over a very youthful king. A suggestion that Katherine was contemplating marriage with Edmund Beaufort, her late husband's cousin, was enough, given the factional politics of the minority, to cause the swift passing of a statute in 1428. This prohibited anyone from marrying a queen-dowager without the king's permission, which could only be given after he reached the age of discretion. Katherine was not prepared to wait another ten years for her son to grow up, nor was she, in the words of a contemporary chronicler, 'able to fully curb her carnal passions'. The result was a secret marriage to a Welsh squire in her household named Owen Tudor. The queen was greatly disparaged by the match, but there were plenty of precedents among noble widows, and her sister-in-law, Jacquetta of Luxembourg, duchess of Bedford, was to follow suit when she married one of her household, Richard Woodville. There is no doubt that the queen's remarriage actually took place. It may not have been common knowledge but the Council certainly knew of it and may even have been relieved that there were unlikely to be political repercussions. The marriage probably took place in 1430, possibly when the queen became pregnant with Owen's first child. She was to give him three sons and a daughter before her early death in 1437. Officially he held the position of clerk to her wardrobe, where he was responsible for the security of her jewels and robes. Shortly before she died, Katherine entered Bermondsey Abbey and in her will refers to 'a long, grievous malady' from which she had been suffering. What it was, we do not know, though it is possible that the affliction was mental rather than physical, given the histories of both her father and her son, Henry. The will appointed the king as her executor and Cardinal Beaufort and her brother-in-law, Humphrey, duke of Gloucester, as supervisors, but it makes no mention of her second family, merely begging the king in guarded tones for the 'tender and favourable fulfilling of mine intent'. In 1452 the king created her sons by Owen, Edmund and Jasper, earls of Richmond and Pembroke. Edmund was to become the father of Henry VII.

None of Katherine's letters are known to have survived and little is known of the queen's tastes and interests, though the well-known story of Owen Tudor first attracting her attention by falling into her lap during a dance suggests that dancing and music may have been among them. Only one instance of queenly intervention on her part is recorded, when at her coronation feast, she pleaded, apparently successfully, with the king for the liberty of his prisoner, James I of Scotland. If she also pleaded for her sister Isabella's widower, Charles, duke of Orleans, then in strict captivity in Pontefract, she was less successful.

MARGARET OF ANJOU, WIFE OF HENRY VI

The marriage of Henry VI and Margaret, daughter of René, duke of Anjou, titular king of Sicily, Naples and Hungary, took place in 1445. As a child, Henry VI was far more isolated than any Plantagenet child before him. He had no siblings and no English cousins, although his Breton cousin, Gilles, grandson of Joan of Navarre and son of his mother's sister, Jeanne, was brought up with him and they were very attached. His mother, Queen Katherine, who had been very close to him in his early childhood virtually abandoned him for her second family when he was eight. This was bound to have had an effect on Henry's emotional development; so too, was the bitter political rivalry between two of his closest surviving male relatives, his uncle, Humphrey of Gloucester and Cardinal Beaufort, his great uncle of the half-blood. Because he was already king, he could not be surrounded by a household full of boys of a similar age as a mere prince would have been. He was instead brought up by ageing, distinguished soldiers. What Henry almost certainly needed was an early marriage. In similar circumstances it had been highly beneficial for Richard II, but Henry was not to be so lucky. Instead of being married at fifteen to a girl of his own age, Henry had to wait until he was twenty-three and his attitude to women was already largely formed. At fifteen he already seemed to a papal envoy in 1437 more like a monk than a king, and he avoided the sight and conversation of women.

When Henry married Margaret of Anjou in 1445, she was sixteen and brought no dowry with her, but she was the living symbol of the truce with France and the hope of future peace. Given the circumstances of her marriage, it is hardly surprising that she did all she could to foster peace, and developed close relations with members of the peace party. Even as a young woman she seems to have had the qualities of firmness and determination which later so characterized her. Henry, on the other hand, was accustomed to being surrounded by dominant figures, and there is no reason to believe that the marriage was not, at the least, averagely happy. The couple spent most of their time in each other's company and the relationship between their two households was close. The queen's influence on Henry was apparent to all, and the only cloud on their personal horizon was the lack of children. As we have seen, a number of earlier queens had taken several years to produce their first child, but in this case the need for a son was urgent for Henry had no close heir presumptive. None of Henry V's three brothers had left legitimate children and the king's nearest English male relative in the royal line was Henry Holland, duke of Exeter, grandson of Richard II's half-brother and Elizabeth, daughter of John of Gaunt. This, however, was to overlook the claims of Richard, duke of York, descended from both the second and fourth sons of Edward III. When Margaret finally gave birth to her son Edward in 1453, Henry had already lapsed into his first bout of mental illness and the arrival of a heir apparent made any political settlement with York much more difficult.

Margaret's father, René, duke of Anjou, was a man as rich in titles as he was poor in worldly goods. She brought only a small entourage with her to England but the embassy sent to France to escort her thither was lavish in the extreme. Headed by the marquess of Suffolk and his lady, it required seventy ships to transport it, and its cost over a period of six months was £5,573 17s 5d. Added to this was the cost of refurbishing royal palaces which had effectively had no queen for twenty years. Like her two Lancastrian predecessors, Margaret was granted a dower of 10,000 marks p.a. The war-drained exchequer did not find this easy to provide. Only about £2,000 worth of lands were available to be settled on the queen; these included the duchy of Lancaster honours of Tutbury, Leicester and Kenilworth, a concentration in the midlands which was later to provide Margaret with a power base. Gradually over the years she also aquired a number of the more traditional dower lands, Havering, Gillingham, Rockingham, Odiham and Hadleigh, with income from the fee farms of Southampton, Devizes, Bristol and Marlborough, among others. In addition to her lands, Margaret was also granted at the time of her marriage a cash annuity of £1,000 from duchy sources and, on the death of Duke Humphrey of Gloucester, a further annuity of 500 marks. The rest of her income was drawn from various cash sources such as the customs of Southampton, over which she and her officials had no control, and as Henry's financial problems worsened they became harder to collect. Following Queen Katherine's example, Margaret employed duchy officials in her own household with the result that her income from duchy sources usually came in promptly, but her income from cash sources was often several years in arrears. It appears that her servants pursued the collection of her revenue with great determination, presumably reflecting the queen's own attitudes.

Despite the financial difficulties of her husband and the problems of collecting her own revenues, Margaret of Anjou's household was larger and more lavish than that of any other medieval queen, save only Isabella of France in the days of her personal rule. For 1451–2, the total household expenditure was £7,539 15s 4¾d, much higher than that of her predecessors. Her chancellor (successively the half-brothers William and Lawrence Booth) had a clerk of the register to assist him, William Cotton, the receiver-general, a clerk of receipt; there was a clerk of the jewels to record her purchases and gifts for the treasurer of her chamber; a clerk of the signet to write her personal letters; a secretary for her council; and so the list proliferated, all offices that were created under Margaret. Her estate officials, as for earlier Lancastrian queens, were usually officials of the duchy of Lancaster. The

Margaret of Anjou, a drawing of a window once in the church of the Cordeliers, Angers

queen's council met daily in the chamber assigned to her for that purpose at Westminster. Its purpose, like the council of any large landowner, was to advise the queen, assist in the administration of her estates and handle her legal business. Besides comprising her senior household officers, it included a number of prominent men of affairs, such as the duke of Somerset and Lord Scales.

Margaret's personal attendants were headed by her chamberlain, Sir John Wenlock. An ordinance for the regulation of the royal household, drawn up in 1445, the year of Margaret's marriage, lists sixty-six persons as the appropriate number of the queen's household. The list was headed by a countess as senior lady, with seven personal staff of her own, followed by a baroness with five attendants, and two other ladies and six damsels. Two chamberers and two launderers made up the distaff side of the household. Under the chamberlain were listed three chaplains and a secretary, three carvers, two ushers, two sewers, four squires, a master of horse, two henchmen, nine valets, four boys and a page. There is no reason to suppose Margaret's household ever conformed exactly to this pattern. In her accounts for 1452–3, for instance, her senior lady was Lady Scales, a baroness, who received a fee of £40 p.a., but she had three ladies: Isabel, Lady Grey (despite the Christian name, this is almost certainly Elizabeth Woodville); Margaret, daughter of Lord Roos; and Isabel, daughter of Lord Dacre; each receiving £20 p.a. Wenlock received £40 for his office of chamberlain and Sir Edward Hull and Sir Andrew Ogard (a naturalized Dane) received £53 6s 8d between them for duties as knights carvers. Slight variations on the regulation size of her household were insignificant, but it is clear that Margaret's household was far bigger than the authorized sixty-six persons. When the king first became ill, the Great Council, called in 1454, attempted some economies and reforms of the royal households. Reiterating the size regarded as proper for the king in 1445, it sugggested 424 servants and officials for the king, but demanded that the size of the queen's household be reduced to 120, that is, to a size twice that regarded as appropriate nine years before. The queen had more than doubled the size of her own household; in 1452–3 she was in fact paying wages to 151 persons, though this included about twenty men who were clerks and administrators rather than personal attendants. The baby prince had his own household of 38 persons. It is certainly possible to see this enlarging of the queen's household as reflecting Margaret's increasing political influence.

Towards those who served her, Margaret proved an indefatigable patron. She was even prepared to compete with the king, as when her pressing recommendation to the Pope on behalf of her chancellor, Lawrence Booth, led him to appoint Booth to the see of Durham, despite the fact that Henry had already nominated his physician, John Arundell. Benefices, offices, profitable marriages, the queen supported her servants' claims to all of them. She was not, of course, always successful, but her energy and determination on their behalf brought her, in return, devoted service. Cotton, her receiver-general, died fighting for her at Towton; Lord Beaumont, her chief steward of lands, at Northampton; and Edward Ellesmere, who rose to be treasurer of her chamber, was attainted after Towton. In 1448, in an attempt to secure the cash parts of her dower, the young queen was licensed to ship wool free of customs, a privilege bitterly resented by the merchant class. In 1453 she was granted royal rights of justice on her lands, that is, the right to exclude the king's officials and impose her own trading tolls. Her presence and power, therefore, were increasingly felt in all parts of the country where she held land.

In political terms the queen soon became a force to be reckoned with. The English royal family, then as now, were expected to be above faction, to dispense justice and patronage even-handedly. Failure to do so risked a political crisis. Margaret's French upbringing was quite different; both her mother and grandmother had had to fight fiercely to protect their family interests in the absence of their husbands, and once in England Margaret soon perceived she might have to take on a similar role to support her husband. The years of Henry's minority saw the rise of two competing parties, one based on the desire to seek a peaceful settlement with France, the other opposed to it. The queen's marriage had resulted from the success of the first party, and it was the one her husband was temperamentally inclined to. She came to England in the company of the duke of Suffolk, the man responsible for the negotiations, determined to do all she could to promote peace. While this was a laudable, indeed queenly, aim in itself, it was a grave political error for the queen to be seen to favour one faction to the exclusion of the other. Her relations with Suffolk remained close; his wife, Alice Chaucer, entered her service and remained a friend. There is no reason to give credence to contemporary rumours of a liaison between the queen and duke, but the fact that such rumours existed reflect the queen's lack of wisdom and increased her unpopularity.

Henry's mental collapse just prior to their son's birth thrust more responsibility on the queen. She was not prepared to hand over the reins of government to the duke of York and politics in England were reduced to a duel between the two for supremacy. In the words of Henry's recent biographer, Ralph Griffiths, 'Contemporaries found her a determined and ruthless woman . . . It was Margaret who had insisted on York's removal as Protector in February 1456, even though the king was far less hostile to him, and it was she who forced the pace in 1459 at a council meeting at Coventry where the Yorkist lords were condemned.' The royal family retreated to a power base in the midlands centred on the duchy of Lancaster honours which were part of Margaret's dower, and close to Prince Edward's hereditary Cheshire lands. From there, as one contemporary put it, 'The queen with such as were of her affinity ruled the realm as she liked.' Her determination to bring York down and to treat him as a rebel was successful in the short term, but led directly to the fall of the house of Lancaster. The defeat and death of York at the battle of Wakefield was followed by the move of the queen's army south. The permission she gave that army to loot and pillage Yorkist towns along the way was a severe political miscalculation and inspired in London, at least, a determination never to let the queen and her army into the city. It was with London's support that York's son, Edward, was able to seize the throne, and his defeat of the queen's army at Towton secured it for him. For the first decade of Edward IV's reign, Margaret never gave up her attempts, either military or political, to regain her husband's throne for him. She traded Berwick to the Scots and married her son to the daughter of one of her greatest political enemies, and though that achieved the brief Re-adeption of Henry VI, it ultimately led to the deaths of both her son and her husband.

Henry was captured in 1463 and from then until his death, after Margaret's defeat of Tewkesbury, the royal couple never saw each other again. With the death of their son after Tewkesbury, Margaret ceased to be a threat to Edward and, although he might have been justified in imprisoning her, he could afford to be lenient and she was placed in the custody of her old friend, Alice Chaucer, duchess of Suffolk, at Wallingford. Now harmless, the former queen might have expected to live the rest of her life in obscure retirement, but fate and politics had not finished with her yet. In 1475, when Edward IV and Louis XI drew up the treaty of Picquigny, it was arranged that Louis should ransom his cousin Margaret for £10,000. The queen, in order to obtain her release, had to agree to renounce all her rights as queen consort in England, including her dower rights, a totally unjust demand on Edward's part. Nor was Louis acting out of chivalry. He wanted Margaret to renounce all claim to the inheritance of her father, René of Anjou, and mother, Isabel of Lorraine. In return he granted her the modest pension of 6,000 crowns p.a. On her father's death in 1480, she retired to a small château near Saumur, where she died two years later. Margaret's political sense and judgment were inappropriate in England, but although she was not a likeable woman she cannot fail to command respect, and ultimately, pity.

Margaret of Anjou was the first medieval queen whose letters are written entirely in English, and while they were not penned with her own hand, presumably she had learned the language well enough to dictate in it. When Queen Margaret's dower was set, £1,000, a large proportion of it, was charged upon the customs of Southampton. She found, as many a queen had before her, that this type of income could not be relied upon. Within two or three years of her marriage, payment of it was in arrears, hence the following letter, and Parliament therefore agreed to the commutation of money payments into lands held of the duchy of Lancaster. Sir John Wenlock, her chamberlain, was later to desert her for the Yorkists. Edward IV raised him to the peerage, but Wenlock changed sides again, supporting the earl of Warwick and Henry VI's Re-adeption. He was killed at Tewkesbury, this time fighting for his erstwhile queen.

Margaret of Anjou, Queen of England, to John Somerton, one of the Custumers of Southampton, 1447/8

By the Queen.

Trusty etc. We desire and pray you and also exhort you and require you, that, of such money as is due to us, at Michaelmas term last past, of our dower, assigned to be paid of the custumers of Southampton by your hands, you will do your pain and diligence that we may be contented and paid in all haste. And of the day of your payment you will ascertain by writing our right well beloved knight, Sir John Wenlock, our chamberlain, which knows in what wise the said money must be employed and bestowed in all possible haste; and that you fail not hereof as we trust, and you think to stand in continuance of the favour of our good grace, and to eschew our displeasure.

Given etc.

(Monro, letter lxxviii.)

Queen Margaret was tireless in the pursuit of the interests of her servants and a great many of her letters written on their behalf survive, seeking a living here, an office there, a wife wherever. Two such examples are shown here, the first on behalf of a servant of her chamber, Thomas Shelford, who had come to her via service with the duke of Suffolk. Presumably, Master Kent's ward, the daughter of Hall of Larkfield (in Kent) was a minor heiress. The second is to the bishop of Durham urging the claim of the king's chaplain, Richard Chester, to the mastership of Gretham Hospital. The telling phrase 'as it is said' indicates that the queen was not entirely sure of the facts of the case. Certainly Chester does not appear among the published list of Masters. The bishop, Robert Neville, was a son of Ralph Neville, earl of Westmorland, and Joan, illegitimate daughter of John of Gaunt, duke of Lancaster. Margaret also wrote to William Scrope, who then occupied the position of Master, instructing him to make restitution of it to Chester.

Margaret of Anjou, Queen of England, to R. Kent, c. 1445–50

By the Queen.

Wellbeloved, we greet etc, and let you weet that our wellbeloved servant, Thomas Shelford, whom, for his virtues, and the agreeable service he hath done us herebefore, and in especial now late in the company of our cousin of Suffolk, we have taken into our Chamber, there to serve us about our person, hath reported unto us that, for the good and virtuous demeening that he hath heard of a gentlewoman being in your governance, which was daughter to one Hall of

Larkfield, he desireth full heartily to do her worship by way of marriage, as he saith;
wherefore we desire and pray you heartily that, setting apart all instances or
labours, that have or shall be made unto you for any other person whatsoever he be,
you will by all honest and lawfull means be wellwilled unto the said marriage,
entreating the said gentlewoman unto the same, trusting to God's mercy that it shall
be both for her worship and avail in time to come. And if you will do your tender
diligence to perform this our desire, you shall therein deserve of us right good and
especial thanks, and cause us to show unto you the more especial favour of our good
grace in time to come.
Given etc.

(Monro, letter lx.)

Margaret of Anjou, Queen of England, to Robert Neville, Bishop of Durham
(c. 1451)

Worshipful father, etc. and we verily suppose that it is clearly in your
remembrance how that now late we wrote unto you for the recommendation
of my lord's clerk and ours, Master Richard Chester unto the restitution of the
hospital of Gretham, and his goods, longing unto him there of right, as it is said.
Wherein as yet you have not accomplished our intention, to our great marvel.
Wherefore we pray you eftsoons that you suffer our said clerk to rejoyse [re-enjoy]
his said hospital with the said goods, as right, law and good conscience require; or
else to certify us the cause in writing why you will not, or ought not, to do so of
right. As you desire to stand in the favour of our good grace in time coming. Given
at W[indsor].

(Monro, letter lxxxix.)

The earl of Northumberland, to whom the following letter was addressed, was the
son of Henry Percy, 'Hotspur', and his wife, Elizabeth Mortimer. He was a
companion in arms to Henry V and one of the executors of the king's will. His
mother married as her second husband, Thomas, Lord Camoys, and therefore,
Roger, Lord Camoys, who is referred to in the letter, was Northumberland's half-
brother. Roger spent much of his time serving the Lancastrian cause in France. In
1436 he relieved the garrison of Calais and in 1443 was captured by the French and
held in various prisons while he made arrangements for the payment of his ransom.
Sir Matthew Gough, a leading figure in the administration of Normandy, negotiated
the ransom, himself standing surety that a large sum would be paid on a certain day.
Camoys' wealthy brother, the earl, was also called in to stand surety and may have

been responsible for the collection of the ransom money from Camoys' lands. In any event the sum was not paid in time and Gough, and probably Camoys himself were put at risk. The queen's letter presumably had some effect since Camoys was released. He was made seneschal of Gascony and captured again after a vain defence of Bordeaux following the English defeat at Castillon in 1453. He eventually supported the duke of York in his rebellion against the king. Gough meanwhile had died in 1450, fighting against the rebels under Jack Cade.

Margaret of Anjou, Queen of England, to Henry Percy, Earl of Northumberland (1445–50)

By the Queen

Right trusty and wellbeloved cousin, we greet you well, letting you wit that, upon truste and surety of your obligation, wherein you were bounden, as we be informed, unto our wellbeloved squire, Mathew Gough, in 2000 saluts [a gold coin worth 25s], for the finance of the lord Camoys, we were the rather inclined and benevolent to desire our said squire, by our letters, to do all his pain and diligence for the deliverance of the said lord. At whose instance and request our said squire took upon him to lay his seal in this matter. And it is now so, that he has ascertained us that the day prefixed of your payment is past and run; so that the charge lies now upon him, and must needs be driven by justice to answer that to himself, and likely, in your default, to be dishonoured and rebuked for ever; the which we suppose you will take right nigh to heart, in especial since he was brought in thereto by your means. Wherefor we desire and exhort you, upon your worship, that, in all goodly haste, you do content your said sum, in saving our said squire harmless, so that we be no more called upon, in lack of your devoir, and true aquittal, in this part. Given at Windsor the viii day of March.

(Monro, letter lxxvi.)

The manor of Hertingfordbury in Hertfordshire formed part of the queen's dower and was a duchy of Lancaster manor. The date of this letter is unclear, but in another, Margaret complained that her bailiff, William Southwood, had been set upon by Edmund Pyrcan. Clearly there was something seriously amiss, and it may be that Pyrcan and Sir John Forester were acting in concert. A riot by the queen's tenants that landed many of them in jail, seemingly as a result of the actions of Forester, himself a tenant, was something that Margaret was unlikely to ignore, but it speaks volumes for the semi-lawless state of the countryside in the mid-fifteenth century that Forester could take such action on a manor of the queen's so relatively close to London.

Margaret of Anjou, Queen of England, to Sir John Forester, knight, n.d.

By the Queen.

Trusty and wellbeloved, We let you weet, that, this same day, there have been before us a great multitude, both of men and women, our tenants of our lordship of Hertingfordbury, complaining them that you have, and yet be, daily, about to destroy and undo them forever; in so far forth that you have do many of them to be wrongfully endicted, now late, of felony, before the coroner, by your own familiar servants and adherents, not knowing the truth of the matter; and many of them you do keep in prison and the remnent of our tenants dare not abide in their houses for fear of death and other injuries, that you daily do them; and all by colour of a farm that you have there of ours, that, as is said, for your own singular lucre, you wrongfully engross towards you all our tenants livelihood there; not only unto great hindering and undoing of our said tenants, but also unto great derogation and prejudice of us, and our said lordship; wherof we marvel greatly; and, in especial, that you that be judge would take so peaceably the wrongful destruction of our said tenants. Wherefore we will and expressly exhort and require you, that you leave your said labours and business, in especial against us and our said tenants, until time that you have communed and declared you in this matter before us; and that the meanwhile, you do suffer our tenants that be in prison to be mainprised, under sufficient surety; and the remnant of our tenants, guiltless, that be fled, for fear of your destruction, may come home unto our said lordship. And if any of our tenants have offended against the law, our intent is that, the truth known, he shall be painfully punished and chastised as the case requires. And how ye think to be disposed therein you will ascertain us, by the bringer of these, whereto we shall trust; as you desire to stand in the tender and favourable remembrance of our grace therefore in time coming. Given etc. at Windsor etc.

(Monro, letter xcv.)

This last letter of Queen Margaret's is not a personal letter, but is addressed to the citizens of London as a propaganda measure. It was written between early January 1461 when the queen learned that her supporters had defeated and killed Richard, duke of York, at Wakefield and 17 February, when the defeat of York's nephew, Warwick, at St Albans allowed the captive Henry VI to be freed and reunited with his wife and son. The letter vilifies York and seeks to counter the warning that the Yorkist party had issued to London against the imminent arrival of the queen and her son, Edward, Prince of Wales, with a horde of wild northerners bent on despoiling the capital. Since London was the centre of pro-Yorkist sentiment and the citizens were well aware that the Lancastrian northern army had plundered and pillaged the late duke's estates as it travelled south, they slammed their gates in the queen's face and prayed for the arrival of York's son, Edward, earl of March. Soon after he reached London he was crowned as Edward IV.

Margaret of Anjou, Queen of England, to the Citizens of London, 1461

Right trusty and well-beloved, we greet you heartily well.

And whereas the late Duke of York of extreme malice, long hid under colours, imagined by divers and many ways and means the destruction of my lord's good grace, whom God of his mercy ever preserve, hath now late, upon an untrue pretence, feigned a title to my lord's crown, and royal estate, and pre-eminence, contrary to his allegience and divers solemn oaths of his own offer made, uncompelled or constrained, and fully proposed to have deposed him of his regality, ne had been [had it not been for] the sad [wise], unchangeable and true dispositions of you and others, his true liegemen, for the which your worshipful dispositions we thank you as heartily as we can. And howbeit, that the same untrue, unsad, and unadvised person, of very pure malice, disposed to continue in his cruelness, to the utterest undoing, if he might, of us, and of my lord's son and ours, the prince, which with God's mercy, he shall not be of power to perform, by the help of you and all other my lord's faithful disposed subjects, hath thrown among you, as we be certainly informed, divers untrue and feigned matters and surmises; and in especial, that we and my lord's said son and ours should newly draw towards you with an unseen power of strangers, disposed to rob and to despoil you of your goods and havings [property]; we will that you know for certain that, at such time as we or our said son shall be disposed to see my lord, as our duty is and so binds us to do, you, nor none of you, shall be robbed, despoiled, not wronged by any person that at that time we, or our son shall be accompanied with, or any other sent in our or his name. Praying you, on our most hearty and desirous wise, that [above] all earthly things you will diligently intend [attend] to the surety of my lord's royal person in the mean time; so that through malice of his said enemy he be no more troubled, vexed, or jeoparded. And, so doing, we shall be unto you such lady as of reason you shall be largely content. Given under our signet, etc.

(BL Harleian MS 543, fol. 147.)

ELIZABETH WOODVILLE, WIFE OF EDWARD IV

One interested observer of the difficulties Margaret of Anjou encountered in collecting that part of her dower not secured on lands was her lady-in-waiting, Elizabeth, Lady Grey. When she became queen of England in 1464, her husband Edward IV ended the Lancastrians' absurdly overgenerous dower of 10,000 marks p.a. and reverted to the old fourteenth-century level of about £4,500 p.a. Elizabeth Woodville was in no position to press for anything more. She was the widow of a Lancastrian, with two small sons. Her parentage was respectable, but no more, since her mother was Jacquetta of Luxembourg, widow of Henry V's brother, John, duke of Bedford, and her father a mere knight, Sir Richard Woodville. She was several years older than her royal husband and was generally believed to have demanded marriage as the price for her virtue. The couple were married secretly, which was to have important repercussions after Edward's death, and in political terms it was a blunder of major proportions. It deprived England of a foreign royal match and brought the queen's family back into politics after 200 years, for the Woodvilles were a numerous, poverty-stricken and ambitious clan. In addition to the two sons of her first marriage, the new queen had five brothers and seven unmarried sisters. The Woodvilles came of respectable gentry stock, but Elizabeth's father had been created Lord Rivers in 1448 and her eldest brother Anthony was Lord Scales in right of his wife. As his council pointed out to the young king when he announced his marriage to them, 'she was not his match, however good and however fair she might be, and he must know well that she was no wife for a prince such as himself'. Although Edward did not lavish lands on the Woodvilles, they were provided for in other ways. Her father was made Treasurer, always a lucrative post, her seven sisters married to the highest ranking available peers or their heirs, temporarily cornering the aristocratic marriage market. The youngest Woodville, John, was married off to the extremely wealthy dowager duchess of Norfolk, a mere forty-five years his senior. While all this was bound to cause resentment, it was, so to speak, legitimate advancement. Tampering with the customary laws of inheritance to provide endowment for the queen's Grey sons, and the king's younger son, Richard, bitterly offended not only the legitimate heirs but the landowning classes in general. The prominence of the Woodvilles at court, their greedy and grasping behaviour and their suspicion and antagonism towards possible rivals for power all added to their unpopularity.

In many ways the new queen proved a good wife and mother. She was fertile and she ran her household efficiently and economically. It is not really fanciful to suggest that Elizabeth, having learned the lesson in Margaret's household, pressed her doting husband into securing all her dower in land. Not for her the income from customs, fee farms or wardships which had proved so troublesome to collect. Her grant of dower lands again included many traditional ones, but also a number of

A portrait of Queen Elizabeth Woodville as foundress of Queens' College, Cambridge

duchy of Lancaster lands south of the Trent and some of the southern lands of the Bohun earldom, both now incorporated in the Crown's holdings rather than the private inheritance of the Lancastrian kings. Unlike her former mistress, and on a smaller income, Elizabeth proved well able to live within her income. Her household account for 1466–7 shows that her household was smaller than that of any of her predecessors for a century, comprising only 100 persons. In the second decade of Edward's reign, when she and the king were separated for longer periods and she had a nursery full of children, her expenses were considerably heavier. Elizabeth has been criticized for many of her actions as queen, but in this she could not be faulted. She lived within her means, providing an able support in her husband's largely successful attempt to make the royal household administratively efficient and solvent yet impressive in appearance and style. A.R. Myers, in his two articles on the household accounts of Elizabeth and Margaret, makes some pertinent comparisons between the two queens. Elizabeth, for instance, had only seven ladies where Margaret had ten, two attornies-at-law compared to Margaret's five and in almost every aspect of their household expenditure Margaret's was higher, often nearly double. Although it may be argued that their real income was a good deal closer than the disparity in the size of their dower suggests, because of Elizabeth's more securely landed endowment, none the less the fact remains that Elizabeth was careful where Margaret was extravagant. As Myers points out, this is made more interesting by the high degree of continuity among the duchy of Lancaster officials who served both queens. In the end it was the queen's personality and policy rather than the efficacy of her officials which determined the financial position of her household.

This is not to deny the efficiency of Elizabeth's officials, particularly her treasurer and receiver-general, John Forster, and his senior assistant Thomas Holbeche, the clerk of receipt, particularly since most of her officials received less generous allowances than Margaret's had done. A number of the new queen's family held positions in her household: her brother John was master of her horse, her sister Anne, Lady Bourchier, and her sister-in-law Elizabeth, Lady Scales, were ladies-in-waiting, as was Alice, wife of her cousin, Sir John Fogge. Lady Bourchier was married to the son and heir of the earl of Essex; Essex's brother, Lord Berners, was the queen's chamberlain and his son, Sir Humphrey Bourchier, was one of her stewards. All, however, served in established household offices and no family members received higher salaries than custom sanctioned. Lady Bourchier and Lady Scales received £40 p.a. each and the more junior ladies £10 p.a. The earl of Essex was married to the king's aunt, Sir John Fogge was treasurer of the king's household and the queen's other two ladies, Jane, Lady Norris, and Elizabeth, Lady Uvedale, were both married to men in royal service. This close-knit connection between the two royal households was common practice. Elizabeth also numbered among her household seven damsels of gentle birth and two other waiting women, three minstrels, a confessor, Edward Storey, who later became bishop of Carlisle, a physician named Domenico de Sirego, who received a fee of £40 p.a., as large as that of Lord Berners, her chamberlain, and her brother John, master of horse.

There can be little doubt that Elizabeth's influence on her young husband was very strong. She had, after all, induced him to commit the imprudence of making her queen. If he ever regretted it, the only indications are the mistresses he took in the second half of his reign. Elizabeth had two sons by her first marriage, but the first three children she bore Edward were girls. If their eldest child, Elizabeth of York, who was seventeen at the time of her father's premature death in 1483, had been a boy, the political situation would have been very different. The future Edward V, born in 1471, and his brother, Richard, duke of York, born in 1473, had three younger sisters as well as three older ones. It was the largest royal family since Edward III's. Despite the king's interest in other women, there is no indication that the queen's influence over him diminished in the later years of their marriage. As the mother of his heir, her position was unassailable. Other rivals for influence, the king's cousin, the earl of Warwick, and his brother, George, duke of Clarence, were removed and his younger brother, Richard, duke of Gloucester, retired northwards from court. Unfortunately, Elizabeth's influence seems not to have been exercised in the traditional queenly roles of mercy and charity, but mainly in order to advance her own family in wealth and power, and on more than one occasion the easy-going king was manoeuvred into actions which were morally and legally dubious. The queen was seen by her husband's subjects as cold and avaricious and looking at her portrait, the first of an English queen, it is difficult not to see the coldness in her undoubted beauty. A Hungarian visitor commented on the splendour and arrogance of the queen. This arrogance, in a queen of humble birth, was politically very ill-judged and repeated on a number of occasions. Yet Elizabeth was not entirely worldly in her attitude. Queen's College, Cambridge, founded by her predecessor but inadequately endowed, might well not have survived without her patronage. She founded the chapel of St Erasmus in Westminster Abbey and was a particular supporter of the Austin Friars at Huntingdon. She also chose to end her days in the religious surroundings of the Cluniac abbey of Bermondsey. The abbey's chief benefactors had been the Clare family, whose last male representative was her husband the king.

If Elizabeth was not solely responsible for the downfall of the House of York, she and her family must bear a good deal of the blame. They alienated many of the peers; Prince Edward was brought up surrounded by his maternal relatives to the virtual exclusion of his paternal ones and, on the king's death, the very real fear of Woodville rule made Richard III's usurpation possible. Like Queen Margaret before her, Elizabeth paid a very heavy price for her actions. The usurpation deprived her elder son of his throne and both he and his brother of their lives. Richard's parliament declared Elizabeth's own marriage invalid and deprived her of her position as queen-dowager. When she and her daughters were finally persuaded to come out of sanctuary a few months later, her erstwhile brother-in-law granted her, as Dame Elizabeth Grey, the not ungenerous annuity of 700 marks. When Henry VII caused the act invalidating her marriage and illegitimating her children to be repealed, Elizabeth was restored to her former position as queen-dowager, but Henry did not restore her dower lands. After his own wedding to her eldest daughter, Elizabeth of York, Henry did, however, grant his new mother-in-law nearly thirty manors, including a number of traditional dower lands she had formerly held, and a cash income from Bristol and a number of other sources. Considering that Henry had a new wife, his own mother and his wife's grandmother, Cecily, duchess of York (whose York lands had reverted to the Crown) to provide for as well, Elizabeth was treated fairly and quite generously in the circumstances.

Just over a year later, the queen-dowager entered Bermondsey Abbey, apparently on the grounds of ill-health. The argument that she was ordered there and stripped of her lands for complicity in the rebellion of the earl of Lincoln is often advanced. Not only does this make little political sense, but it is contradicted by the favour the king continued to show her. With her sons dead and her daughter queen she was unlikely to jeopardize everything on behalf of a mere nephew of her late husband, albeit the male heir of York, and it is certainly unlikely that she believed Lambert Simnel to be the earl of Warwick. On the contrary, she stood godmother at the christening of Henry's heir, a signal honour, and was proposed as a wife for the widowed James III of Scotland and continued to receive gifts of money made to 'the right dear and right well beloved Queen Elizabeth'. The income from the lands she surrendered, and later the lands themselves, were made over to her daughter, the queen. In return Elizabeth accepted a pension of 400 marks, later increased by a third to £400, ample to secure her a comfortable retirement at Bermondsey until her death in 1492 at the age of fifty-five. One possible explanation is that Elizabeth was persuaded to surrender her lands by a financially embarrassed Henry.

One of the reasons that Queen Elizabeth was able to live within her means was a determination to uphold her rights. Her dower lands were largely those of the Duchy of Lancaster and administered by its officials, but there is no doubt of the queen's active interest. When she discovered that one of her husband's knights of the body, Sir William Stonor, was usurping her rights in the forest of Bernwood, Buckinghamshire, she wrote him a stinging letter of rebuke, threatening to sue for remedy in the courts and demanding to be shown any commission he had received from her husband. Yet despite the arrogance and rudeness of the letter, Stonor remained loyal to the queen and her sons and was later to be one of the body of Edward's servants who joined Buckingham's rebellion against the usurping Richard III.

Elizabeth Woodville, Queen of England, to Sir William Stonor, n.d.

Trusty and wellbeloved, we greet you well. And whereas we understand, by report made unto us at this time, that you have taken upon you now of late to make masteries within our forest and chace of Barnwood and Exhill, and there, in contempt of us, uncourteously to hunt and slay our deer within the same, to our great marvel and displeasure; we will you wit that we intend to sue such remedy therein as shall accord with my lord's laws. And whereas we furthermore understand that you purpose, under colour of my lord's commission, in that behalf granted unto you, as you say, hastily to take the view and rule of our game of deer within our said forest and chace; we will that you show unto us or our council your said commission, if any such you have, and in the mean season, that you spare of hunting within our said forest and chace, as you will answer at your peril. Given under our signet, at our manor of Greenwich, the first day of August.

(PRO SC 1/46/151. Wood, vol. i, letter xliv.)

The following letter, from the Paston collection, reflects the unstable state of local politics in East Anglia. The earl of Oxford, who was about twenty-five at the time, had recently been allowed to succeed to his father's honours, after the former earl and his eldest son had been executed for treason in 1462. The young earl had officiated as the queen's chamberlain at her coronation. He married the earl of Warwick's sister at about this date, and later joined Warwick and Clarence in their attempt to restore Henry VI. Thereafter he remained an unrepentant Lancastrian spending the second decade of Edward's reign partly in prison at Hammes, near Calais, and, after he had escaped from there, in exile. He joined Henry VII's invasion in 1485 and was one of the leaders of the victorious army at Bosworth. In 1467, the Pastons were part of Oxford's clientele in Suffolk and it was they, not Oxford himself, who were in possession of the disputed manor of Hemnals. This was all part of the great lawsuit over the will of Sir John Fastolf, about which readers may be referred to the *Paston Letters* themselves for further details. Simon Bliaunt, on the other hand, who was a very minor player in the game, seems to have been a supporter of the Norfolk/Howard group of active Yorkists. It was very probably Sir John Howard, later duke of Norfolk, who induced the queen to write on Bliaunt's behalf. His steward was named John Bliant and Simon Bliaunt later became his retainer. After receiving the queen's letter, Oxford wrote to Paston, warning him that he feared Howard and Sir Gilbert Debenham were likely to take the manor back by force. Howard and the Pastons had recently fallen out over a disputed parliamentary election.

Elizabeth Woodville, Queen of England, to John de Vere, Earl of Oxford, c. 1467

Right trusty and entirely beloved cousin, we greet you well, letting you weet how it is come unto our knowledge that whereas you newly entered upon our wellbeloved Simon Bliaunt, gentleman, into the manor of Hemnals in Cotton, descended and belonging unto him by right of inheritance, as it is said, you thereupon desired the same Simon to be agreable for his part to put all matters of variance then depending between him and one Sir John Paston, knight, pretending a title unto the said manor, into the award and judgement of two learned men, by you named and chosen as arbitrators between them; and in case that the same arbitrators of and upon the premises neither gave out nor made such award before the breaking up of Paschal [Easter] term now last passed, you of your own offer granted and promised unto the said Simon, as we be informed, to restore him forthwith thereupon unto his possession of the said manor. And how it be that the same Simon, at your motion and for the pleasure of your lordship, as he saith, agreed unto the said compromise, and thereupon brought and showed his evidence concerning, and sufficiently proving his right in the said manor unto the said arbitrators, and that they have not made nor holden out between the said parties any such award; nor have you restored the same Simon unto his possession of the said manor, but continually keep him out of the same, which, if it so be, is not only to his right great hurt and hindrance, but also our marvel. Wherefore, we desire and pray you right affectuously that you will the rather at the contemplation of these our letters, show unto the said Simon, in his rightful interest and title in the said manor, all the favourable lordship that you goodly may, doing him to be restored and put into his lawful and peaceable possession of the same, as far as reason, equity and good conscience shall require and your said promise, in such wise that he may understand himself herein to fare the better for our sake, as our very trust is in you. Given under our signet at my Lord's Palace of Westminster, the xxv day of June.

(Paston Letters, *vol. vi, no. 1020, wrongly dated 1487–1502.*)

ANNE NEVILLE, WIFE OF RICHARD III

Anne Neville was the younger of the two co-heiresses of Richard Neville, earl of Warwick and Salisbury and Anne Beauchamp, sole heiress of the earls of Warwick. Her father and Edward IV were first cousins, and the king's younger brother, Richard, created duke of Gloucester, was brought up in Warwick's household. It is quite clear that Warwick intended to match his two daughters with the king's two brothers, not least because the Woodville sisters of the new queen had virtually cornered the market in eligible noble heirs. Isabel, his elder daughter was married in 1469 to George, duke of Clarence; the ceremony took place at Calais, where her father and new husband were in revolt against the king. Unsuccessful, in 1470 they were forced into exile in France, where necessity forced Warwick into alliance with his archenemy, Queen Margaret of Anjou. This unlikely union was sealed with the marriage of Margaret's son, Edward, Prince of Wales, and Warwick's younger daughter, Anne. 1471 saw the death of Anne's father at Barnet and her husband at Tewkesbury. George of Clarence succeeded in winning a pardon from his brother, but he proved extremely reluctant to share his wife's inheritance with her sister, particularly when his younger brother Richard indicated his desire to marry the widow. Whether, as romance has it, there was a youthful attachment between the two and Clarence attempted to thwart his brother by hiding Anne away, disguised as a kitchen maid, or not, the whole episode was an unedifying spectacle of two royal brothers squabbling over the inheritance of a traitor. The final result was a triumph for Gloucester, largely because his loyalty meant he had the king's backing. He married Anne, who was still only sixteen, in July 1472 and arbitration by the king settled the territorial dispute, with Richard receiving the heartland of the Neville inheritance in the north and Clarence lands in the midlands. The only difficulty lay in the fact that most of the midland lands were the property of the widowed countess of Warwick in her own right. It was resolved by treating the countess as though she were dead and her lands thus free to be divided among her daughters.

Anne Neville therefore brought her second husband a power base in the north which was later to make his usurpation possible. Nothing is known of any formal dower arrangements made for her, and given the behaviour of Clarence and Gloucester, her interests were probably ignored. The lordships of Abergavenny and Glamorgan, which were the inheritance of Anne's maternal grandmother, Isabel Despenser, should have passed by law to George Neville, Lord Abergavenny, who was the heir male, but they were retained by Gloucester and treated as though they were his wife's. They may have provided her with a source of income both as duchess and queen, since there is no evidence that Richard made any additional provision for her dower when she became queen.

Richard and Anne had a joint coronation, the first of its kind since that of Edward II and Isabella, for which detailed accounts survive. The queen, wearing a mantle of crimson velvet, furred with miniver, was bareheaded, with her hair loose to her shoulders and kept in place by a richly jewelled circlet of gold. A drawing of her thus apparelled is contained in the *Rous Roll*. Her train was probably borne by Margaret Beaufort, countess of Richmond and her senior attendant was the king's sister, Elizabeth, duchess of Suffolk. Also in attendance were no fewer than three duchesses of Norfolk and the countesses of Surrey and Nottingham, all gowned in blue velvet with crimson cloth of gold. The Great Wardrobe accounts for the coronation which detail the robes for all the senior members of the queen's household are the only records which survive to throw any light on Anne's household; there are none from any of her officers for the brief period of her queenship. Nor is there any indication of the sources of her income. It seems likely that her household was run along lines similar to that of her Yorkist predecessor. The royal couple's only child, Edward, later Prince of Wales, was born in 1473 and died in April 1484. The *Croyland Chronicle* describes the king and queen at Nottingham after the death of their son as 'almost bordering on madness by reason of their sudden grief', grief compounded by the fact that they had not had sufficient notice of his illness to be with him when he died. Personal feeling was less important than the demands of the state. Richard needed an heir of his body and Queen Anne seemed unlikely to give him another child. Croyland reported that at the Christmas festivities of 1484 the king had ordered similar gowns for his queen and for his niece, Elizabeth of York. This, coupled with the queen's ill health and the king's decision to shun her chamber, gave rise to the very strong rumour that Richard was planning to strengthen his title to the throne by marriage to his brother's heiress either after the death of the queen or an annulment of his marriage, for which he had conveniently not obtained a dispensation. He had not reckoned with the loyalty of his northern supporters to the daughter of Warwick. It was as her husband he had commanded their loyalty and they were not about to countenance her discarding. In the face of this opposition and that of the Church against the marriage of an uncle and niece he was forced into the publicly humiliating position of having to deny that he had any such intention. Nobody believed him. On 16 March 1485 Anne died, probably of tuberculosis, but rumours that he had poisoned her abounded. It is not necessary to believe the rumours, the important fact is that they existed, together with the equally strong belief that Richard had murdered his nephews, innocent children to whom he should have been a protector.

Very little is known of Anne, who at best remains a shadowy figure. She seems to have shared a love of books with her husband, and remained extremely proud of her Warwick inheritance; she signed herself Anne Warwick in her books, but it was pride in her Beauchamp blood, not that of the Nevilles, which she shared with her husband. It was almost certainly she who commissioned the illuminated biography of her grandfather, known as *The Pageant of Richard Beauchamp, Earl of Warwick* which was written in about 1483. A second glorification of the great earl and his family, *The Rous Roll*, ended with the accession of his granddaughter as queen.

No letters from Anne are known to survive.

CECILY NEVILLE, DUCHESS OF YORK, MOTHER OF EDWARD IV AND RICHARD III

It is appropriate now to turn from queens consort to queen mothers, or rather, to the mothers of kings, and to two of the most remarkable English women of the fifteenth century, Cecily Neville and Margaret Beaufort. Cecily was the youngest daughter of Ralph Neville, first earl of Westmoreland by his second wife, Joan Beaufort, daughter of John of Gaunt. Known as the 'Rose of Raby' (Raby was her family's main seat in Durham), she was married to her father's ward, Richard, duke of York in 1438. Thereafter she was parted from him only by circumstance. They lived in France, which the duke was governing in Henry VI's name during the early 1440s, and where three of her surviving children were born, and in Ireland where he was sent as Lieutenant in 1449 as a form of political exile. In the factional struggles of the English court of the 1450s, to which York returned after Cade's rebellion in an attempt to restore some form of good government, his hand was strengthened by the fact that after the death of the king's uncle, Humphrey, duke of Gloucester, he himself became heir apparent. Indeed, descended as he was from both Edward III's second son in the female line and his fourth son in the male line, it could be argued that his hereditary claim to the throne was stronger than Henry's. In 1453 Henry went mad; three months later Queen Margaret was delivered of a son. York was no longer heir, but he was appointed Protector of the Realm. When Henry recovered his sanity, York and his ministers were dismissed. The country descended into civil war.

Throughout this time Duchess Cecily's main residence was the castle of Fotheringay, where three more of her children were born. In 1459 she and her two youngest sons, George and Richard were captured by the Lancastrians at Ludlow, while her husband, her sons Edward and Edmund, and her brother Salisbury, and his son Warwick, escaped by flight. She was taken to Coventry, where a Lancastrian parliament attainted her husband and brother. Cecily herself was granted an annuity of 1,000 marks by the king 'for the relief and sustention of her and her young children that have not offended against us', and placed in the custody of her sister Anne, duchess of Buckingham. On her husband's return from exile, she hurried off to join him. The following battle of Northampton left Buckingham dead, the king captured and the Yorkists triumphant. York then made a fatal mistake. He claimed the throne by hereditary right. After protracted debate it was agreed that Henry should remain king until his death and be succeeded by York who was named heir and protector. The queen was certainly not prepared to accept the disinheritance of her son and, with her northern supporters massing, York and his supporters moved north to meet them. At Wakefield York and Salisbury were surprised and killed, and so, too, was York's second son, Edmund, earl of Rutland. Cecily had lost a husband, a son and a brother in a single day. A few months later the wheel of fortune had turned again and her eldest son Edward was crowned king at the age of nineteen.

Cecily Neville (second from front right behind the countess of Westmoreland), duchess of York and mother to two kings (Edward IV and Richard III), in a detail from a miniature of the Neville family at prayer

We know Cecily to have been beautiful, we also have evidence of her pride. Her husband may never have occupied the throne he claimed, but Cecily was routinely to describe herself as wife of the rightful inheritor of the realm of England. She undoubtedly exerted a strong influence on her son in the early days of his reign, and indeed it was believed that she could rule Edward as she pleased. She was reportedly furious when Edward announced his marriage to an obscure Lancastrian widow, and who can blame her? Her London home, Baynard's Castle, remained a family centre. It was there that Edward was reunited with his wife and children after his return from exile in 1471, and undoubtedly Cecily played a part in reconciling Clarence with his brother. Her feelings over Clarence's final fall and judicial death are unknown. When her youngest son Richard was planning to usurp the throne of his nephew, Edward V, one contemporary observer, Dominic Mancini, says that he claimed that his brother Edward IV 'was conceived in adultery and in every way was unlike the late duke of York, whose son he was falsely said to be, but Richard, duke of Gloucester, who altogether resembled his father, was to come to the throne as his legitimate successor'. If Edward was a bastard, then his son could not legitimately be king of England. If it were true that Richard put about this claim, then he was echoing doubts about Edward's paternity which had been raised by the earl of Warwick in 1469 during his rebellion, and again by Clarence shortly before his downfall. According to Mancini, the story dates back to the time of Edward's marriage, when, on learning of it, the duchess of York fell into such a frenzy that she offered to submit to a public enquiry and assert that Edward was not her husband's son, but conceived in adultery. No shred of evidence to support the rumours was produced, but kings born outside England – Edward was born in Rouen – were vulnerable to such chauvinistic charges. If the rumours that Richard made such a claim were true, it seems strange that at the time he made them, he was a frequent visitor to his mother's London residence, and there is no evidence at all of any rift between the two.

In her later years, Cecily was famed for her piety. Her life at Baynard's Castle and her other principal residence, Berkhamsted, was monastic in all save vows. The great fluctations of fortune in her life had left her with a deep humility as well as a consciousness of the responsibilities of her rank and she was drawn to the mystical form of contemplative piety exemplified by the two female saints, St Catherine of Siena and St Bridget of Sweden. The cult of St Bridget was particularly strong in England, where its centre was the great double Bridgettine abbey of Syon, a few miles west of London. The abbey had been founded by Henry V but, led by Cecily, the York family had made it the centre of their devotional life. Edward IV was regarded as the abbey's second founder, and while not noted for his piety, the king was prepared to name his seventh daughter Bridget, a name hitherto almost unknown in England. Her grandmother stood sponsor for her and may well have always intended the child for the Church, and in due course, after her father's death, Bridget entered the Church, not at Syon but at Dartford, another centre of mysticism. The royal connection at Syon was maintained by another of Cecily's granddaughters, Anne de la Pole, who eventually became abbess there.

The following letter is one where Cecily, standing on her dignity, describes her husband as the rightful inheritor of England. Her son, the king, took a special interest in Windsor Castle, building St George's Chapel and greatly enhancing the splendour of its college in the second half of his reign. It is likely, therefore, that the mayor took the rebuke from the king's mother seriously and hastened to ensure the restoration of her servant to his former office.

Cecily, Duchess of York, to the Mayor of Windsor, n.d.

By the rightful inheritor's wife of the realm of England and of France, and lordship of Ireland, the king's mother, Duchess of York.
Trusty and well-beloved, we greet you well. And forasmuch as our beloved servant Richard Foster hath had the occupation of your steward, and done you good service in the same, and desireth to do in time coming, albeit he hath been hindered and put from the said office, we, desiring his promotion and furtherance, pray you that you will have the said Richard preferred unto your said office of your steward, and the rather at the contemplation of this our especial writing, wherein you shall do unto us right especial pleasure, and shall cause us to show you the favour of our good ladyship therefore, in such things as we may do for you in time coming. Given under our signet, at the Priory of Merton, the 23rd day of November.

(BL Harl. MS 787, fol. 2. Wood, vol. i, letter xl.)

In her second letter, the duchess was again taking someone to task, this time the surveyor of her estates in Suffolk, Essex, Cambridge, Huntingdon and Hertford, who had been neglecting his duties. William Wolflete was dean of the college of Stoke by Clare in Suffolk, a foundation associated with the York family, who were the heirs of the Clares. The duchess may have been noted for her piety, but that did not mean that she neglected her more worldly interests.

Cecily, Duchess of York, to Dean William Wolflete, n.d.

The king's mother, Duchess of York.
Right Trusty and wellbeloved, we greet you well. And forasmuch as it is come unto our knowledge that our livelihood within the counties of Suffolk, Essex, Cambridge, Huntingdon and Hertford, is not duly surveyed nor approved to our

behalf as it ought to be; we, putting our trust in you in that behalf, considering you to be our surveyor and great officer in that country, charge you therefore straightly, as you will have our good ladyship, to put you in faithful and true devoir to see it amended. And that you fail not hereof as you will avoid the awful peril that may ensue with our great displeasure and heavy ladyship. Given under our signet in our place at Baynard's Castle, in London, the 19th day of August.

Superscription: To our right trusty and wellbeloved master William Wolflete, dean of our college of Stoke, and surveyor of our lands within the counties of Suffolk, Essex, Cambridge, Huntingdon and Hertford.

(Wood, vol. i, letter xli.)

The Tudor Queens

MARGARET BEAUFORT, COUNTESS OF RICHMOND AND DERBY, MOTHER OF HENRY VII

Margaret, one of the most formidable women of the late Middle Ages, was to exert a far greater influence over a king than most crowned queens consort. She was the only child and heiress of John Beaufort, duke of Somerset, and thus a great-granddaughter of John of Gaunt. Her mother was a minor heiress, Margaret Beauchamp of Bletsoe, who already had children by a former marriage to Oliver St John. Her father died in political disgrace when she was an infant, and may possibly have committed suicide. Her mother's third husband was Lionel, Lord Welles, by whom she had a son. Margaret herself, born on 31 May 1443, was a considerable heiress, and was married as a child to the duke of Suffolk's son, though the marriage was dissolved three years later, when she was nine, in order that she might be married to Edmund Tudor, earl of Richmond, the king's half-brother. The ceremony took place in 1455 when she was twelve and her bridegroom was twenty-six. It was normal in such cases for consummation of the marriage to be delayed until the bride was a little older, but Tudor's desire to secure an heir and thus a life interest in his wife's lands should she die, was greater than his interest in her health and well-being and he quickly made her pregnant, only, ironically, to die of plague himself a few months later. Margaret was a widow and a mother before she was thirteen. The birth was reportedly a difficult one and both mother and child nearly died. Certainly Margaret never bore another child despite a happy third marriage to Henry Stafford, younger son of the duke of Buckingham. The wardship of her son Henry, earl of Richmond, was granted by Edward IV to his close ally, William Herbert, whom he had created earl of Pembroke, and Henry was brought up at Herbert's castle of Raglan, and not in his mother's household.

The Beaufort family had, of course, been ardently Lancastrian, but the Staffords were more inclined to favour the Yorkist cause. Margaret's third husband died of wounds after fighting for Edward IV at Barnet, but when her former brother-in-law, Jasper Tudor, fled into exile again after the Re-adeption of Henry VI, he took his nephew, Henry, with him, and Margaret acquiesced out of concern for her son's safety. Edward had broken his promise of a pardon to her mother's stepson, Richard, Lord Welles, with whom she had grown up, and broken sanctuary to take her cousin, the duke of Somerset, prisoner after Tewkesbury. Both were executed. Margaret's fears for her son condemned him to grow up in Brittany apart from her, and prevented his absorption into the life of Yorkist England. Margaret protected herself by a marriage to Thomas, Lord Stanley. This move, into the heart of the Yorkist court, enabled her to secure all her west-country estates and some of her mother's lands for her son, provided Henry returned from exile. Henry himself had never taken arms against the king and all was arranged with Edward IV's agreement. The possibility of a match between Henry and Elizabeth of York, the king's eldest daughter, was also raised, but not in any very serious manner. On the usurpation of Richard III, Margaret's chief concern initially was for the new king's agreement to these arrangements, but she soon became aware of the opposition to the new king and took the highly risky course of joining it. The first aim was to rescue Edward V from the Tower, but when they increasingly came to believe the princes were dead, Margaret and Queen Elizabeth Woodville, in concert with the queen's son Dorset and her brother the bishop of Salisbury, altered course to promote the earlier idea of a marriage between their children and their accession to the throne. The collapse of the rebellion in 1483 was to be the lowest point in Margaret's fortunes. She was saved only by the fact that her husband, Stanley, had stayed loyal, but she lost all title to her lands and Stanley was ordered to imprison her. Two years later the wheel of fortune had turned full circle: her son was crowned Henry VII, having owed his victory at Bosworth in large part to the treachery of the Stanleys to Richard III, and was married to Elizabeth of York.

The devotion between Henry and his mother was extraordinary. They had barely seen each other since he was a small child and their relationship had been sustained solely by letter. Margaret held her son to be 'my own sweet and most dear king and all my worldly joy', while Henry wrote, having granted a request from her, 'all of which things according to your desire and pleasure, I have, with all my heart and goodwill given and granted unto you; and, my dame, not only in this but in all other things that I know should be to your honour and pleasure, and weal of your soul, I shall be glad to please you as your heart can desire it, and I know well, that I am as much bounden so to do, as any creature living for the great and singular motherly love and affection that it hath pleased you at all times to bear me'. It was she, rather than Henry who had grown up abroad, who set the tone for court procedure and etiquette, and she was treated exactly as a queen-dowager would have been. Indeed, she spent more time with her son and his queen than any dowager would have been likely to. Her outstanding influence over the king was quickly recognized and they acted in concert throughout the reign. In the life of the royal family, her husband was quickly marginalized. Margaret was declared a 'femme sole' as far as her property was concerned; that is, she had total control over it. In 1499 she took a vow of chastity and removed her household to Collyweston in Northamptonshire, where she proceeded to transform a modest manor house into a palace. Stanley was welcomed there and had his own suite of rooms, but it was a welcome granted to a friend and not a husband. It was a novel solution to a situation without precedent in England, but it was an assertive action initiated by Margaret and not the king.

We know Margaret to have been slight in build, and her features, best illustrated in Torrigiano's masterpiece of sculpture from her tomb in Westminster Abbey, were those of a handsome woman with high cheekbones, slightly hooded eyes and high-arched brows. She was undoubtedly highly intelligent but her well-attested ability to weld together and control a household comprising very different men of talent indicates a personality both forceful and charming. There is no doubt that she could inspire devotion, yet this was a woman who did not scruple to take legal action against the widows of her servants for debt, and whose ruthless pursuit of legal and financial rights, often over many years, finds echoes in the avarice of her son's later years. Her estates were administered with outstanding efficiency and many of her most talented

An effigy on the tomb of Margaret Beaufort by P. Torrigiano, Westminster Abbey

officers came from the Manchester area and were recruited when she and Stanley were living chiefly on his Lancashire estates at Lathom and Knowsley. The order of her household and of the administration of her estates was a reflection of the discipline of her personal routine. While not as deeply pious as her predecessor, Cecily, duchess of York, Margaret was devoted to the Church, but her piety was always blended with practicality. Her benefactions almost always required a specific personal return, usually prayers for herself and her family. She identified very strongly with her mother's family and constantly promoted the interests of her half-siblings, the St Johns and the Welles, including obtaining as a wife for her half-brother John, Lord Welles, the queen's sister Cecily. For the most beautiful of Edward IV's daughters this was hardly an appropriate match, but of course nobody would have dared to say so. Margaret and Cecily, in fact, seem to have got on rather well: Cecily spent time at Collyweston and when, as a widow, she married an undistinguished knight, Sir Thomas Kyme, Margaret protected her from the repercussions and even paid some of her funeral expenses. Her relationship with the queen was, not surprisingly, less easy. While there was no question of any open breach, Elizabeth would not have been human if she had not felt uneasy about the influence Margaret had over the king and about her controlling role at court. Margaret and the queen's grandmother Cecily of York, however, held each other in great respect and in her will Cecily left the countess a beautiful breviary bound in gold.

At Collyweston and her London house of Coldharbour, Margaret enjoyed entertaining, playing chess, and recitals by her choir when she was not pursuing business or her devotions. She patronized Caxton, encouraged book production and translated books from the French for publication, and was punctilious over her visits to the poor and sick. After the king and queen, she was the greatest landowner in the country and her expenditure greater than that of the richest peers, the duke of Buckingham and the earl of Oxford. She maintained a household of about 230 persons and on her death her moveable wealth was calculated at £15,000. Much of this was to be spent continuing what was the outstanding achievement of her life, her patronage of the university of Cambridge. The concentration on the younger university after an initial patronage of both was a result of her relationship with John Fisher, bishop of Rochester from 1503, who held office in the university and who was her confessor. She first gave help to the existing colleges of Jesus and Queen's and then went on to transform the modest royal foundation of God's House into Christ's College. She turned from this success to the improvement of St John's Hospital, but her death in 1509 left most of the work to her executors and it was they who were responsible for the foundation of St John's College. Her patronage of the universities was to a very great degree a reflection of the two strands of piety and practicality so evident in her own life, and ensured, perhaps more than any of the medieval queens, her continuing influence on successive generations.

The most striking feature of Margaret's letters to her son, Henry VII, is their passionate devotion, which was in every sense reflected in the king's feelings for his mother. There is a very touching reference to the king's birthday at the end of the second letter. Mother and son rarely disagreed about anything, and certainly not over their 'great matter' to which both the following letters refer. It concerned a large ransom due to Margaret from the French house of Orleans, the rights to which she had inherited from her grandfather, John, earl of Somerset, and which dated back to 1412. Much of the ransom was in fact paid, but it was the outstanding part which concerned Margaret. On her son's accession she had all the weight of the Crown behind her. Her claim was tested in the French courts, but proceedings had come to a halt and even pressure from the French king, Charles VIII, had failed to secure a favourable verdict in the Paris parlement. Since Henry VII would be the ultimate beneficiary, his mother was able to make use of the Crown's legal advisors, ambassadors and even the king's French secretary, Jean Meautis. The matter was finally settled in 1514 when Louis XII, himself a member of the Orleans branch of the French royal family agreed payment to Henry VIII.

In the first of the two letters, the cardinal referred to is John Morton, archbishop of Canterbury, chancellor, and Henry's leading minister. Dr Whitstone, one of the king's chaplains, had clearly been briefed in the matter and both Margaret and her son were familiar with the documentation of the case. The fact that the claim they were making was far in excess of the sum still owing is an illustration of the avarice and determination to pursue their rights to the last which were unattractive features of their characters, but in this, as in everything, their hearts and minds were as one.

In the second, longer letter, Margaret went on to refer to other matters of interest. The lordship of Kendal was part of the lands granted to her father at the time he was created duke of Somerset and had been the core of her dower lands as countess of Richmond. Her rights to it had been disputed by the Parr family but she had regained a lifetime interest in it during the previous reign, and with her son as king she was determined to have her full rights restored. At this time she also achieved her desire to be treated as a 'femme sole'. Her husband's financial rights were scrupulously respected but she took over the practical management of her estates. In Kendal, perhaps to soothe Stanley's feelings, she agreed to the appointment of his chaplain, William Wall, as her receiver. He was to deliver Stanley's share of the proceeds to him and the rest to Margaret's own receiver general, Reginald Bray. In 1501 the unfortunate chaplain failed to render satisfactory accounts and was dismissed. Her stepson, Edward Stanley, who held other posts in the lordship, had been pursuing a policy of retaining Margaret's tenants to himself and Margaret proposed to her son an appropriate way of dealing with him. Henceforth Margaret would be ordered by her son to ensure that she employed in Kendal only those retained in the name of the king's younger son, Henry, duke of York. This, she felt, would provide an excuse for her to her husband.

The bastard of Edward IV to whom the king had just shown his pleasure, was Arthur, created Viscount Lisle in 1523; his mother was unknown, but was possibly Elizabeth Waite. At some point during Henry's reign he was appointed an esquire of the body, a position he filled at the king's funeral. He was the last male Plantagenet and for many years was Governor of Calais. He died without heirs in 1542, shortly after being released from the Tower, where he had been imprisoned on suspicion of treason. What Henry VII had requested his mother to do for Arthur is unspecified. Nor do we know anything of the gentleman, Fielding, for whom Margaret was soliciting the king's good lordship. The newly elected bishop of Ely was Richard Redman, previously bishop of Exeter, and the marquis who unsuccessfully tried to retain Fielding was probably Thomas Grey, marquis of Dorset, the queen's half-brother, who died only a few months later, in September 1501.

Margaret Beaufort, Countess of Richmond, to her son Henry VII, 14 January (1499)

My own sweet and most dear King and all my worldly joy, in as humble a manner as I can think, I recommend me to your Grace and most heartily beseech our Lord to bless you; and my good heart where that you say that the French king hath at this time given me courteous answer and written . . . letter of favour to his court of Parlement for the true expedition of my matter which so long hath hanged, the which I know well he doth especially for your sake, for the which my . . . ly beseech your Grace that . . . to give him your favourable . . . thanks and to desire him to continue his . . . And, given it so might like your Grace, to do the same to the Cardinal, which as I understand is your faithful true and loving servant. I wis my very joy, as I often have showed, and I fortune to get this or any part thereof, there shall never be that or any good I have but it shall be yours, and at your commandment as surely and with as good a will as any you have in your coffers, as would God you could know it as verily as I think it. But my dear heart, I will no more encumber your Grace with further writing in this matter, for I am sure your chaplain and servant Doctor Whitston hath showed your Highness the circumstance of the same. And if it so please your Grace, I humbly beseech the same to give further credence also to this bearer. And Our Lord give you as long good life, health and joy, as your most noble heart can desire, with as hearty blessings as our Lord hath given me the power to give you.
At Colyweston, the 14th day of January, by your faithful true bedewoman, and humble mother, Margaret R

(Cotton MS, Vespasian F XIII, fol. 60. Holograph. Ellis, Original Letters, *vol. i, letter xxii.)*

Margaret Beaufort, Countess of Richmond, to her son Henry VII, 28 January 1501

My dearest and only desired joy in this world,

With my most hearty loving blessings and humble commendations I pray our Lord to reward and thank your grace, for that it hath pleased your highness so kindly and lovingly to be content to write your letters of thanks to the French king, for my great matter, that hath so long been in suit, as Master Welby hath showed me your bounteous goodness is pleased. I wish, my dear heart, an my fortune be to recover it, I trust you shall well perceive I shall deal towards you as a kind, loving mother; and, if I should never have it, yet your kind dealing is to me a thousand times more than all that good I can recover, an all the French king's might be mine withal. My dear heart, an it may please your highness to license Master Whitstone, for this time, to present your honourable letters, and begin the process of my cause – for that he so well knoweth the matter, and also brought me the writing from the said French king, with his other letters to his parlement at Paris – it should be greatly to my help, as I think; but all will I remit to your pleasure. And if I be too bold in this, or any my desires, I humbly beseech your grace of pardon, and that your highness take no displeasure.

My good king, I have now sent a servant of mine unto Kendall, to receive such annuities as be yet hanging upon the account of Sir William Wall, my lord's chaplain, whom I have clearly discharged; and if it will please your majesty's own heart, at your leisure, to send me a letter, and command me that I suffer none of my tenants be retained with no man, but that they be kept for my lord of York, your fair, sweet son, for whom they be most meet, it shall be a good excuse for me to my lord and husband; and then I may well, and without displeasure, cause them all to be sworn, the which shall not after be long undone. And where your grace showed your pleasure for the bastard of King Edward's, sir, there is neither that, nor any other thing, I may do by your commandment, but I shall be glad to fulfill to my little power with God's grace. And, my sweet king, Fielding, this bearer, hath prayed me to beseech you to be his good lord in a matter he sueth for to the Bishop of Ely, now (as we hear) elect, for a little office nigh to London. Verily, my king, he is a good and wise, well-ruled gentleman, and full truly hath served you well, accompanied as well at your first as all other occasions, and that causeth us to be the more bold and gladder also to speak for him; howbeit, my lord marquis hath been very low to him in times past, because he would not be retained with him; and truly, my good king, he helpeth me right well in such matters as I have business with in these parts. And, my dear heart, I now beseech you of pardon of my long and tedious writing, and pray Almighty God to give you long, good, and prosperous life as ever had prince, and as hearty blessings as I can ask of God.

At Calais town, this day of St Anne's, that I did bring into this world my good and gracious prince, king, and only beloved son.

By your humble servant, bedeswoman and mother.

(Wood, vol. i. letter xlviii.)

In 1497, when the following letter was written, England was trying to normalize both its political and commercial relationship with Burgundy after the latter had ceased to support Perkin Warbeck, the pretender to Henry's throne who claimed to be the younger of Edward IV's two sons, Richard, duke of York. One of the English ambassadors was the earl of Ormond, the queen's chamberlain, a lifelong Lancastrian supporter. In thanking him for a gift of gloves she had solicited, Margaret's tone seems to be sardonic in its reference to the great ladies of Burgundy, for the greatest of them all was her enemy, the Duchess Margaret of York, who had for so long recognized her supposed nephew, Perkin. A touch of pride in the smallness of her own aristocratic hand can also be detected. In expressing her concern for the queen's health, the term she uses, 'crazed', should be read to mean delicate. Margaret is the first of our ladies for whom a letter exists written entirely in her own hand.

Margaret Beaufort, Countess of Richmond, to Thomas Butler, Earl of Ormond, Chamberlain to the Queen, 25 April 1497

My lord chamberlain, I thank you heartily that you list so soon remember me with my gloves the which were right good save they were too much for my hand. I think the ladies in that part be great ladies all, and according to their great estate they have great personages. As for news here I am sure you shall have more surety than I can send you. Blessed be God, the king, the queen and all our sweet children are in good health. The queen has been a little crazed but now she is well God be thanked. Her sickness is [?not] so good as I would but I trust hastily it shall with God's grace, wherein I pray give you good speed in your great matter and bring you next and safe home. Written at . . . the xxv day of April. M Richmond

(SC 1/51/189. Holograph.)

The following letter illustrates one of the perennial problems of the court, that of supply. The royal right of purveyance, by which officers of the household purchased supplies at fixed low prices, was extremely unpopular. Not only did the court consist of large numbers of people, it also housed large numbers of animals, particularly horses; a point neatly made in Margaret's letter to her bailiff at Ware in Hertfordshire. At the time of the king's expedition to France in 1492, quite apart from her very large financial contribution to the costs, his mother also supplied large quantities of grain from her estates. Shirley was from a family with several members serving the countess. As well as being bailiff of Ware he was keeper of the park there reserved for her horses.

In about 1500 Margaret altered the style of her signature. Up to that date she used the common aristocratic style where the title had pre-eminence, M Richmond. Then she changed to the royal style using her Christian name, Margaret R. It was a lucky coincidence that her title began with the letter usually taken to mean reine, or queen. Although she did style herself countess of Richmond and Derby, it was the older, royal title she continued to use in her signature after her marriage to Stanley.

Margaret Beaufort, Countess of Richmond, to Richard Shirley (c. 1501)

Margaret R

To our servant Richard Shirley, Bailiff of our town of Ware.
Richard Shirley we send unto you at this time the king's servant, clerk of the market, this bearer, for ordinance and devising of victuals as well for man as beast within our town there, willing you to help and assist him in the same the best you can and thereupon to do the execution thereof as you tender our pleasure. Written at the manor of Hatfield the xxiii day of July.

(BL Cotton MS, Vespasian F XIII, f. 61. Wood, vol. i, letter xlvii.)

ELIZABETH OF YORK, WIFE OF HENRY VII

As the eldest daughter of Edward IV and Elizabeth Woodville, Elizabeth of York's marriage was a useful diplomatic card for her father. He considered offering her as a wife to Henry Tudor, the exiled earl of Richmond, as an inducement to come home and make his peace with the new regime, but at the conclusion of his military expedition to France in 1475 she was contracted to marry Louis XI's son, the dauphin Charles, who was four or five years her junior. It was, incidently, the first time that an English princess had been deemed worthy of a match likely to make her queen of France. A certain portion of the tribute Louis paid her father was set aside for her use and she was taught to speak and write French and Spanish. In 1482 Louis rejected the English match in favour of a Burgundian marriage for his son in the Treaty of Arras. No new match had been arranged for Elizabeth at the time of her father's death.

On the presumed death of her brothers in 1483, Elizabeth became the heiress of the house of York. Her mother had taken her younger son and her daughters into sanctuary at Westminster on learning of Richard of Gloucester's *coup d'état* against her brother, Earl Rivers, at Stony Stratford, which had delivered the young king into his uncle's hands. Once the usurpation was an accomplished fact, Queen Elizabeth, as we have seen, came to terms with the situation and brought her daughters to court. This did not prevent her from plotting with Lady Margaret Beaufort, countess of Richmond, and mother of one of the few remaining Lancastrian claimants to the throne. A successful invasion by Henry Tudor would win him the princess as a wife, and unlikely as this initially seemed, it is precisely what happened in August 1485. The marriage took place in January 1486 and their eldest son, Arthur, was born exactly nine months later. A number of their children died in infancy but four, Arthur, Henry, Margaret and Mary, survived to adulthood.

Not only was the new queen the heiress of York, she and her sisters, Cecily, Anne, Katherine and Bridget, were the co-heiresses under English law to the Mortimer-Clare inheritance, which did not technically form part of the Crown's holdings. Under Henry the lands were quietly subsumed by the Crown. Elizabeth, it is true, was granted some of them as part of her dower and some were used to support her mother and grandmother, but her sisters, daughters of a king, went portionless to their husbands. In 1487 the queen was granted the lands her mother had received in 1485 and then surrendered, and in 1492 was granted more lands and the reversion of those held by her grandmother. Cecily, duchess of York, outlived almost everybody, dying in the same year as the queen, 1503. It is, however, reasonable to suppose that in the end Elizabeth's disposable income was similar to that of her mother as queen. Unlike her, she did not leave any household accounts by which her income and expenditure can be checked. What do exist are her privy purse accounts for the last year of her life. These show her chamber receipts as being £3,585 19s 10½d and her expenditure as £3,411 5s 9¼d, a balance of which Mr Micawber would have been proud. It gives rather a false picture, however, for certainly in the past the queen's revenue had not always proved sufficient for the demands made on it and she had been forced to borrow money on occasion. The king had sometimes come to her aid, but had expected her to pledge her plate as security.

If Elizabeth of York became pecuniarily embarrassed, it was not through extravagance on her part. Her household was run on economical lines, and compares well even with that of her mother. The highest salary paid to any of her ladies was £33 6s 8d in comparison to the £40 paid by both her mother and Margaret of Anjou. Her own habits were modest, but she had a number of extraordinary charges upon her income. The marriages arranged for her three sisters (the youngest, Bridget, became a nun) while not disparaging, were not advantageous either; Henry VII had no intention of impoverishing the Crown to provide them with dowries, a factor which ruled out foreign matches. The queen, however, would not allow her sisters to go to their husbands completely penniless and paid each of them £50 annuities for their privy expenses and their husbands £120 p.a. each for their support. In addition she seems later to have supported her Courtney nephews and niece, children of her sister Katherine, after their father, William, heir to the earl of Devon, was imprisoned and attainted and his property seized, for alleged complicity in the earl of Suffolk's rebellion. The children were in the care of Margaret, Lady Cotton, and the queen paid for all their clothes and necessities. In other respects her privy purse expenses were predictable: rewards for people bringing her gifts, servants' wages, repairs to her barge and litters, purchase of household articles, cloth for her own and her ladies' use, jewellery, furs, religious offerings and payments to her physicians and apothecaries. Elizabeth seems to have been very fond of music. She had her own minstrels and purchased a pair of clavicords, which she may have played herself. Certainly her daughters were instructed in the lute, and her son Henry, of course, was a highly accomplished musician. These accounts for the last year of the queen's life, during which time she was pregnant, give a vivid picture of the peripatetic life of the court. As well as a progress to Wales, Elizabeth moved up and down the Thames valley between Greenwich and Windsor, staying at Westminster, Hampton Court, Richmond and her own York town house of Baynard's Castle.

Despite the somewhat unappealing picture generally painted of Henry VII as a person, he and Elizabeth seem to have been happy together. If the king did not treat the queen with as much honour as he should have done in the early years, delaying first his wedding and then her coronation until after the birth of an heir, it was because he had strong political reasons rather than personal ones for doing so. They led a full court social life together, spending much time in each other's company. The references to his wife in Henry's privy purse expenses and the manner in which he referred to her in his letters indicate tenderness and affection. Elizabeth seems to have been easy to love. A contemporary described her as very handsome (her sister Cecily was regarded as the beauty of the family), of great ability and beloved for her charity and humanity. She did not inherit her mother's domineering or grasping qualities and in many ways more closely resembled her pious and learned grandmother Cecily, duchess of York. Although it is nowhere spelled out, one of her outstanding qualities seems to have been one she shared with her father, the common touch, a combination of personal charm and accessibility. The same

Detail of a gilt-bronze effigy of Elizabeth of York by P. Torrigiano, Westminster Abbey

contemporary observer (the Spanish ambassador) suggested that the primary influence on Henry was that of his mother and that the queen did not like it. While the first part of the observation may be correct, there is no evidence as to the second. Certainly Elizabeth made no attempt to interfere in political affairs, but there is no indication that she wished to. Nor is it ever possible to quantify the influence a beloved wife may have on her husband behind the scenes. In some ways Elizabeth was very powerful indeed. Her gentle, pious and good nature together with her beauty and her lineage gave Henry's reign the one key dimension which he could not supply, namely popularity. Like that earlier queen of English lineage, Matilda of Scotland, and rivalled among the foreign queens only by Philippa of Hainault, Elizabeth of York was beloved by her husband's subjects.

The death of Prince Arthur shortly after his marriage to the Spanish infanta, Katherine of Aragon, was a devastating blow to his parents on both a personal and a dynastic level. An anonymous account of what happened at court when the news arrived is one of the few glimpses we have of the relationship between the king and queen. Henry immediately sent for his wife, who sought to comfort him with 'full great and constant comfortable words', saying among other things that 'God had left us yet a fair prince and two fair princesses and that God is where he was, and we are both young enough'. Having left Henry and returned to her own chamber, Elizabeth then collapsed with grief and it was Henry's turn to come and comfort her. True to her word, the queen conceived again within a few weeks of her son's death, and died ten months later on her thirty-eighth birthday following the birth of a short-lived daughter. Henry, grief-stricken, 'privily departed to a solitary place and would no man should resort unto him'. Hardly the reaction of an indifferent husband. He never remarried, though he toyed with the idea for political purposes, and was succeeded by his second son, Henry of York. How great the effect of his mother's death was on the eleven-year-old Henry and how great an influence she would have been on his adolescence and early reign is impossible to judge, but one cannot help feeling that Henry's personal relationships would have been a good deal more stable had she lived.

A marriage between his heir, Prince Arthur, and a daughter of Ferdinand of Aragon and Isabella of Castile was one of the central tenets of Henry VII's foreign policy. While the pretender, Perkin Warbeck, was recognized at foreign courts as Richard, duke of York, the rightful king of England, Henry knew such a marriage would never be negotiated, but in the summer of 1497 Perkin left Scotland and after an abortive trip to Ireland and a hopeless landing in Cornwall, he surrendered to Henry. Shortly afterwards, the Spanish monarchs agreed to the betrothal of Arthur to their youngest daughter, Katherine. Queen Elizabeth's subsequent letter to Queen Isabella is couched in the extravagant terms of such courtly correspondence, but beneath it is a genuine expression of English relief and delight at the outcome. The actual marriage took place four years later, but Elizabeth died only a year after Katherine's arrival in England. If she had lived longer, poor Katherine's unhappy time as Arthur's widow would undoubtedly have been alleviated by the queen's kindness.

Elizabeth of York, Queen of England, to Isabella, Queen of Castile,
3 December 1497

To the most serene and potent princess, the Lady Elizabeth [Isabella], by God's grace queen of Castile, Leon, Aragon, Sicily, Granada etc., our cousin and dearest relation, Elizabeth by the same grace, queen of England and France, and lady of Ireland, wishes health and the most prosperous increases of her desires. Although we before entertained singular love and regard to your highness above all other queens in the world, as well for the consanguinity and necessary intercourse which mutually take place between us, as also for the eminent dignity and virtue by which your majesty so shines and excels that your most celebrated name is noised abroad and diffused everywhere; yet much more has this love increased and accumulated by the accession of the most noble affinity which has recently been celebrated between the most illustrious Lord Arthur, prince of Wales, our eldest son, and the most illustrious princess the Lady Catherine, the infanta, your daughter. Hence it is that, amongst our other cares and cogitations, first and foremost we wish and desire from our heart that we may often and speedily hear of the health and safety of your serenity, and of the health and safety of the aforesaid most illustrious Lady Catherine, whom we think of and esteem as our own daughter, than which nothing can be more grateful and acceptable to us. Therefore we request your serenity to certify of your estate, and that of the aforesaid most illustrious Lady Catherine our common daughter. And if there be anything in our power which would be grateful or pleasant to your majesty, use us and ours as freely as you would your own; for, with most willing mind, we offer all that we have to you, and wish to have all in common with you. We should have written you the news of our state, and of that of this kingdom, but the most serene lord the king, our husband, will have written at length of these things to your majesties. For the rest may your majesty fare most happily according to your wishes.

From our palace of Westminster, 3rd day of December 1497.

(BL Egerton MS 616, fol. 7, Latin. Wood, vol. i, letter xlvi.)

Virtually none of Elizabeth's letters survive, and the one here following must serve as typical of large numbers which she undoubtedly wrote. It is a simple request to the prior of Christ Church, Canterbury, to honour a promise to allow the queen the right of presenting one of her chaplains to the next vacancy in the living of All Saints, Lombard Street, of which the monastic cathedral held the advowson. Queens, and kings, relied on the goodwill of their subjects in these matters to be able to reward and support their household servants. A royal chaplain might amass several livings in the course of his career, but only the most able would aspire to a deanery or bishopric.

Elizabeth of York, Queen of England, to the Prior of Christ Church, Canterbury, 6 June 1499

To our Right Trusty and well beloved in God the prior of the monastery of Christ's Church at Canterbury.

Right Trusty and well beloved in God, we greet you well, and as we recently in other letters desired you to grant unto us the living of the parish church of All Saints in Lombard Street in my lord's city of London, whenever it should fall vacant through the death of Sir Marques Husy, the late incumbent; whereupon it pleased you, out of your loving and kindly heart, to grant us freedom of the said benefice in writing, to nominate it for whichever of our chaplains we should choose at its next vacancy, for which we heartily thank you; we have been informed that it is now the case, the said Sir Marques being recently departed out of this transitory life into the mercy of God, so that the said benefice is now vacant.

We therefore request and require you, that in honouring the said promise, you shall send us under your usual seal the giving of the said benefice, with a blank space on it, with the intention that we shall enter the name of whichever of our chaplains we shall think able and suitable to have charge of the curacy there. We sincerely trust that you will effect this desire of ours, whereby you will greatly deserve our special thanks, to be recalled in connection with any reasonable desires of your own concerning your well-being or that of your office in time to come.

Given under our signet at my lord's city of London the sixth day of June.

(Moriarty, pp. 80–1.)

KATHERINE OF ARAGON, FIRST WIFE OF HENRY VIII

Katherine was born on 16 December 1485, the youngest child of two reigning monarchs, Ferdinand of Aragon and his wife, Isabella of Castile. She was named after Isabella's grandmother, Catherine of Lancaster, daughter of John of Gaunt. Katherine and her sisters were not only educated in the way thought proper for fifteenth-century princesses, in music and dancing, housewifery, and above all, in their devotions, but were also given tutors in the classics, in Latin history, and in civil and canon law; Katherine could reply in fluent extempore Latin to the speeches of ambassadors, and seemed to Erasmus a miracle of feminine learning. Her only brother John died without heirs and the succession of the Spanish thrones descended to Charles V, the only son of her elder sister Joanna, who had married Philip of Austria, son of the Emperor Maximilian and Mary of Burgundy. Katherine was betrothed to Arthur, eldest son of Henry VII, when she was three and Arthur not quite two, and throughout her childhood she was referred to as the Princess of Wales. In 1501, at the age of fifteen, she set off for England, where the match was warmly welcomed. After the wedding the young couple travelled to Ludlow where Arthur, as titular head of the Council of Wales, had his main residence. Four months later he was dead of the sweating sickness and Katherine installed as a widow in the vacant palace of the bishop of Durham in the Strand.

The death of his daughter's husband was a devastating blow to the plans of Ferdinand, who needed the English alliance as a counterpoise to the threat of the French aggression against Italy, where a branch of the house of Aragon ruled in Naples. Ferdinand sent a formal request for the return of his daughter and her dowry and the payment of her widow's dower from the revenues of the Principality of Wales, but he was in fact quite willing for a marriage to be arranged for her with Henry's surviving son Henry, duke of York. Henry VII was reluctant to abandon so advantageous a match and even more reluctant to repay that part of Katherine's dowry he had already received, claiming that the payment of her dower depended on the full payment of her dowry. It was at this point that the question of the consummation of Katherine's marriage to Arthur was first raised, since if it had in fact taken place a dispensation from Rome would be required before a match with young Henry could be contemplated. Dona Elvira Manuel, Katherine's duenna, and Katherine herself, were adamant that no such consummation had taken place and Henry VII accepted it. It is perhaps worth noting that Katherine's sister Maria had married her sister Isabella's widower, the king of Portugal, after the appropriate dispensation had been acquired. A suggestion that she marry the king himself after the death of Queen Elizabeth was rejected by Spain, and in June 1503 a new marriage treaty was signed. In it Ferdinand agreed to the payment of the rest of her dowry, while Katherine renounced her claim to her widow's jointure in return for a similar settlement on her marriage to Henry, which would take place in two years time when he was fifteen. Until then, she would be dependent on the bounty of the king.

In 1504 Katherine's mother died and Ferdinand began to lose control over Castile, threatened by Maximilian and Philip's claim to rule on behalf of Philip's small son. An economic treaty with England was repudiated by the Castilians to Ferdinand's chagrin and English commercial loss. Nor could Ferdinand manage to raise the money for the rest of Katherine's dowry. Katherine and her small suite of Spaniards were desperate for money; her father could not supply it and counselled patience; her father-in-law would not and began to wonder if he might not find a better match for his heir. For four years the two wily, parsimonious old men circled each other, while Katherine, in the middle, suffered and well-nigh starved. But she hung on with patience, courage and faith, isolated in Durham House, seeing almost nobody, never invited to court, but always hoping for a successful conclusion to her troubles. Henry's fifteenth birthday came and went. His father, the king, signed a treaty of alliance with Philip, and discussed a match between his heir and Philip's daughter, Eleanor. Katherine pawned the jewels and plate that were supposed to form part of her dowry with great reluctance and only after repeated appeals to her father. On the recall of her father's ambassador, De Puebla, whom Katherine had always felt (unjustly) was not diligent enough on her behalf, Ferdinand sent his daughter formal credentials as his ambassador and for the next two years she struggled singlehandedly to keep the Anglo-Spanish alliance and the prospect of her remarriage alive. And then on 21 April 1509 Henry VII died, assuring his son on his deathbed, so it was said, that he was free to marry whom he chose. Henry, to his eternal credit, chose Katherine. Overnight her position was transformed, and for the rest of her life she never ceased to love, honour, and in all save matters of conscience, obey the golden young king who had rescued her from the seven long years of her widowhood which she had endured almost alone. Henry, in turn, adored and depended on his wife, both personally and politically. When he invaded France in 1512, he made his wife regent and captain of all his home forces, empowering her to raise loans for the defence of the kingdom. Although Henry knew a threat from the Scots to be real, he could hardly have foreseen that the queen's forces, led by the aged earl of Surrey, would win at Flodden the greatest of all English victories over the Scots.

The happy state of the royal marriage lasted for a number of years, marred only by their failure to produce a surviving son. Their daughter Mary was born in 1516 when Henry was twenty-five, the queen thirty-one, and as befitted a daughter of Isabella of Castile, Katherine began to train Mary for the position of queen regnant. The king continued to treat his queen with every mark of affection and respect, though his eye had begun to stray. Katherine, once well-regarded for her personable

Katherine of Aragon as a young girl by Michael Sittow

appearance, for she had grey eyes and russet-gold hair, a sturdy and dignified body, with small hands and feet, was beginning to show her age, and numerous pregnancies had taken their toll on her looks. In public she and Henry were still much together, but privately they were less in each other's company. The queen spent even more time at her devotions than the king, took a large share in the management of the royal household, even caring for and embroidering her husband's linen. She supervised her own estates, presiding over meetings of her council of officials in person, insisting on the recognition of her smallest rights, but fulfilling all her duties with equal diligence. Charities began to take up more and more of her time. It was said of her that the poor of England loved her because she fed them; she could not prevent the economic changes that were taking place but she did her best to mitigate some of their consequences. She also took a lively interest in English education. The humanist Thomas Linacre, once Prince Arthur's physician, was appointed Mary's Latin tutor, and his friends, such as John Colet and Thomas More, began to find places at court. When he visited England Erasmus himself was impressed by her exceptional learning. She became a patron of her countryman, the humanist Juan Luis Vives, whom she commissioned to produce a scheme of education which would equip her daughter Mary for rule as well as for private life. She endowed lectureships at Oxford and Cambridge, supported poor scholars there and favoured Wolsey's policy of suppressing decayed religious foundations in order to endow his new college at Oxford. Her father, Ferdinand, died only a few weeks after the birth of Princess Mary, and Katherine's most immediate concern with international politics abated somewhat. She was quite content to let the king's minister Cardinal Wolsey take over her role as Henry's chief confidante and adviser, though she often did not approve of the grandiose foreign plans he and the king adopted.

In 1518 the Emperor Maximilian died, leaving his grandson, Katherine's nephew Charles V, as heir to the Hapsburg lands in northern Europe as he already was to the kingdoms in Spain. There were now only three kings of any significance in Europe: Charles V, Francis I of France and duke, by conquest, of Milan, and very much third in all eyes but his own, Henry VIII of England. Rivalry between the three was to dominate politics for years to come and only Henry could hope to hold the balance of power between the other two. Katherine, of course, wanted the balance tilted towards her nephew, though she did not object to friendship with France provided it was not aimed at Spain. Wolsey, however, tended to favour the French. In 1520 Charles V visited his English relatives and the possibility of him as a husband for Princess Mary was first broached; sixteen years difference in age was not looked on as an insurmountable obstacle. Henry went on to meet Francis at the Field of the Cloth of Gold, but the meeting could hardly be described as a success and in fact the Anglo-Imperial alliance lasted almost until the royal divorce. In 1525 Charles broke off his betrothal to Mary in order to marry a Portuguese cousin who could provide him with a cash dowry and an immediate heir. The humiliation felt by Henry was vented on the queen. He created his six-year-old bastard son duke of Richmond, bestowing on him all the titles and offices normally held by the heir to the throne except that of Wales. Katherine's outrage at the insult to her daughter was punished by the removal of all her women who were not tools of Wolsey and the nine-year-old Mary was ordered to go to Ludlow and take up her duties as Princess of Wales. Yet the king and queen still spent, and enjoyed, time in each other's company. For Wolsey, working towards a French alliance and a French marriage, Katherine remained a constant obstacle until a way of removing her presented itself.

It is not exactly clear when doubts about the validity of his marriage first crossed Henry's mind, but once planted they took firm hold. If God did not see fit to give him a legitimate son, it must be because he had offended in some way; either the dispensation to marry Katherine was invalid or the Pope had no power to grant it. The most urgent spur, as all the court knew by July 1527, was his increasing infatuation with Anne Boleyn. It is possible that if Henry had approached Katherine with a request for a divorce in order that he might marry again and beget a legitimate male heir she might just have reluctantly agreed, and retired to a convent. There were certainly continental precedents for such action. Henry, however, made the fatal error of attacking the validity of his marriage from the beginning and claiming that the dispensation for it was insufficient. Katherine's opposition to this was unswerving, partly because she knew her first marriage to have been unconsummated and therefore void, but chiefly because if her marriage to the king was not valid, then the legitimacy of her daughter was in question and this she refused to countenance. She refused to admit the competence of a papal court which opened in London to try the case and maintained her moral certainty of the rightness of her cause throughout the years that followed, despite the danger to the Church that her intransigence threatened. In this she had the sympathy of the great majority of her husband's subjects, but unfortunately for the queen, she did not have the active support of the papacy. Wolsey, unable to deliver a verdict from the Church that gave the king what he wanted, was dismissed from his posts and died a broken man, leaving the way open to a far more radical solution than the cardinal would have proposed. His erstwhile man of business, Thomas Cromwell, was to obtain the king's divorce, solve his financial problems, and destroy the independence of the Church.

In the meantime, Henry's final parting from Katherine came in July 1531 and he did not have the courage to tell her face to face. She was asked to retire to Wolsey's former house, the More, but was permitted to retain a court of some two hundred persons. This situation could not last; under pressure to renounce the title of queen and submit to the king over the question of her marriage, Katherine was retired to the Bedfordshire manor of Ampthill, nominally a prisoner in the custody of her former chamberlain, Lord Mountjoy, where she learned of her husband's marriage to the pregnant Anne Boleyn in January 1533. The emperor's ambassador, Eustace Chapuys, who had become Katherine's trusted counsellor and friend, was eager to urge the emperor to war on behalf of his aunt, confident that there would be a popular revolt in England in her favour. Katherine would have none of it, nor would she accept the title princess dowager of Wales and an appropriate dower estate; to have done so would have been to deny the legitimacy of her daughter. She was moved further from London, to the bishop of Lincoln's palace at Buckden in Huntingdon, but at first was neither ill-treated or ill-lodged and her suite, though small, was adequate. Buckden, however, was unhealthy, and Katherine's request to move somewhere drier led to her transference to Kimbolton in the charge of Sir Edmund Bedingfield, where she remained until her death in January 1536. Henry refused to allow her to see their daughter, or to honour the dispositions of her will. He had loved her, respected her and in the end feared her, but he had been unable to break her.

The following three letters, part of a series written by Katherine of Aragon to her father during the period when she was the widowed princess of Wales, are the earliest holograph letters of a queen of England. They are naturally written in Spanish; Katherine learned English properly after her marriage to Henry, and all the subsequent letters are in the language of her adopted country. Katherine spent seven long years as Arthur's widow, deprived of her dower and dependent on the parsimonious bounty of her father-in-law, Henry VII. Not only did she have insufficient money to live in the state appropriate for a princess but she literally lacked the funds to buy clothing and other necessities for her small household, let alone pay them wages; the meagre sum allowed her by her father-in-law was sufficient only for food.

Dr De Puebla, the Spanish ambassador, had negotiated the new treaty for Katherine's marriage to young Henry and in doing so had no reason to suppose that the two-year period stipulated before Henry was old enough to marry would condemn her to such poverty, or that the king's bounty would prove so extremely frugal. De Puebla, a non-aristocratic lawyer, who had long served as resident Spanish ambassador, had won the confidence of both Henry and Ferdinand, but after her mother's death Katherine's trust in him was undermined by her powerful duenna, Dona Elvira Manuel, whose brother was one of a group of leading Castilians who wished to limit Ferdinand's role in their country and who were actively intriguing for an alliance between Philip of Austria, father of the heir to Castile, and England. Dona Elvira's supposed need to go to Flanders had nothing to do with her health. De Puebla finally managed to convince Katherine that she and her father were being duped and her duenna was speedily dismissed into exile in Flanders. Thereafter the princess took charge of her own household until Henry VII dismissed it and ordered her to reside at court. The Infanta Isabella to whom Katherine referred was her elder sister Isabella, briefly the wife of Alfonso of Portugal and then married to his successor, Manoel.

The second letter to her father was written by Katherine after the shipwreck which brought her sister Joanna, queen of Castile and her husband, Philip of Austria, to England on their way to Spain. There Philip and King Henry had negotiated a treaty aimed against Katherine's father. Don Pedro d'Ayala, the Spanish ambassador to the court of Burgundy, was an old and valued acquaintance of Henry, having earlier been ambassador to England and Scotland. Katherine refers to him as De La Membrilla; he was a commander of an order of that name. An aristocratic and witty courtier, despite the fact that he was bishop of the Canaries, D'Ayala had constantly sought to undermine De Puebla's position and had taught Katherine to despise him also. The letter paints a graphic description of Katherine's poverty and refers to an illness which she had had for six months; this was a tertian fever, not uncommon at the time, in which fever recurred every third day. Her request for a confessor was almost certainly not the first she had made. Don Allesandro Geraldini, her former tutor, had come to England with her as confessor, but had been sent back to Spain in disgrace because he had told De Puebla that Katherine's marriage had been consummated. Dona Elvira, in correcting the mistaken assumption, had seized the chance to get rid of a man who had always wielded a considerable influence over the princess. Thereafter Katherine confessed to Dona Elvira's chaplain. After the departure of that lady she was left bereft until she found Fray Diego Fernandez in 1507, one of the order of Observant Franciscans to whom Katherine, like her mother before her, was most attached. He remained one of her few confidants for a number of years, despite the fact that he was disliked and distrusted by other Spaniards.

In contrast, the third letter, written after she and Henry had been married only a few weeks, is full of happiness, despite the tact with which she tells her father that the strongest reason for her loving Henry is his devotion to Ferdinand. In the months before Henry VII's death, all her Spanish suite were desperate to return to Spain, and the Spanish ambassador hoped at best to extricate the princess and as much of her dowry as he could from England. Only Katherine herself, supported by her confessor, clung determinedly to the belief that against all the odds her marriage would take place. Her stubbornness was regarded as due to Fray Diego's bad influence. Once her marriage had taken place, she was content for her Spaniards to return home, trusting that her father would compensate them for their long, unhappy exile. Her favourite maid, Maria de Salinas, had married an Englishman, Lord Willoughby.

Katherine of Aragon, Princess of Wales, to her father, Ferdinand II of Aragon,
1505

Most high and most puissant lord,

Hitherto I have not wished to let your highness know the affairs here, that I might not give you annoyance, and also thinking that they would improve; but it appears that the contrary is the case, and that each day my troubles increase; and all this on account of the doctor de Puebla, to whom it has not sufficed that from the beginning he transacted a thousand falsities against the service of your highness, but now he has given me new trouble; and because I believe your highness will think I complain without reason, I desire to tell you all that has passed.

Your highness shall know, as I have often written to you, that since I came into England, I have not had a single maravedi, except a certain sum which was given me for food, and this such a sum that it did not suffice without my having many debts in London; and that which troubles me more is to see my servants and maidens so at a loss, and that they have not the wherewith to get clothes; and this I believe is all done by hand of the doctor, who, notwithstanding your highness has written, sending him word that he should have money from the king of England, my lord, that their costs should be given them, yet, in order not to trouble him, will rather intrench upon and neglect the service of your highness. Now, my lord, a few days ago, donna Elvira de Manuel asked my leave to go to Flanders to be cured of a complaint which has come into her eyes, so that she lost the sight of one of them; and there is a physician in Flanders who cured the infanta donna Isabel of the same disease with which she is affected. She laboured to bring him here so as not to leave me, but could never succeed with him; and I, since if she were blind she could not serve me, durst not hinder her journey. I begged the king of England, my lord, that until our donna Elvira should return his highness would command that I should have, as a companion, an old English lady, or that he would take me to his court; and I imparted all this to the doctor, thinking to make of the rogue a true man; but it did not suffice me – because he not only drew me to court, in which I have some pleasure, because I had supplicated the king for an asylum, but he negotiated that the king should dismiss all my household, and take away my chamber-[equipage], and send to place it in a house of his own, so that I should not in any way be mistress of it.

And all this does not weigh upon me, except that it concerns the service of your highness, doing the contrary of that which ought to be done. I entreat your highness that you will consider that I am your daughter, and that you consent not that on account of the doctor I should have such trouble, but that you will command some ambassador to come here, who may be a true servant of your highness, and for no interest will cease to do that which pertains to your service. And if in this your highness trusts me not, do you command some person to come here, who may inform you of the truth, and then you will have one who will better serve you. As for me, I have had so much pain and annoyance that I have lost my health in a great measure; so that for two months I have had severe tertian fevers, and this will be the cause that I shall soon die. I supplicate your highness to pardon me that I presume to entreat you to do me so great favour as to command that this doctor may not remain; because he certainly does not fulfil the service of your highness, which he postpones to the service of the worst interest which can be. Our Lord guard the life and most royal estate of your highness, and ever increase it as I desire. From Richmond, the second of December.

My lord, I had forgotten to remind your highness how you know that it was agreed that you were to give, as a certain part of my dowry, the plate and jewels that I brought; and yet I am certain that the king of England, my lord, will not receive anything of plate nor of jewels which I have used; because he told me himself that he was indignant that they should say in his kingdom that he took away from me my ornaments. And as little may your highness expect that he will take them in account and will return them to me; because I am certain he will not do so, nor is any such thing customary here. In like wise the jewels which I brought from thence [Spain] valued at a great sum. The king would not take them in the half of the value, because here all these things are esteemed much cheaper, and the king has so many jewels that he rather desires money than them. I write thus to your highness because I know that there will be great embarrassment if he will not receive them, except at less price. It appears to me that it would be better if your highness should take them for yourself, and should give to the king of England, my lord, his money. Your highness will see what would serve you best, and with this I shall be most content.

The humble servant of your highness, who kisses your hands.

(BL Cotton MS Vespasian, c. XII, fol. 207, holograph, Spanish. Wood, vol. i, letter lii.)

Katherine of Aragon, Princess of Wales, to her father, Ferdinand II of Aragon,
1506

[The first folio of this letter has not survived]

. . . [I cannot] speak more particularly, because I know not what will become of this letter, or if it will arrive at the hands of your highness; but when don Pedro d'Ayala shall come, who is now with the king and queen in the harbour, your highness shall know all by ciphers. I have written many times to your highness, supplicating you to order a remedy for my extreme necessity, of which [letters] I have never had an answer. Now I supplicate your highness, for the love of our Lord, that you consider how I am your daughter, and that after Him I have no other good nor remedy, except in your highness; and how I am in debt in London, and this not for extravagant things, nor yet by relieving my own [people], who greatly need it, but only for food; and how the king of England, my lord, will not cause them [the debts] to be satisfied, although I myself spoke to him, and all those of his council, and that with tears: but he said that he is not obliged to give me anything, and that even the food he gives me is of his goodwill; because your highness has not kept promise with him in the money of my marriage portion. I told him that I believed that in time to come your highness would discharge it. He told me that that was yet to see, and that he did not know it. So that, my lord, I am in the greatest trouble and anguish in the world. On the one part, seeing all my people that they are ready to ask for alms; on the other, the debts which I have in London; on the other, about my own person, I have nothing for chemises; wherefore, by your highness' life, I have now sold some bracelets to get a dress of black velvet, for I was all but naked; for since I departed thence [from Spain] I have nothing except two new dresses, for till now those I brought from thence have lasted me, although now I have nothing but the dresses of brocade. On this account I supplicate your highness to command to remedy this, and that as quickly as may be; for certainly I shall not be able to live in this manner.

I likewise supplicate your highness to do me so great a favour as to send me a friar of the order of San Francesco de Osservancya, who is a man of letters, for a confessor; because, as I have written at other times to your highness, I do not understand the English language, nor know how to speak it: and I have no confessor. And this should be, if your highness will so command it, very quickly; because you truly know the inconvenience of being without a confessor, especially now to me, who, for six months have been near death: but now, thanks to our Lord, I am somewhat better, although not entirely well. This I supplicate your highness once again that it may be as soon as possible. Calderon, who brings this letter, has served me very well. He is now going to be married. I have not wherewith to recompense him. I supplicate your highness to do me so great a favour as to command him to be paid there [in Spain] and have him commended; for I have such care for him that any favour that your highness may do him I should receive as most signal.

Our Lord guard the life and most royal estate of your highness, and increase it as I desire.

From Richmond, the 22nd April. The humble servant of your highness, who kisses your hands.

(BL Egerton MS 616, art. 55, fol. 17, holograph, Spanish. Wood, vol. i, letter liii.)

Katherine of Aragon, Queen of England, to her father, Ferdinand II of Aragon, 1509

Most high and puissant lord,

I received your highness' letter which this courier brought me, with which I rejoiced so much, that your highness will scarcely be able to believe how much pleasure I had in knowing that I have ever been held and esteemed by your highness as your true daughter and servant. And it is the greatest favour that your highness can do me and most conformed to my will, since I know that in this life I have no other good except that of being your daughter; although (by) your highness so well married, that more cannot be said, except that it is the work of those hands of your highness which I kiss for so signal a favour.

As to the king my lord, amongst the reasons that oblige me to love him much more than myself, the one most strong, although he is my husband, is his being the so true son of your highness, with desire of greater obedience and love to serve you than ever son had to his father. I have performed the office of ambassador as your highness sent to command, and as was known by the king my lord, who is, and places himself entirely, in the hands of your highness, as of so entire a father and lord. And your highness may believe me, that he is such in keeping obedience to your highness as could never have have been thought, from which I increase in infinite pleasure as much as reason requires.

The news from here is that those kingdoms of your highness are in great peace, and entertain much love toward the king my lord and to me. His highness and I are very hearty to the service of your highness. Our time is ever passed in continual feasts. I supplicate your highness, as to the favour which you have always bestowed upon me, in which you have shown me the greatest favour, henceforth to bestow it on me, by showing that you esteem the king my lord and me as your true children.

. . . [this passage in cypher] . . . favour. I feel assured your highness, having received my good will with the desire which I have for your service with which I write this, and believing that you have given and will give credit to my letters, although you have not chosen to send an answer to all that which was in them – since it so greatly concerned my honour and estate that, by the life of your highness, it could not be thought how much the commandant De la Membrilla, being here as ambassador, did me disserve, by having said what he did, and by taking up the topics which he took up. Supposing my confessor were the worst man in the world, yet, for the sake of giving the lie to the said ambassador, I should have kept him in my service, and made him a great prelate. So much the more being such a person, and so sufficient, as I believe your highness knows, since I have him in my service; and I hope to keep him all the time that I shall be able, if your highness may thus be served. If I believed not that your highness would hold him in the same office, as reason is, I should think myself much annoyed and disfavoured by your highness.

My mistress, Janina de Cuer, my chamberlain, with my other servants, set off from hence to their homes. I commanded to pay all their salaries, in the form and quantity as every year the same officials are paid in the house of your highness: to Alonzo de Esquivel for six years and to all the others for eight; and all the help I gave them was for the service of your highness, besides other things which by my command they have received from my chamber; this not for the service which they have done me, but only for that your highness had commanded them to come here. Wherefore, if you should wonder at the boldness of them, and of the ambassador, I would supplicate your highness to command to chastise him and them; but afterwards, by reason that they can call themselves mine, I supplicate your highness to pardon them, commanding that they should be regarded as persons who have been in my house.

Our Lord keep the life and royal estate of your highness, and increase it, according to my desire. From Greenwich, the 29th of July.

The humble servant of your highness, who kisses your hands,

I supplicate your highness to do me so signal a favour as to send to the king my lord three horses, – one a jennet, and the other from Naples, and the other a Sicilian; because he desires them much, and has asked me to beg your highness for them: in which I shall receive a great favour from your highness; and also to command them to be sent by the first messenger that comes here.

(BL Egerton MS 616, art. 56, fol. 25, holograph, Spanish. Wood, vol. i, letter lviii.)

Katherine's reliance on her husband's busy servant and almoner, Thomas Wolsey, was considerable during the campaign in Flanders in 1513. The first letter is largely concerned with one of her former maids of honour, Francesca de Carceres, who had been one of her favourites as princess of Wales, but who was one of those among her household who had been anxious for a return to Spain since the future in England without money or the prospect of a husband looked bleak. She intrigued with the Spanish ambassador against Katherine's confessor, lost Katherine's confidence and finally eloped with an elderly Genoese banker. Two months later Katherine was queen of England and Francesca had lost her chance of a fine English marriage but she continued to try and scheme her way back into Katherine's good graces. Wolsey's plan to introduce her into the household of the duchess of Savoy was firmly vetoed by the queen, for Louise of Savoy was the mother of Francis I.

While applying herself to the business of regent of England in her husband's absence, she none the less found time to write frequently to France, counting on Wolsey to send her news of the king even when Henry was too absorbed in the delightful business of war to find time to write himself. She worried about her husband's health, writing to her former sister-in-law, Philip's sister, Margaret of Austria, asking her to send the best physician she could find to the king; Margaret had been married briefly to Katherine's short-lived only brother John. While delighting in the English cavalry victory, the queen found it a little troublesome to deal with the illustrious French prisoner, Louis d'Orleans, duc de Longueville, whom Henry sent home in triumph to her while she and the council were attempting to raise forces against the Scots with most of the military leaders away with their king. In her letter to Wolsey there is little indication of the serious threat posed by a large Scottish army, led by the king's brother-in-law, James IV; just a prayer for good luck against them at the end. Reinforcements had already been despatched to the aged earl of Surrey in the north and Katherine was gathering a reserve army at Buckingham, while at the same time responding to Henry's needs for men and money. Lord Mountjoy, her own chamberlain, was sent with men to Calais. A week after the letter was written, Surrey and his forces won the overwhelming victory of Flodden. Katherine's own letter to Henry about it is a monument of tact, calling the victory his, and sending, in return for the French banners he had so romantically sent her, a piece of King James's coat by the hands of the herald, Rougecross. 'My Lord Howard' was Surrey's son, later the third duke of Norfolk. She tactfully ends the letter by referring to Walsingham, famed as a place of pilgrimage for women wishing for a child, thus distancing herself from the affairs of war and state.

Katherine of Aragon, Queen of England, to Thomas Wolsey, the King's Almoner, 1513

Maister Almoner, thinking that the King's departing from Calais shall cause that I shall not so often hear from his Grace for the great business in his journey that every day he shall have, I send now my servant to bring me word of the King, and he shall tarry there til another cometh, and thi[s w]ay I shall hear every week from thence and so I pray you to take the [pains] with every of my messengers to write to me of the king's health, and w[hat] he intendeth to do, for when you be so near our enemies I shall be never in [rest] til I see often letters from you; and doing this you shall give me cause to thank you, and I shall know that the mind that you have had ever to me continues still as my trust always has been. The brief that the Pope sent to the King I was very glad to see, and I shall be more to hear that he is the means either to make an honourable peace for the King, or else help on his part as much as he can, knowing that all the business that the King hath was first the business of the Church, and with this and the emperor together I trust to God that the King shall come home shortly with as great victory as any Prince in the world; and this I pray God send him without need of any other Prince. Mr Almoner, touching Frances de Cassery's matter, I thank you for your labour therein; true it is she was my woman before she was married, but now since she cast herself away I have no more charge of her. For very pity to see her lost I prayed you in Canterbury to find the means to send her home to her country. Now you think that with my letter of recommendation to the Duchess of Savoy she shall be content to take her into her service. This Mr Almoner is not meet for her, for she is so perilous a woman that it shall be dangerous to put her in a strange house. And you will do so much for me to make h[er] go hence by the way with the ambassador of the King my father, it should be to me a great pleasure, and with that you shall bind me to you more than ever I was. From hence I have nothing to write to you. But everybody here is in good h[ealth], thanked be God, and the council very diligent in all things concerning the expedition of the King's service. And you will do so much to pray the King['s grace to] be so good lord as to write to them that he is informed by me, so well . . . is done by them that he is very well content therewith and give them [thanks for it], bidding them so to continue. And with this I make an end. At R[ichmond the] 26th day of July.

[Mr Al]moner, after the writing of this letter my lord Admiral [Lord Howard] sent hither . . . which was taken with his ship and brought to him as the said . . . from Depe [? Dieppe] towards Flanders, and he hath shewn . . . things as be specified in a bill . . . a true man in his words. Inform the K[ing] . . . his pleasure shall be, for I am assured the same sh. . . .
Katherine the Queen

(Cotton MS Caligula D vi, fol. 92. The original damaged by fire. Ellis, vol. i, letter xxviii.)

Katherine of Aragon, Queen of England, to Mr Almoner Wolsey, 1513

Master almoner,

I received your letter by the post, whereby I understand of the coming hither of the duke, and the king is content that he shall be in my household. Touching this matter, I have spoken with the council to look and appoint what company shall be meet to attend upon him. Here is none that is good for it but my lord Mountjoy, who now goes to Calais as chief captain of the 500 men. And for this cause, and also that I am not so well accompanied as were convenient for his keeping here, it is thought to me and my council that it should be better the said duke be, as soon as he comes, conveyed to the Tower; especially the Scots being so busy as they now be, and I looking for my departing every hour, it should be a great incumbrance to me to have this prisoner here; seeing that, according to the king's mind, he must be conveyed to the Tower at my going forward. I pray you shew this to the king, and with the next messenger send me an answer of his pleasure.

Mr Almoner, I am sorry, knowing that I have been always so bound unto you, that now you shall think that I am miscontent without a cause, seeing that my servant asked of you no letter, nor brought you none from me. The cause was, that two days before I wrote unto you by Copinger, and at that time I had nothing further to write, – and with my servant's unwise demeanour I am nothing well content; for one of the greatest comforts that I have now is to hear, by your letters, of the king's health and of all your news. And so I pray you, Mr Almoner, to continue as hitherto you have done: for I promise you that from henceforth you shall lack none of mine, and before this you should have had many more, but I think your business scantly gives you leisure to read my letters. From hence I have nothing to write to you more than I am sure the council informs the king; praying God to send us as good luck against the Scots as the king had there.

At Richmond, the 2nd day of September.

(PRO SP 1/5, f. 28. Wood, vol. i, letter lx.)

Katherine of Aragon, Queen of England, to Henry VIII, 16 September 1513

Sir,

My Lord Howard hath sent me a letter open to your Grace, within one of mine, by the which you shall see at length the great Victory that our Lord hath sent your subjects in your absence; and for this cause there is no need herein to trouble your Grace with long writing, but, to my thinking, this battle hath been to your Grace and all your realm the greatest honour that could be, and more than you should win all the crown of France; thanked be God of it, and I am sure your Grace forgetteth not to do this, which shall be cause to send you many more such great victories, as I trust he shall do. My husband, for hastiness, with Rougecross I could not send your Grace the piece of the King of Scots coat which John Glynn now brings. In this your Grace shall see how I keep my promise, sending you for your banners a king's coat. I thought to send himself unto you, but our Englishmens' hearts would not suffer it. It should have been better for him to have been in peace than have this reward. All that God sends is for the best.

My Lord of Surrey, my Henry, would fain know your pleasure in the burying of the King of Scots' body, for he has written to me so. With the next messenger your Grace's pleasure may be herein known. And with this I make an end, praying God to send you home shortly, for without this no joy here can be accomplished; and for the same I pray, and now go to Our Lady of Walsingham that I promised so long ago to see. At Woburn the 16 September.

I send your Grace herein a bill found in a Scotsman's purse of such things as the French King sent to the said King of Scots to make war against you, beseeching you to send Mathew hither as soon as this messenger comes to bring me tidings from your Grace.

Your humble wife and true servant, Katherine.

(BL Cotton MS Vespasian F III, fol. 15. Ellis, vol. i, letter xxxii.)

Katherine's letter to Queen Claude was written at some point between 1518 when the princess Mary, still only a toddler, was betrothed to the dauphin, and 1521 when the match was broken off in favour of one with Katherine's nephew, the Emperor Charles V. At this point Wolsey and Henry were trying to act as the peacemakers of Europe, and while a French match was not considered an ideal one by Katherine, as long as the Anglo-French alliance was not aimed at Spain, she was able to accept it. Claude was the daughter of Louis XII of France and Anne of Brittany and had married her distant cousin, Francis, who was the male heir to the throne and became Francis I; her son Francis, the dauphin, predeceased his father and her younger son became Henry II. One of Queen Claude's ladies at this time was an English girl named Anne Boleyn. Katherine and Claude met at the Field of the Cloth of Gold in 1521 and the queens' natural liking for each other did much to diffuse the tensions created by their husbands' rivalry. Claude died in 1524.

Katherine of Aragon, Queen of England, to Claude, Queen of France, c. 1521

[My good sister and cous]in,

I have by your esquire of the stable [received your good and] affectionate letter, and I assure you that [I have been much] and very greatly consoled at having heard [the good] news, health, estate and prosperity in [which is my] very dear and most beloved good son and yours the dauphin. A[nd believe] what by your said esquire you will similarly hear, not only of the good health, estate and prosperity, and news of the king my husband, of me and of my daughter the princess, [but also] the affection, goodwill and very great desire that the king my said lord and husband and I have to the good and [continuance] of the good love, friendship, and fraternal intelligence and alliance which now is between the two kings our husbands, and their kingdoms, which I hold inseparable, and ever pray God that it may continue, which I desire above all things, and for my part shall exert myself for it as I have always done and shall do. However, I will cease writing you a longer letter, except praying you that from time to time I may be participant of your good news, and those of my said son the dauphin. Also, if there be anything in which I could do you pleasure, I will do it with very good heart, as she who considers herself and wishes ever to continue,

Your good sister and cousin.

(BL Cotton MS Caligula E1, fol. 1, French, a draft, badly burned. Wood, vol. i, letter xcii.)

Katherine wrote the following letter to Wolsey in 1533. Although the date of the letter gives no year, the queen was at Ampthill only for six months, from the end of 1532 until July 1533 when she was moved to Buckden. At this point Henry still hoped that she might be willing to renounce her title of queen and submit to his will over the question of her marriage, and his agreement in the matter of the marriage of one of her maids may perhaps be seen as part of an attempt to indicate how generous he might be if she aquiesced. She still had eight or ten maids of honour in her household, some of them Spanish, and it is one of these to whom the letter refers. The Arundel concerned may have been the son and heir of Sir Thomas Arundel, the only man of that name prominent at court, and who was an aide of Wolsey's, but it seems slightly surprising since Arundel himself had just married a cousin of Anne Boleyn. Katherine was acting on behalf of her maid who had no family or friends in England to act for her; her dowry was a gift from the queen. Despite all her own worries for the future, Katherine was concerned to secure that of one of her dependents and was willing to approach Wolsey to ensure that something the king had sanctioned was carried out.

Katherine of Aragon, Queen of England, to Cardinal Wolsey (1533)

My lord,

It hath pleased the king to be so good lord unto me as to speak unto Arundel the heir for a marriage to be had between him and one of my maids; and upon this I am agreed with him, having a sum of money that is offered unto him, he shall make her sure jointure during her life, the which she cannot be sure of without the licence and goodwill of his father, being on life: for the which case I beseech you, good my lord, to be good and gracious lord unto the said Arundel, for business which he hath now to do before you; so that with right you will make a short end, to the intent that he may have a time to go to his father, and make me sure of this said jointure in this present term-time. And if this be painful unto you, I pray you, my lord, pardon me; for the uncertainty of my life and the goodness of my woman causes me to make all this haste, trusting that she shall have a good husband and a sure living. An God would call me the next day after, the surer it shall appear before him that I intend to help them that be good, and take labour doing me service. And so I make an end, recommending me unto you. At Ampthill, the 25th day of January.

(Private collection. Wood, vol. i, letter c.)

The following letters all relate to Katherine's daughter Mary, the only one of the queen's children to live. Katherine took a very close concern in her upbringing and education. She herself had been highly educated by a mother who was a queen regnant. If God willed it so, Katherine saw no reason why her daughter should not reign as well. In 1525, however, the queen's nephew, Charles V, broke off his engagement to the youthful Mary in order to marry a Portuguese princess and Henry's fury led him to punish his wife. First he created his illegitimate son duke of Richmond and then ordered his daughter to take up her duties as princess of Wales at Ludlow Castle. For the first time, mother and child were separated. Mary had a suitable household, headed by the queen's friend, the countess of Salisbury (Margaret Pole was the daughter of Edward IV's brother, George, duke of Clarence). The queen's letter, conveyed by Charles, her courier, is sad and resigned, but encouraging her daughter, aged nine, to keep up her studies. Her new Latin tutor was Dr Richard Fetherstone, who was imprisoned in the Tower in 1534 to punish his pupil and in 1540 was put to death for popish treason.

The next letter was written to Mary six months after the birth of Anne Boleyn's daughter Elizabeth. Henry's demand that his elder daughter take the oath to the Act of Succession which denied her mother's marriage and branded herself illegitimate was met with stubborn resistance by the princess. In consequence she was stripped of most of her household, threatened with physical violence and ultimately with death. Lady Salisbury had been sent away and she was put in the charge of Anne, wife of Sir John Shelton, and aunt of Anne Boleyn. Her mother's letter is full of quiet advice. Katherine was only too well aware of the dangers facing her daughter, and the line she advised her to take was that which she followed herself. Obey the king in everything except where obedience meant offence to God and the loss of her own soul. Henry had promised Mary that if she took the oath, then there would be nothing preventing her marriage to either a Scottish prince or a French one. The last paragraph of the queen's letter states quite explicitly that she feared that ultimately she and Mary faced death at Henry's hands. Mary took precautions against poisoning by the Boleyn faction, but when she fell ill Henry was worried enough not only to send his own physician but to allow Katherine to send hers and ultimately to allow Mary to be moved near to Kimbolton where Katherine then was. The two were not to be allowed to meet, but Mary would be safe from threats of poison. In allowing this, Henry was implicitly accepting that he feared for his daughter's safety at the hands of his second wife.

The third letter was written to the Imperial ambassador, Chapuys, who was Katherine's staunchest ally and close confidant. He had taken the risk of approaching Henry with the request that Mary go to her mother, and had informed Katherine of Henry's qualified approval. He had also reported Henry's fear that if Mary was sent to a lonely place it would be easy for her to be spirited out of the country. Chapuys was certainly doing his best to ferment a plot that would lead to a general uprising on behalf of Katherine and her daughter, and was well aware of the strength of popular feeling on their behalf. His plans faltered on the rock of

Katherine's refusal to countenance any such action. Her horror of war, her reluctance to have any action taken on her own behalf and her sense of obedience to the king left her in no doubt of where her duty lay. As she wrote to Chapuys, she would offer her own person as surety to the king that what he feared would never come to pass. Her plea to see Mary, from whom she had been parted for four years, was ignored and Mary was not allowed to visit her mother, though she was permitted to retire to the country. Mother and daughter were never to meet again.

Katherine of Aragon, Queen of England, to her daughter, Princess Mary, n.d.
(1525)

Daughter,

I pray you think not that any forgetfulness hath caused me to keep Charles so long here, and answered not your good letter, in the which I perceive you would know how I do. I am in that case that the long absence of the King and you troubleth me. My health is meetly good; and I trust in God, he that sent me the last doth it to the best, and will shortly turn it to the first to come to good effect. And in the meantime I am very glad to hear from you, especially when they show me that you be well amended. I pray God to continue it to his pleasure. As for your writing in Latin I am glad that you shall change from me to Master Federston, for that shall do you much good, to learn by him to write right. But yet sometimes I would be glad when you do write to Master Federston of your own inditing when he hath read it that I may see it. For it shall be a great comfort to me to see you keep your Latin and fair writing and all. And so I pray you to recommend me to my Lady of Salisbury. At Oborne [Woburn] this Friday night.

Your loving mother, Katherine the Queen.

(BL Cotton Ms Vespasian F XIII, fol. 72. Ellis, vol. ii, letter cvii.)

Katherine of Aragon, formerly Queen of England, to her daughter Princess Mary,
April 1534

Daughter, I heard such tidings today that I do perceive if it be true, the time is come that Almighty God will prove you; and I am very glad of it, for I trust He doth handle you with a good love. I beseech you agree of His pleasure with a merry heart; and be sure that, without fail, He will not suffer you to perish if you beware to offend Him. I pray you, good daughter, to offer yourself to Him. If any pangs come to you, shrive yourself; first make you clean; take heed of His commandments, and

keep them as near as He will give you grace to do, for then you are sure armed. And
if this lady [Shelton] do come to you as it is spoken, if she do bring you a letter from
the King, I am sure in the self same letter you shall be commanded what you shall
do. Answer with few words, obeying the King, your father, in everything, save only
that you will not offend God and lose your own soul; and go no further with
learning and disputation in the matter. And wheresoever, and in whatsoever
company you shall come, observe the King's commandments. Speak you few words
and meddle nothing. I will send you two books in Latin; the one shall be De Vita
Christi with a declaration of the Gospels, and the other the Epistles of St Jerome
that he did write to Paula and Eustochium, and in them I trust you shall see good
things. And sometimes for your recreation use your virginals or lute if you have any.

But one thing I especially desire you, for the love that you do owe unto God and
unto me, to keep your heart with a chaste mind, and your body from all ill and
wanton company, [not] thinking or desiring any husband for Christ's passion;
neither determine yourself to any manner of living till this troublesome time be past.
For I dare make sure that you shall see a very good end, and better than you can
desire. I would God, good daughter, that you did know with how good a heart I do
write this letter unto you. I never did one with a better, for I perceive very well that
God loveth you. I beseech Him of His goodness to continue it; and if it fortune that
you shall have nobody with you of your acquaintance, I think it best you keep your
keys yourself, for howsoever it is, so shall be done as shall please them.

And now you shall begin, and by likelihood I shall follow. I set not a rush by it; for
when they have done the uttermost they can, then I am sure of the amendment. I
pray you, recommend me unto my good lady of Salisbury, and pray her to have a
good heart, for we never come to the kingdom of Heaven but by troubles.

Daughter, wheresoever you come, take no pain to send unto me, for if I may, I
will send to you.
Your loving mother,
Katherine the Queen

(BL Arundel 151, f. 194, Letters and Papers, vi, no. 1126, Mattingly, pp. 292–3.)

Katherine of Aragon, formerly Queen of England, to Eustace Chapuys, Imperial ambassador, 1535

Mine especial friend,

You have greatly bound me with the pains that you have taken in speaking with
the king my lord concerning the coming of my daughter unto me. The reward
you shall trust to have of God; for (as you know) in me there is no power to gratify

that you have done, but only with my goodwill. As touching the answer which has been made you, that his highness is contented to send her to some place nigh me, so as I do not see her, I pray you vouchsafe to give unto his highness mine effectual thanks for the goodness which he shows to his daughter and mine, and for the comfort that I have thereby received; and as to my seeing of her, you shall certify that, if she were within one mile of me, I would not see her. For the time permitteth not that I should go about sights, and be it that I would I could not, because I lack provision therefor.

Howbeit, you shall always say unto his highness that the thing which I desired was to send her where I am; being assured that a little comfort and mirth, which she should take with me, should undoubtedly be half a health to her. I have proved the like by experience, being diseased of the same infirmity, and know how much good it may do that I say. And, since I desired a thing so just and reasonable, and (that) so much touched the honour and conscience of the king my lord, I thought not it should have been denied me.

Let not, for my love, to do what you may that this may yet be done. Here have I, among others, heard that he had some suspicion of the surety of her. I cannot believe that a thing so far from reason should pass from the royal heart of his highness; neither can I think that he hath so little confidence in me. If any such matter chance to be communed of, I pray you say unto his highness that I am determined to die (without doubt) in this realm; and that I, from henceforth, offer mine own person for surety, to the intent that, if any such thing should be attempted, that then he do justice of me, as of the most evil woman that ever was born.

The residue I remit to your good wisdom and judgment as unto a trusty friend, to whom I pray God give health.

(BL Cotton MS CX, fol. 176, much burnt. Wood, vol. ii, letter lxxxii. Mattingly, pp. 297–8.)

On the day of her death, Katherine wrote two letters, one to the emperor and this to her husband, which speaks for itself. When he heard of her death, Henry gave a ball to celebrate the news.

Katherine of Aragon, formerly Queen of England, to Henry VIII, 7 January 1536

My most dear lord, king and husband,

The hour of my death now drawing on, the tender love I owe you forceth me, my case being such, to commend myself to you, and to put you in remembrance with a few words of the health and safeguard of your soul which you ought to prefer before all worldly matters, and before the care and pampering of your body, for the which you have cast me into many calamities and yourself into many troubles. For my part, I pardon you everything, and I wish to devoutly pray God that He will pardon you also. For the rest, I commend unto you our daughter Mary, beseeching you to be a good father unto her, as I have heretofore desired. I entreat you also, on behalf of my maids, to give them marriage portions, which is not much, they being but three. For all my other servants I solicit the wages due them, and a year more, lest they be unprovided for. Lastly, I make this vow, that mine eyes desire you above all things.

(Mattingly, p. 308.)

ANNE BOLEYN, SECOND WIFE OF HENRY VIII

There is some controversy about the year of Anne's birth and whether or not she was the elder or younger daughter of Sir Thomas Boleyn and his wife, Elizabeth, daughter of Thomas Howard, second duke of Norfolk, but it is reasonable to suppose, as does her biographer Eric Ives, that it was about 1501 and that she was younger than her sister Mary. Her family was one of the upper landed gentry, whose fortunes had been founded by her great-grandfather, Geoffrey, who had been a successful mercer and lord mayor of London and who had purchased estates at Blickling in Norfolk where Anne herself was born, and at Hever in Kent. His wife was the co-heiress of Lord Hoo and their son married the daughter and co-heiress of Thomas Butler, earl of Ormond. Anne's father, therefore, was the prospective heir to great wealth, but until he inherited he needed a position at court to survive. He became a squire of the body and a successful courtier. He was a skilled linguist and negotiator, intelligent, resourceful and loyal only to the king and himself. He was well-educated and ensured that his children, particularly the two younger, Anne and George, were also. His elder daughter, Mary, was established at court, where she caught the king's eye. Henry VIII's first mistress, Elizabeth Blount, had borne him a son, recognized as Henry Fitzroy, but there is no reason to believe that Mary's children were not those of her husband, William Carey. The affair lasted for approximately three years, from about 1522 to 1525.

Anne, meanwhile, had been sent to Europe when she was about twelve to thirteen years old. This not only marked her out in later life from other court ladies but indicated that already her father had recognized that she was exceptional. She was sent to be a maid of honour to Margaret of Austria, regent of Burgundy for her nephew, the emperor Charles V. Margaret had been briefly married to Queen

Katherine's brother John, and had taught Katherine French. Thomas Boleyn had been sent to her court on his first diplomatic posting and had got on well with the regent. In Burgundy Anne perfected her French, learned dancing, music, deportment, the art of conversation and grew up amid a culture far more sophisticated than was to be found in England. When diplomatic changes led to the breaking of the betrothal of Henry's sister Mary and Charles V and her marriage to the aged Louis XII of France, Anne was called from the regent's household at Mechelen to act as a companion and interpreter for Mary. When the widowed queen returned to England after a few months, Anne stayed in France and entered the household of the new queen of France, Claude, wife of Francis I, where she stayed until 1521. She returned to England on the death of her great-grandfather, the earl of Ormond, for there was a family plan to marry her to the male Butler heir.

Anne was an immediate success at court. She was slim, black-haired and with striking eyes; though not conventionally beautiful, she was elegant and sexually challenging, witty, lively and above all, independent. At twenty she had already proved she could make her way in the the courts of Europe. The Butler match was never finalized and it is hardly surprising that Anne went her own way and entered into some form of contract with Henry Percy, the earl of Northumberland's heir. This was scotched by his father and Wolsey, in whose household he served, and Percy was hurriedly married off to Mary Talbot, to whom he had long been betrothed. Anne was then involved with Sir Thomas Wyatt, a Kentish neighbour, but there was almost certainly a good deal more on his side than hers and it may have been the pursuit of her by Sir Thomas and some of his fellow-courtiers that first aroused the king's interest. It is the view of Ives that Henry fell seriously in love during 1526. He and Queen Katherine had been drifting apart for years and the queen had ignored his mistresses in a dignified manner, but in 1524 he started to think seriously about ending the marriage in order to beget a legitimate son. In 1525 he created his bastard son, Henry, duke of Richmond and by the following year his deteriorating diplomatic relationship with the emperor meant he had less to fear on the international front by setting aside Charles' aunt Katherine. In the first instance, early in 1527, Henry offered Anne the position of official mistress. She refused him. It was only gradually that Henry came to see that Anne offered a solution to both his matrimonial and sexual problems and offered her marriage once his divorce had been obtained. They expected the divorce to be quick but in the end it took six years.

After 1527 Anne became an important focus of patronage, for the king was only too eager to give her what he could. At this point Henry and Anne still believed that Wolsey, master of the diplomatic arts, could obtain the divorce, and Wolsey believed that he could work with Anne as queen even if he would have preferred a French match for the king. By early 1529 it was clear that Wolsey would never be able to persuade Pope Clement VII to rule that his predecessor had exceeded his powers in granting the dispensation that had permitted the marriage of Henry and Katherine, and that his political enemies, led by Norfolk (Anne's uncle), Suffolk (the king's brother-in-law) and Rochford (Anne's extremely able brother), were closing in on him. The failure of the legatine court at Blackfriars under Cardinal Campaggio to resolve the question of the legitimacy of the royal marriage was the beginning of the end for Wolsey. Anne was now his enemy and her influence with Henry was very great. Wolsey no longer had the king's ear exclusively, but he might have survived if he had not failed Henry in the area where his expertise should have been greatest – foreign affairs. He mishandled the treaty of Cambrai and allowed Francis I to deceive him, and thus Henry, totally. His fall was largely Anne's success, but the faction which supported her still had no answer to the question of the divorce.

Several radical ideas came from the Boleyn faction, including Cranmer's approach to the universities and Tyndale's view that the ruler was answerable only to God and not the Church and that the matter could be settled by the English Church without reference to the Pope. There was, however, strong resistance to the radical alternative. A number of people who had supported Anne against Wolsey were still in favour of Katherine; some who would accept Anne as queen would not countenance a break with Rome. There is no doubt that Anne made enemies. She was too clever, too forceful and her influence over Henry too great, for her to be popular, while the strain of waiting made her lash out from time to time. As the years passed she became increasingly tense. If the birth date of 1501 is correct, she was already nearly thirty, very old in sixteenth-century terms, to bear her first child. Until 1531 Katherine was still at court and still regarded by all as queen. Finally Henry left her for good, lacking even the courage to say goodbye, and fearful of the effect on public opinion. For the king the great breakthrough came with the advent of Thomas Cromwell. He brought Anne to the throne and in doing so, brought himself into high favour. While not a radical thinker, he was a first-rate politician who could put other people's ideas into effect. The Submission of the Clergy in 1532 was the first step, and the death of Archbishop Warham, who had surrendered to the king only because he knew he had no choice, left the way open for the elevation of Cranmer, a Boleyn protégé, to the see of Canterbury.

In the autumn of 1532 Henry was preparing for a state visit to France that signalled the end of the Imperial alliance. He took Anne with him as a way of introducing her as his next queen. He spent large sums of money on her to ensure she dressed as befitted her new station. He took the unprecedented step of creating her marquess of Pembroke in her own right but Francis' second wife (a niece of Katherine's) and his sister, the Queen of Navarre, refused to meet Anne, and even among the English, only ladies from her own faction were willing to attend her. It was during the visit to France that Henry and Anne seem finally to have consummated their long relationship. Anne conceived almost immediately and they were married at the end of January 1533. The

Anne Boleyn by an unknown artist

fact was kept secret while Convocation ruled on the validity of the Pope's dispensation for Henry's first marriage. Anne was finally acknowledged as queen at Easter and crowned on Whit Sunday with the fullest pageantry the king could command and the limited time span allowed. Henry had won at last. All Anne's opponents had acquiesced and accepted her openly, no matter what their private feelings. Elizabeth was born on 7 September. If she had been a boy, Anne would have been secure and nothing could have touched her. Even Katherine and Mary would have accepted the prior claim of a boy, but as it was, Mary's claim was kept alive and Anne was never safe. She miscarried of a boy at five to six months in July 1534.

As queen, Anne continued to be unpopular. Much of the feeling against her was based on resentment of the king's repudiation of Katherine and Mary, but she was also blamed for the break with Rome, the royal policies on tax, the deaths of Sir Thomas More and the Carthusian martyrs in 1435 and the new alliance with France. None of this would have mattered if she had been the mother of a male heir. As it was, even some of her former supporters abandoned her. Her uncle, Norfolk, who had hoped to succeed Wolsey as the king's chief minister, saw himself ousted by Cromwell, despite the fact that the queen had obtained the king's bastard son, Henry Richmond, for him as a son-in-law.

The new queen's jointure was settled on her as soon as the marriage was acknowledged. The grants made to her as marquess of Pembroke were confirmed and two further grants were made in March 1533 of lands formerly held by Katherine. Much was in the form of fee farms, but part came from estates in which Anne took an active interest. Her total income was about £6,400 p.a. A report by one of her chaplains tells of Anne calling all her council and other officers together as soon as she set up her household and instructing them in their duties; her first requirements were honour, equity, justice and value for money. It is hardly surprising that she saw the importance of style, and the ostentation required of royalty ideally suited her. She knew that in order to play the part of queen she must look it – a trait developed to the finest pitch by her daughter. She had always been a woman of artistic taste, much influenced by French ideas, but as queen she also patronized Holbein and Flemish craftsmen.

In her early period as queen her supporters expected to reap rewards and they were not disappointed. Her influence over the king was very great and, at this stage, Cromwell was still her loyal supporter. Her patronage was seen chiefly in religious matters, where she supported and protected reform. She pushed Henry into asserting his leadership of the Church in England because that was the only practical way to obtain his divorce, and without her to stiffen his sinews he would never have taken that step. She did not do it purely for personal gain. There is no doubt that Anne had a genuine belief in reform, and the grass-roots movement in England for such reform was given an irresistible push by her support at the top. Over this, she and Cromwell were in more or less total agreement. Of the ten elections to bishoprics between 1532 and 1536, seven were reformers who were her clients and, once in post, she expected them to promote reform and rebuked them if they failed to do so. She did not act in isolation, but was the leader of a group of powerfully placed individuals, including Cromwell himself and the new archbishop, Cranmer. Her central religious conviction was of the overriding importance of the Bible. She kept an English version in her suite available to anyone who wished to read it and was ready to protect the illegal trade in English Bibles even though she herself preferred to read it in French. She was opposed to the total secularization of the dissolved religious houses and felt that many should be turned into places of study or hospitals to preserve the best features of the monastic inheritance. She was a generous patron of scholars and was lavish in her relief of the poor and needy.

On 7 January 1536 Katherine of Aragon died, probably of cancer, but then on 29 January Henry had a serious accident in the tiltyard and in her anxiety over his safety Anne miscarried of another son. It was the beginning of the end. Henry now felt that God was still denying him a son and this time the reason was because Anne had seduced him into marriage by witchcraft. He had been playing the courtly game of love with one of her ladies, Jane Seymour, but Anne's emotional relationship with Henry, coupled with her insecurity, meant she was unable to turn a blind eye as Katherine had done, and with his first wife now dead, the king could reject Anne without having to return to Katherine. It was not long before Anne's enemies saw the potential in the passive tool of Jane. Mary could be recognized again as heir until Henry had a son; a reconciliation with the emperor would then be possible, thus lessening the reliance on France in international affairs, never popular in England, and the power of the religious reformers could be reduced, if not destroyed. Cromwell was actively working to bring the emperor and the king together, but in the end, to give Henry the reconciliation he demanded without Charles having publicly to climb down over Anne, Cromwell knew he would have to sacrifice the queen, despite all their shared interests and beliefs. In doing so he had also to get rid of her chief supporters. At this point Anne played into his hands and Cromwell improvised a brilliant coup from her mistake.

It was a measure of Anne's desperate insecurity that she acted as she did. The catalyst was a well-publicized romantic quarrel she had with Sir Henry Norris. While the king played games of courtly love with his wife's ladies, so the queen had her suiters among the gentlemen of his Privy Chamber. Norris was probably the king's closest friend, but Anne so far forgot herself as to accuse him in public of wishing to marry her after the king's death. At the same time, the court had been amused by the sight of one of her musicians, Mark Smeaton, making a fool of himself over the queen. He was talented and had been made a pet of, but he was not a gentleman and he did not know the rules of courtly games. Cromwell knew that Anne's brother Rochford, who was close to the king, had to be gathered in as well to prevent recovery or counterattack by the Boleyn faction. For good measure two more of the king's gentlemen, Sir Francis Weston and William Brereton, who had the misfortune to be in the wrong place at the wrong time, were arrested also and all five men were charged with adultery with the queen. Smeaton confessed after torture, the others protested their innocence up to and on the scaffold. The judicial process was speedy, and the jury was made up of hand-picked opponents of the queen. The outcome was never in doubt, despite the fact that adultery, even with a queen, was not a common-law crime, though rape of the queen was high treason. The real charge was treasonable conspiracy to bring about the king's death, so that Norris could marry Anne. At the time probably few believed the charges; there is certainly no need for us to do so. Anne swore her innocence twice on the sacrament.

When she was first arrested the queen seems to have had some sort of nervous collapse, but by the time of her trial she was well in command of herself. The common view was that 'she made so wise and discreet answers to all things laid against her', but it did her little good. Her uncle, Norfolk, as senior peer, pronounced the verdict, weeping as he did so, probably as much in fear for himself as in grief for his niece's fate. The trial of George Boleyn followed. Like his sister, he used the Boleyn brains and wit to demolish the case against him and like her, to no avail. Anne's biographer says their performance showed their calibre and why Cromwell had to ensure their deaths. In her speech from the scaffold Anne acquiesced in the travesty of justice and prayed for the king, for to have done otherwise would have endangered both her daughter and her surviving family and she died with the courage and dignity that might have been expected of her. Her marriage was immediately declared invalid and Elizabeth bastardized. Henry had lost three of the people he had loved best in the world to save Cromwell's skin, and his comfort was left to the Seymours.

Cromwell's assessment of Anne was that she had intelligence, courage and spirit, and he was in a position to know. The king had fallen in love with her because of her strength and independence, and it was that strength that enabled him to get where he wanted to be. She played a crucial and controversial role in the English Reformation but it was certainly not a passive one.

The letters here from Anne to Cardinal Wolsey, written in her own hand before she became queen, show just how much she and Henry relied on the Cardinal to obtain the king's annulment and their disillusion when he failed. Wolsey had good reason to fear that the aristocratic opposition to his policies would seek to use Anne in the battle against him, but, initially at least, Henry, and Anne as well, truly believed that he could obtain what they wanted; indeed, against any other combination of factors in European politics, he probably could have done; kings had not usually failed to rid themselves of unwanted wives before. Wolsey himself had initially little doubt that he could eventually achieve it and believed that once Henry had recovered from his infatuation with the Lady, he could be found a suitable French wife. If the relationship with Anne continued, then in order to retain power, Wolsey would almost certainly have accepted her as the future queen, but in the meantime he believed that a little delay might weaken her influence if the king's affections were fading.

The first letter can be safely dated to the summer of 1528 because of its reference to the sweating sickness, a virulent form of influenza which often proved fatal. Henry was always fearful for his health and on learning that a servant of Anne had succumbed to it he reluctantly decided to send her away. She returned home to Hever and this absence from court was the occasion of most of Henry's letters to her. She, in fact, caught the sweat but recovered. Her letter to Wolsey was in thanks for the gift and kind letter he had sent her on her recovery. The illness had broken out in his household too, but the Cardinal himself was not affected.

The second letter may have been written as late as the spring of 1529, but probably dates from the previous year. While Anne and the Cardinal were each aware of the threat the other posed, they were also realistic enough to know that neither could afford to offend the other. The third letter was written later in 1529. By then Anne was sure that Wolsey was trying to frustrate, not advance, the cause of the divorce, and among the body of his opponents she became an equal partner, no longer a tool of her father or uncle. The fiasco of the legatine court at Blackfriars in May 1529 finally convinced Henry that the Cardinal could not obtain a divorce for him.

Anne Boleyn to Cardinal Wolsey, c. July 1528

My Lord,

In my most humble wise that my poor heart can think, I do thank your grace for your kind letter, and for your rich and goodly present, the which I shall never be able to deserve without your help, of which I have hitherto had so great plenty, that all the days of my life I am most bound of all creatures, next the king's grace, to love and serve your grace, of the which I beseech you never to doubt that ever I shall vary from this thought, as long as any breath is in my body. And as touching your grace's trouble with the sweat, I thank our Lord that them that I desired and prayed for are escaped; and that is the king's grace and you, not doubting that God has preserved you both for great causes known alonely of His high wisdom. And as for the coming of the legate, I desire that much. And if it be God's pleasure, I pray him to send this matter shortly to a good end; and then I trust, my lord, to recompense part of your great pains. In the which I must require you, in the mean time, to accept my goodwill in the stead of the power; the which must proceed partly from you, as our Lord knoweth, whom I beseech to send you long life, with continuance in honour. Written by the hand of her that is most bound to be your humble and obedient servant, Anne Boleyn.

(BL Cotton Otho C x 218, Strickland, vol. ii, p. 202.)

Anne Boleyn to Cardinal Wolsey, 1528/9

After my most humble recommendations, this shall be to give unto your grace, as I am most bound, my humble thanks for the pain and travail that your grace doth take in studying, by your wisdom and great diligence, how to bring to pass honourably the greatest wealth that is possible to come to any creature living, and in especial remembering how wretched and unworthy I am in comparing to his highness. And for you, I do know myself never to have deserved by my deserts that you should take this great pain for me; yet daily of your goodness I do perceive by all my friends, and though that I had not knowledge by them, the daily proof of your deeds doth declare your words and writing toward me to be true.

Now good my lord, your discretion may consider as yet how little it is in my power to recompense you, but all only with my goodwill, the which I assure you, that after this matter is brought to pass you shall find me, as I am bound in the mean time, to owe you my service, and then look what thing in this world I can imagine to do you pleasure in, you shall find me the gladdest woman in the world to do it. And next unto the king's grace, of one thing I make you full promise to be assured to have it, and that is my hearty love unfeignedly during my life; and being fully determined, with God's grace, never to change this purpose, I make an end of this my rude and true-meaning letter, praying our Lord to send you much increase of honour, with long life.
Written with the hand of her that beseeches your grace to accept this letter as proceeding from one that is most bound to be
Your humble and obedient servant,

(*BL Cotton MS Vespasian F XII, art. 92, fo. 80, Wood, vol. ii, letter xvii.*)

Anne Boleyn to Cardinal Wolsey, 1529

My lord,

Though you are a man of great understanding, you cannot avoid being censured by every body for having drawn on yourself the hatred of a king who had raised you to the highest degree to which the greatest ambition of a man seeking his fortune can aspire. I cannot comprehend, and the king still less, how your reverent lordship, after having allured us by so many fine promises about divorce, can have repented of your purpose, and how you could have done what you have, in order to hinder the consummation of it. What, then, is your mode of proceeding? You quarrelled with the queen to favour me at the time when I was less advanced in the king's good graces; and after having therein given me the strongest marks of your affection, your lordship abandons my interests to embrace those of the queen. I acknowledge that I have put much confidence in your professions and promises, in

which I find myself deceived. But, for the future, I shall rely on nothing but the protection of Heaven and the love of my dear king, which alone will be able to set right again those plans which you have broken and spoiled, and to place me in that happy station which God wills, the king so much wishes, and which will be entirely to the advantage of the kingdom. The wrong you have done me has caused me much sorrow; but I feel infinitely more in seeing myself betrayed by a man who pretended to enter into my interests only to discover the secrets of my heart. I acknowledge that, believing you sincere, I have been too precipitate in my confidence; it is this which has induced, and still induces me, to keep more moderation in avenging myself, not being able to forget that I have been
Your servant,

(Leti, Vita de Elisabetha, *vol. i, p. 60. Wood, vol. ii, letter xix.)*

Seventeen of Henry's love-letters to Anne survive and are now in the Vatican archives, but their most recent editor erroneously states that none of Anne's to Henry still exist. The following is one that does, but it was also missed by Anne's biographer, Ives. It is undated and is probably the first that she wrote. At this stage in their relationship, the king had clearly begun to take an interest in her, perhaps initially because of the devotion to her of one of his gentlemen, Thomas Wyatt. It also contains the only evidence that Anne owed her official place at court to the king himself. She had probably first met him at the Field of the Cloth of Gold, where she had been in attendance on Queen Claude of France and, one presumes, in demand as an interpreter. Anne returned to England at the end of 1521 and was certainly present at court from that date onwards, but what position, if any, she held is not clear. Her marriage to James Butler was the reason for her return and it may be that, in light of her proposed removal to Ireland, she was not initially, at least officially, employed. It is also possible that she held the post of maid of honour on two separate occasions. The first from 1522, when she returned to England, until the ending of her attachment to Henry Percy when, at the Cardinal's instance, she was dismissed from court and returned to her parents at Hever, towards the end of 1523. From 1522 to 1525, Anne's father was treasurer of the royal household and there may well have been occasions when Henry encountered Anne, whose sister Mary was his mistress. Her return to court may have been at Henry's insistence.

Her letter of thanks to the king for the warrant of maid of honour, however, clearly states that Henry had already declared his love for her, and while initially this may only have been an element in a game of courtly love, it must be closer in time to the period when the game changed to something much more serious, and that makes the dating likely to be mid- or later 1526.

Anne Boleyn to Henry VIII, n.d. (?1526)

Sire,

It belongs only to the august mind of a great king, to whom Nature has given a heart full of generosity towards the sex, to repay by favours so extraordinary an artless and short conversation with a girl. Inexhaustible as is the treasury of your majesty's bounties, I pray you to consider that it cannot be sufficient to your generosity; for, if you recompense so slight a conversation by gifts so great, what will you be able to do for those who are ready to consecrate their entire obedience to your desires? How great soever may be the bounties I have received, the joy that I feel in being loved by a king whom I adore, and to whom I would with pleasure make a sacrifice of my heart, if fortune had rendered it worthy of being offered to him, will ever be infinitely greater.

The warrant of maid of honour to the queen induces me to think that your majesty has some regard for me, since it gives me means of seeing you oftener, and of assuring you by my own lips (which I shall do on the first opportunity) that I am, Your majesty's very obliged and very obedient servant, without any reserve,

(Leti, Vita de Elizabeth, vol. ii, p. 50. Wood, vol. ii, letter vii.)

The following letters illustrate not only Anne's strong interest in religious reform, but also her use of patronage to further such reform. Of the ten elections to bishoprics between 1532 and 1536, seven were reformers who were her clients and supporters, but her influence was also felt lower down the ecclesiastical scale. Edward Crome was one of a number of Cambridge men whom she favoured and she secured for him the benefice of St Mary Aldermary, but when she learned that he was slow to take up the new position and begin promoting the cause of reform, she wrote a very strong reprimand, which Crome was presumably not foolish enough to ignore.

Anne's role in the debate over the future of the monastic houses is well documented, among others by her chaplain, William Latimer. She was fully behind the policy of reform, but not that they be dissolved. She wanted them to be converted to places of study and education, and if she had remained queen it is entirely possible that the waste of all that was good in the monasteries, particularly their charitable aspect, would have been considerably less. Her view that such places should become centres for learning is illustrated by her letter to the abbot of St Mary's, York, William Thornton. Thornton had been elected in 1530 and Anne had persuaded him to permit Eldmer, the unsuccessful candidate for the post, to study in Cambridge and to support him there. After a few years, Eldmer was recalled to York and expected to take up his duties at St Mary's. The administrative tasks prevented him from studying and he appealed to Anne; presumably her letter had the desired result.

Anne's attitude to the Bible was quite clear: she read it, and she liked to discuss it with Henry when he dined with her. In defiance of ecclesiastical rules, she kept an

English version in her rooms for anyone who wished to read. Richard Herman, the Antwerp merchant who had been expelled from the English society of merchants there in Wolsey's day for assisting the trade in English bibles, sought her help, knowing it would be forthcoming. Cromwell was also in sympathy with her aims, and Anne continued to regard him as her loyal dependent. The brief note she sent him when his associate, the attorney-general, Christopher Hales, interfered with a wardship she had been granted by the king, is indicative of their easy working relationship. The boy was a Pointz, one of a family who numbered several among her servants.

Anne Boleyn, Queen of England, to Dr Edward Crome, c. 1535

Trusty and well-beloved,

We greet you well, marvelling not a little that, albeit heretofore we have signified unto you at sundry times our pleasure concerning your promotion unto the parsonage of Aldermary, within the city of London, which we have obtained for you, yet you have hitherto deferred the taking on you of the same; by which your refusal, we think that you right little regard or esteem your own weal or advancement. We, minding nothing more than the furtherance of virtue, truth, and godly doctrine, which we trust shall be not a little increased, and right much the better advanced and established, by your better relief and residence there, signify therefore to you, that our express mind and pleasure is that you shall use no farther delays in this matter, but take on you the cure and charge of the said benefice of Aldermary, as you tender our pleasure in any behalf.

Given under our signet, at my lord's manor of Richmond, the 20th of May.

(BL Lansdowne MS 1045, art. 64, fol. 79b. Wood, vol. ii, letter lxxvii.)

Anne Boleyn, Queen of England, to the Abbot of St Mary's, York, 13 May 1535

Trusty and well-beloved in God, we greet you well. And albeit at the time of your preferment to be head and governor of that my lord's monastery of St Mary beside his city of York, we then made request unto you for one dom John Eldmer, batchelor of divinity, a man, as we [be] credibly informed, of good learning, and sad demeanour, and virtuous governance, who then for the same his elect qualities stood in election (as you did) to be abbot, like as we doubt not but you remember right well, that the same dom John Eldmer should apply and continue his study and learning at my lord's university of Cambridge for the increase of virtue and learning: wherewith at that time you were well content. Yet notwithstanding the same, you, contrary to our said request (as we be credibly informed), have not only recalled him from his learning at the said university, but also have intricate and charged him with sundry rooms and offices in your said monastery, to the no little disturbance and inquietation of his mind, and to alienate him as much as may be from his said study and learning: to our no little marvel. We, considering the good affection and desire of the said dom John Eldmer has to the increase of virtue and learning, desire and heartily pray you, that you will permit and suffer him to repair again to the university for the intent aforesaid, giving unto him sufficient exhibition to the maintenance of his study there, or else to signify unto us in writing, by this bearer, a cause reasonable why you defer to accomplish our said request made unto you in that behalf.

Given under our signet, at my lord's manor of Westminster, the 13th day of May.

(PRO SP 1/92, Wood, vol. ii, letter lxxix.)

Anne Boleyn, Queen of England, to Thomas Cromwell, n.d.

Trusty and right wellbeloved, we greet you well. And whereas we be credibly informed that the bearer hereof Richard Herman, merchant and citizen of Antwerp in Brabant, was in the time of the late lord Cardinal put and expelled from his freedom and fellowship of and in the English house there for nothing else (as he affirms) but only for that he did both with his goods and policy, to his great hurt and hinderance in this world, help to the setting forth of the New Testament in English. We therefore desire and instantly pray you that with all speed and favour convenient you will cause this good and honest merchant, being my Lord's true, faithful and loving subject, restored to his pristine freedom, liberty and fellowship aforesaid and the sooner at this our request, and at your good leisure to hear him in such things as he hath to make further relation unto you in this behalf.

Given under or signet at my Lord's manor of Greenwich the 14th day of May.

(BL Cotton MS Cleop. E V, fol. 330b. Ellis, vol. ii, letter cxvi.)

Anne Boleyn, Queen of England, to Thomas Cromwell, n.d. (1535)

Master Secretary, I pray you despatch with speed this matter, for mine honour lies much on it, and what should the king's attorney do with Pointz's obligation, since I have the child by the king's grace's gift, but only to trouble him hereafter, which by no means I will suffer, and thus fare you well as I would ye did. Your loving mistress, Anne the Queen

(BL Add. MS 19,398, f. 48. Letters and Papers, viii, 1057; Ives p. 261.)

Anne Boleyn's first letter to Henry VIII has already been quoted; her last one follows here. It has always been surrounded by controversy and, indeed, may not have been written by her at all. Tradition says that a copy of it was found among the papers of Thomas Cromwell, and many people, including Ives, regard it as a forgery intended to discredit her, putting the view that no political prisoner of her time would have addressed the king in those terms. Conversely, the one person who might have done so was a wife. Her nearest family and friends seemed already likely to pay the ultimate penalty, and Henry might declare their daughter a bastard, but he was unlikely to harm her physically. Perhaps she felt she had nothing more to lose and gave herself the satisfaction of saying what she thought. Readers may make up their own minds.

Anne Boleyn, Queen of England, to Henry VIII, May 1536

Your grace's displeasure and my imprisonment are things so strange to me, that what to write, or what to excuse, I am altogether ignorant. Whereas you send to me (willing me to confess a truth and so obtain your favour), by such a one, whom you know to be mine ancient professed enemy, I no sooner received this message by him, than I rightly conceived your meaning; and if, as you say, confessing a truth indeed may procure my safety, I shall with all willingness and duty, perform your command. But let not your grace ever imagine that your poor wife will be brought to acknowledge a fault, where not so much as a thought ever proceeded. And to speak a truth, never a prince had wife more loyal in all duty, and in all true affection, than you have ever found in Anne Bulen – with which name and place I could willingly have contented myself, if God and your grace's pleasure had so been pleased. Neither did I at any time so far forget myself in my exaltation or received queenship, but that I always looked for such alteration as I now find; for the ground of my preferment being on no surer foundation than your grace's fancy, the least alteration was fit and sufficient (I knew) to draw that fancy to some other subject.

You have chosen me from low estate to be your queen and companion, far beyond my desert or desire; if, then, you found me worthy of such honour, good your grace, let not any light fancy or bad counsel of my enemies withdraw your princely favour from me; neither let that stain – that unworthy stain – of a disloyal heart towards your good grace ever cast so foul a blot on me, and on the infant princess your daughter.

Try me, good king, but let me have a lawful trial, and let not my sworn enemies sit as my accusers and as my judges; yea, let me recieve an open trial, for my truth shall fear no open shames. Then you shall see either my innocency cleared, your suspicions and conscience satisfied, the ignominy and slander of the world stopped, or my guilt openly declared. So that, whatever God and you may determine of, your grace may be freed from an open censure; and my offence being so lawfully proved, your grace may be at liberty, both before God and man, not only to execute worthy punishment on me as an unfaithful wife but to follow your affection already settled on that party

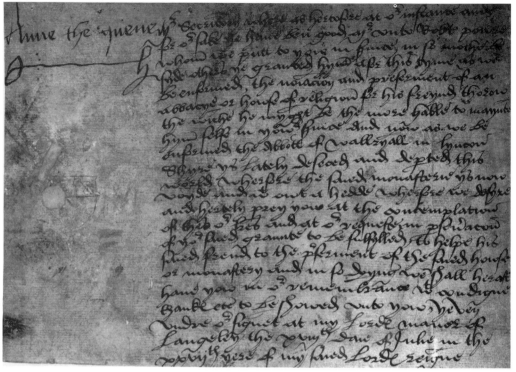

Letter from Anne Boleyn to Thomas Cromwell (1535) (BL Add. MS 19,398, f. 48)

[Jane Seymour] for whose sake I am now as I am, whose name I could some while since have pointed unto – your grace being not ignorant of my suspicion therein. But if you have already determined of me, and that not only my death, but an infamous slander must bring you the joying of your desired happiness, then I desire of God that he will pardon your great sin herein, and likewise my enemies, the instruments thereof; and that he will not call you to a strait account for your unprincely and cruel usage of me at his general judgement-seat, where both you and myself must shortly appear; and in whose just judgement, I doubt not (whatsoever the world may think of me), mine innocency shall be openly known and sufficiently cleared.

My last and only request shall be, that myself only bear the burden of your grace's displeasure, and that it may not touch the innocent souls of those poor gentlemen, whom, as I understand, are likewise in strait imprisonment for my sake. If ever I have found favour in your sight – if ever the name of Anne Bulen have been pleasing in your ears – then let me obtain this request; and so I will leave to trouble your grace any further, with mine earnest prayer to the Trinity to have your grace in his good keeping, and to direct you in all your actions.

From my doleful prison in the Tower, the 6th May.

(BL Otho C x 228; Letters and Papers, x, 808; and Strickland, vol. ii, p. 251.)

JANE SEYMOUR, THIRD WIFE OF HENRY VIII

Unlike his first two queens, who were both women of outstanding character and ability, Henry VIII's third wife was a quiet, unassuming nonentity, a willing tool remembered only for the fact that she bore his legitimate son. Jane was the eldest child of Sir John Seymour of Wolfhall in Wiltshire and his wife, Margaret Wentworth. The Seymours were respectable country gentry, but Jane had none of Anne Boleyn's aristocratic connections. She was probably born about 1509 and her early years were obscure. She may have been one of Mary Tudor's attendants on the bridal trip to France and she was certainly one of Queen Katherine's ladies and then moved on to the same position under Queen Anne. Her younger brother, Edward, a protegy of Wolsey and a man of some military talent, became a squire of the body in 1530 and accompanied Henry and Anne on the trip to Calais in 1532. In other words, the Seymours were familiar figures at court long before Henry began to show any amorous interest in Jane. This seems to have begun early in 1536 and probably earlier than this had been no more than ritual courtly love. It has always been believed that Jane's attraction for Henry was her difference from Anne: fair and gentle, of no great wit and about eight years younger than her predecessor. Chapuys described her as 'of middle stature and no great beauty, so fair that one would call her rather pale than otherwise'. In short, it is difficult to see wherein lay her appeal if it was not in the contrast with Anne.

Katherine's death altered the situation, a factor that was seized on, not just by Edward Seymour, advanced to the Privy Chamber in March, but by Mary's supporters, who thought that if Queen Anne were to be discarded and the king to enter into a legitimate third marriage, the princess might be rehabilitated. Jane was told to proclaim her virtue and hold out for nothing less than marriage, a ploy which had the expected results. Henry declared he would see her only in the company of her relations and then turned Cromwell out of his rooms in Greenwich, which had a private passage to the royal apartments and installed Edward Seymour and his wife instead. The court was treated to the unappetizing spectacle of the king's pursuit of Jane while having his wife tried for adultery. Anne was executed on 19 May, the king and Jane were betrothed on the 20th and on the 30th the marriage took place in the queen's closet at Whitehall. It was followed by an outburst of public celebrations and a week later, Edward Seymour was elevated to the peerage.

A rapid act of Parliament repealed the act in favour of Anne's issue and entailed it on Jane's future offspring, whether male or female. Until such time as the new queen bore a child, the king was given the unprecedented right to name his own successor. He now had three children: a son always accepted as illegitimate and two daughters, each of whom in turn had been accepted as legitimate and treated as the heir to the throne before being rejected. A few weeks after the act which would have enabled Henry to name Richmond as his heir, the young man died. A little later, Mary finally made peace with her father. She was a popular figure, regarded by many as the rightful heir and recognized overseas, but the previous few years had been very difficult ones. She had been refused access to both her parents – Henry's refusal to let her see her dying mother was particularly cruel – moved from house to house, forced to give Elizabeth precedence and humiliated by the latter's household. After the death of her mother she sought Jane's intercession with her father and the new queen was glad to give it. Richmond's death at least meant that failing heirs by Jane, Mary was likely to be named as heir. Henry still demanded complete submission from his daughter and in the end, browbeaten, alone and ill, Mary gave in. She recognized the Act of Succession, the invalidity of her mother's marriage and her own illegitimacy. Once he had obtained his daughter's submission, Henry was pleased to be gracious and generous, and Jane was able to offer real friendship to her stepdaughter, who was only seven years her junior and much in need of the love and support the queen could offer.

Jane's coronation was planned but postponed, first because of an outbreak of plague and then because of her pregnancy. In a letter announcing the queen's condition (ironically it was written to Norfolk), Henry announced his intention of not travelling more than sixty miles away from her in case irrational fears for his safety should disturb her and endanger the infant. Hampton Court was chosen for her lying-in and she was delivered of her son on 12 October 1537 after a two-day labour. So great were the rejoicings that the queen's death twelve days later passed almost unnoticed. No doubt Henry grieved for her, but he was quite capable of writing to Francis I announcing the birth of his son and acknowledging at the end that though the death of his queen cost him some grief, yet that grief was far exceeded by the joy of his son. He wore mourning for three months, he who had previously refused to receive anyone at court who wore it, but was considering remarriage within a month.

Jane Seymour was queen only for eighteen months and her character was not such as would have quickly made its mark at court. Her dower consisted of some 104 manors spread throughout nineteen counties, but there are few details of her administration. We know that she insisted that her ladies wore dresses that were more modest than had recently been the fashion and that life at court became more staid. The king was to look back on this period as the happiest of his married life, conveniently forgetting all the early, happy years with Katherine. The new queen had a very English love of gardening and her head gardener at Hampton Court was called Chapman. Princess Mary used to send presents of cucumbers to Jane and similar gifts to Chapman. A slight clue as to her religious leanings are given in the fact that on her deathbed she received full Catholic rites. Another indication is that she apparently begged the king on her knees to restore the dissolved abbeys and was told sharply to mind her own business if she wished to avoid the fate of her predecessor. Cardinal Pole had heard 'good things' about her, which suggests that despite the direction taken by her family in later years, the queen was certainly not a supporter of the reformers.

Jane Seymour by Hans Holbein

Jane Seymour was queen for little more than a year and we are therefore lucky that letters survive for this brief period. While well brought up and educated for service at court, Jane's letters do not have the style or elegance of those of some of Henry's other wives, and they have a slightly breathless tone, just as she dictated them. The first in date, addressed to the king's chief minister, is an example of her kind-heartedness, which enabled her to make a friend of her elder stepdaughter, Mary. The Thomas Dudley concerned has not been positively identified but was apparently not, as might have been supposed, a close connection of Henry VII's minister, Edmund Dudley, executed by Jane's husband when he first came to the throne, or his son John, later earl of Warwick and duke of Northumberland. Whoever he was, Jane's letter seems to have had the desired result, for a few months later he was granted a cottage in the parish of St Katherine Coleman, London, worth thirty shillings per annum. The second letter, bearing her signature 'Jane the Quene', was a routine order to one of her officials, typical of scores that must have issued from her household. The gentlemen of the Chapel Royal were the king's choir, which suggests that Jane, like most of her contemporaries at court, loved music. The manor of Havering, with its park, had almost invariably formed part of the dower of successive queens.

Jane Seymour, Queen of England, to Thomas Cromwell, 23 November 1536

Trusty and right wellbeloved, we greet you well desiring and in our right hasty wise, praying you that you, for our sake and at this our instance will be so good and favourable unto our trusty and wellbeloved Thomas Dudeley, squire, this bearer, as not only to hear such good causes as he hath to show you for sundry injuries to him committed and done, but also in such discreet wise to speak, write and order him and his said causes and adversaries as you shall serve to be according to equity and good justice whereby we think verily considering that he is now in extreme necessity and a younger brother destitute of all aid or sorrow of his elder brother you cannot do a better deed for the increase of your eternal reward in the world to come.

Given under our signet at my lord's castle of Windsor, the 23rd day of November.

(BL Vesp. F III, f. 16 (no. 35).)

Jane Seymour, Queen of England, to the Parker of Havering, 28 June 1537

To the keeper of our park of Havering and in his absence, to his deputy there.

We will and command you forthwith upon sight hereof and by warrant of the same, to deliver or cause to be delivered unto our wellbeloved the gentlemen of the Chapel Royal of my sovereign lord the king or to the bringer hereafter in their name, two bucks of this season to be taken unto them of our gift within our park of Havering at Bower any restraint or other commandment had or given to the contrary hereof in any wise notwithstanding. Given under our signet at my lord's manor of Hampton Court the 28th day of June the 29th year of the reign of my said lord king Henry the eighth.

(BL Vesp. F III, f. 16 (no. 36).)

Whether or not Jane was personally responsible for the wording of this letter sent in her name on the day she gave birth to the future Edward VI after a very long labour, its sentiments would have been very much hers. In particular, there is the very firm statement that her son had been conceived in lawful matrimony, when both the king's former wives were dead, and in contrast to Elizabeth whose mother had been pregnant at the time of her marriage. The sense of relief at the final settling of the succession, with all that that implied for the peace of the kingdom, is very strong, as is the sense of trepidation over the future health of the longed-for heir. At the time the letter was sent there was no immediate fear for the life of the queen, who did not succumb to puerperal fever until several days later, dying on 24 October.

Jane Seymour, Queen of England, to the Council, 12 October 1537

Right trusty and wellbeloved, we greet you well, and for as much as by the inestimable goodness and grace of Almighty God, we be delivered and brought in childbed of a prince, conceived in most lawful matrimony between my lord the king's majesty and us, doubting not but that for the love and affection which you bear unto us and to the commonwealth of this realm, the knowledge thereof should be joyous and glad tidings unto you, we have thought good to certify you of the same. To the intent you might not only render unto God condign thanks and prayers for so great a benefit but also continually pray for the long continuance and preservation of the same here in this life to the honour of God, joy and pleasure of my lord the king and us, and the universal weal, quiet and tranquillity of this whole realm. Given under our signet at my lord's manor of Hampton Court the 12th day of October.

(BL Harl MS 283, f. 155.)

ANNE OF CLEVES, FOURTH WIFE OF HENRY VIII

Anne, daughter of John, duke of Cleves and Marie, heiress of William, duke of Juliers, married Henry in January 1540, more than two years after the death of Jane Seymour, but the search for a fourth wife for the king began before Jane had been dead a month. This time he was free to look for a royal wife abroad and intense diplomatic manoeuvring encompassed at least nine possible candidates, including Mary of Guise (who married James V of Scotland) and the duchess of Milan. One major difficulty was that Henry, romantically accustomed now to choosing his own wife, refused to consider anyone without either seeing her first or at least having a picture of her. He even attempted to get several French candidates to Calais so that he could inspect them and select one; needless to say this idea was indignantly rejected by the French. One of the English diplomatic aims was to avoid being totally sidelined following an alliance between France and the Emperor. The duke of Cleves had connections with Lutheran states, was at loggerheads with the Emperor over Gelderland which he had just inherited, and had two eligible sisters, Anne and Amelia. Hans Holbein was despatched to bring back portraits and, on the strength of them, Henry selected Anne, the elder sister. The marriage treaty was concluded and she set out for England.

On her journey from Deal to London, Anne was met at Rochester by the king who had dashed down in disguise to have a look at his bride. He was bitterly disappointed: 'I am ashamed that men have so praised her as they have done, and I like her not', was his judgement. According to the two portraits of her that have survived, Anne was, if not a beauty, certainly as pleasant looking as Henry's other wives, but Henry had worked himself up into a state of romantic excitement and then found himself bitterly disappointed because he felt no physical attraction to her. He could not, however, find an excuse for not marrying her and the wedding went ahead. Henry's comments on his new wife's person after the wedding night were even less complimentary than his comments about her face. The marriage was never consummated, though there is no doubt that Henry tried, and it was declared null and void six months later on the grounds of a former contract between Anne and the duke of Lorraine which had been formally renounced long since.

Anne's docility in accepting, first the humiliation of a marriage that her husband spent all his time trying to wriggle out of and then divorce proceedings, which she assisted by confirming the non-consummation, astonished the court. It was, however, a docility based on shrewdness, not stupidity. Her dower as queen-consort, which had been settled on her by Parliament in April 1540, was naturally rescinded, but in relief at his freedom Henry offered her two houses, an appropriate household, an annuity of £500 and the right to address him as 'brother', provided she remained in England. Despite anxious pleas from her brother to return home, she decided to settle in England rather than face an ignominious return to Cleves.

Anne of Cleves, attributed to Barthel Bruyn the Elder, *c.* 1239

Queen Anne's fault may well have lain in her personality rather than her looks. It had certainly been reported to Henry that his proposed bride was not highly educated, spent most of her time sewing and could neither sing, nor play, since these were not required of royal ladies at German courts. A dull, shy young woman (twenty-three at the time of her marriage) who could speak neither English nor French, was unlikely to captivate Henry, nor, indeed, a court dominated by French culture. On the other hand, presumably Anne felt she had escaped lightly from matrimony, and certainly those who offered her the terms were astonished at her alacrity in acceptance. Her continued presence in England prevented her outraged brother from taking any action against Henry and, since it was unlikely that anyone else would have been willing to accept her as a wife, she was almost certainly better off in England with a secure income and an adequate household, though obviously reduced in size from that of 126 persons she had had during her brief time as queen. She had brought several ladies with her from Cleves, together with her own physician and cook. She had little interest in politics and had the good sense never to become embroiled in them. Henry was willing to pay the occasional visit to her at Richmond and she spent several days staying with him and his fifth queen at Hampton Court. After the fall of Katherine Howard, the duke of Cleves attempted to raise the question of a reconciliation, without, needless to say, any success.

Henry's death left Anne free to return home if she wished, but by that time she had learned English, acquired English habits and was respected and accepted by her former husband's subjects. After the queen and the royal daughters, she was the first lady in the land, and her life was akin to that of a rich widow. Her brother may have resented the slight to Cleves, but there is ample evidence that Anne, indifferent to it, was cheerful and even joyous. She had also formed an affectionate relationship with her two stepdaughters, particularly with Mary to whom she was close in age, and her last public appearance was at Mary's coronation when she rode in procession with the Princess Elizabeth. After Henry's death removed her protector, she experienced money troubles and was forced to constantly petition the Council for her annuity. She seems even to have finally wished to return home, but although her brother persuaded the Council to pay some of her debts, she had lost the opportunity to be received back in Cleves. She died at the age of forty-one of a lingering illness in July 1557 at Chelsea, for she had been granted the manor where Thomas Seymour courted Katherine Parr. She was buried at the queen's order in Westminster Abbey near the high altar. When she made her will, Anne bequeathed jewels to her sister, her brother and his wife and to Queen Mary, whom she appointed overseer of the will, and to Elizabeth. The duchess of Suffolk and the earl and countess of Arundel were also remembered and every member of her household received an additional year's wages. She still had eight of her own countrymen with her, who were all given £10 apiece to defray the cost of their journey home. Nor were the poor forgotten; money was set aside for the education of poor children and for distribution to the poor on her various estates.

The following letter is Anne's submission to Henry's desire for an annulment of their marriage. As far as the king was concerned it was the perfect response and from it sprang his desire to be equally generous in his turn. On Anne's side, it is difficult to judge whether it was a genuine reflection of her feelings or an answer calculated to please and remove her safely from a very difficult situation, with loss of face the only price she had to pay. Her reward was financial security, a gentle domestic life in England and the liking amounting to affection felt by Henry and his family towards her, which assured her a welcome at court if she wished to visit it. Anne continued to reside at Richmond after the separation, from whence this letter had been written. The French ambassador reported to his master that 'Madame of Cleves has a more joyous countenance than ever. She wears a great variety of dresses, and passes all her time in sports and recreations.'

Anne of Cleves, Queen of England, to Henry VIII, 11 July 1540

Pleaseth your most excellent majesty to understand that, whereas, at sundry times heretofore, I have been informed and perceived by certain lords and others of your grace's council, of the doubts and questions which have been moved and found in our marriage; and how hath petition thereupon been made to your highness by your nobles and commons, that the same might be examined and determined by the holy clergy of this realm; to testify to your highness by my writing, that which I have before promised by my word and will, that is to say, that the matter should be examined and determined by the said clergy; it may please your majesty to know that, though this case must needs be most hard and sorrowful unto me, for the great love which I bear to your most noble person, yet, having more regard to God and his truth than to any worldly affection, as it beseemed me, at the beginning, to submit me to such examination and determination of the said clergy, whom I have and do accept for judges competant in that behalf. So now being ascertained how the same clergy hath therein given their judgement and sentence, I acknowledge myself hereby to accept and approve the same, wholly and entirely putting myself, for my state and condition, to your highness' goodness and pleasure; most humbly beseeching your majesty that, though it be determined that the pretended matrimony between us is void and of none effect, whereby I neither can nor will repute myself for your grace's wife, considering this sentence (whereunto I stand) and your majesty's clean and pure living with me, yet it will please you to take me for one of your humble servants, and so determine of me, as I may sometimes have the fruition of your most noble presence; which as I shall esteem for a great benefit, so, my lords and others of your majesty's council, now being with me, have put me in comfort thereof; and that your highness will take me for your sister; for the which I most humbly thank you accordingly.

Thus, most gracious prince, I beseech our Lord God to send your majesty long life and good health, to God's glory, your own honour, and the wealth of this noble realm.

From Richmond, the 11th day of July, the 32nd year of your majesty's most noble reign.

Your majesty's most humble sister and servant, Anne the daughter of Cleves.

(PRO SP 1/161, f. 97, Wood, vol. iii, letter lxxxiii.)

Anne's relations with her two erstwhile stepdaughters remained very good; Mary had stayed for several days with her on more than one occasion, and when Anne's marriage was dissolved the only favour she asked of Henry was that she might continue to see Elizabeth, a request Henry was graciously pleased to grant. Her distress over the apparent muddle made by Edward VI's council over Westhorpe clearly springs from the fear that it might damage her friendship with Mary. Her letter to Mary as queen was written a week after Mary's marriage to Philip of Spain. Bletchingley, from where the first letter was written, was another property the council forced her to exchange, this time for Penshurst in Kent (at that time a medieval house, later rebuilt by the Sidney family), though she retained some lands at Bletchingley, for her tenant there was later Sir Thomas Carden, her man of affairs and former Master of the Revels to King Henry. Another favourite house of Annes was the former nunnery at Dartford which had been turned into a hunting lodge by Henry. She had received it, along with Penshurst, as part of the exchange for Bletchingley. Her 'poor house at Hever', from where she wrote to Queen Mary was the original Boleyn home which had been granted to her by the king in 1540 on the death of Thomas Boleyn, Anne's father, without male heirs.

Anne of Cleves to Princess Mary, 8 January 1553

Madam,

After my most hearty commendations to your grace, being very desirous to hear of your prosperous health, wherein I very much rejoice, it may please you to be advertised that it hath pleased the king's majesty to have in exchange my manor and lands of Bisham, in the county of Berkshire, granting me in recompense the house of Westropp [Westhorpe] in Suffolk, with the two parks and certain manors thereunto adjoining; notwithstanding, if it had been his highness' pleasure, I was well contented to have continued without exchange. After which grant, for mine own assurance in that behalf I have travailed, to my great cost and charge, almost this twelve months; it hath passed the king's majesty's bill, signed, and the privy seal, being now, as I am informed, stayed at the great seal, for that you, madam, be minded to have the same, not knowing, as I suppose, of the said grant. I have also received at this Michaelmas last passed, part of the rent of the aforesaid manors. Considering the premises, and for the amity which hath always passed between us (of which I most heartily desire the continuance), that it may please you therefore to ascertain me by your letters or otherwise, as it shall stand with your pleasure. And thus, good madam, I commit you unto the everliving God, to have you in merciful keeping. From my house in Bletchingley, the 8th day of January, 1553.

Your assured loving friend to her little power to command, Anne the daughter of Cleves.

(Strickland, vol. ii, pp. 329–30.)

Anne of Cleves to Queen Mary, 4 August 1554

To the Queen's Majesty

After my humble commendations unto your majesty, with thanks for your loving favour showed to me in my last suit, and praying of your highness your loving continuance, it may please your highness to understand that I am informed of your grace's return to London again; and being desirous to do my duty to see your majesty and the king, if it may so stand with your highness' pleasure, and that I may know when and where I shall wait on your majesty and his. Wishing you both much joy and felicity, with increase of children to God's glory, and to the preservation of your prosperous estates, long to continue with honour in all godly virtue. From my poor house at Hever, the 4th of August.

Your highness' to command, Anne the daughter of Cleves

(PRO SP 11/4, Strickland, vol. ii, p. 330.)

KATHERINE HOWARD, FIFTH WIFE OF HENRY VIII

Katherine Howard was a first cousin of Anne Boleyn and the second niece of Thomas Howard, duke of Norfolk, to become queen of England. Her father was Edmund, third son of the second duke, who suffered all his life from landless poverty. He was a good soldier and distinguished himself at Flodden, but although he was the same age as the king, Henry seems never to have liked him and he was unable to get a post at court although he held local office, chiefly in Surrey and Sussex where the Howards held large estates. Finally his niece, Anne Boleyn, obtained the controllership of Calais for him in 1531. Naturally an advantageous marriage was arranged for him, but although Joyce Culpeper was both an heiress and the widow of Ralph Legh, it does not seem to have solved his financial problems. Katherine was one of their younger children, born about 1520–1, and was still a small child when her mother died. Edmund married two other wealthy but otherwise undistinguished widows, but living in the style he expected without access to court patronage meant that he was always in debt. On the death of her mother, Katherine was sent initially to join the nursery of her cousin Thomas, son and heir of Sir John Culpeper, at Hollingbourne. When she was ten she joined the household of her father's stepmother, Agnes, dowager-duchess of Norfolk, first at Horsham and then at Lambeth.

The aim of entering another household was to teach a young girl the accomplishments necessary for her future; these included reading, writing, music, deportment and how to run a household. Unfortunately for Katherine she learned rather more than was to be good for her. All that we know of her life at Lambeth comes from hostile sources and was used as evidence against her at her trial. In a large household, members mixed closely together regardless of exact rank, and youthful escapades could hardly have been unusual, but under the eyes of relatives and neighbours was generally harmless enough. We know of an early flirtation by Katherine with her virginals teacher, Henry Manox, which was followed by a love affair with Francis Dereham, who, though a gentleman, was hardly likely to be approved of by her family. There is no doubt that she slept with Dereham, and possibly even consented to become secretly betrothed to him. When the liaison came finally to the ears of the duchess, Dereham fled to Ireland and Katherine was severely beaten, but the scandal was naturally hushed up. He seems to have remained loyal to her memory but Katherine's passions, though intense, were short-lived. The arrival of Anne of Cleves to become Henry's fourth queen early in 1540 meant a jostling for positions in her new household; of the six posts for maidens deemed necessary, the duke of Norfolk secured two, on behalf of Katherine and her cousin, Mary Norris. Dereham was forgotten as she hurried off to take her place at court.

It is not necessary to believe that Norfolk had any design to throw his niece in Henry's way, but in contrast to the plain, dull queen it is hardly surprising that the king took an immediate interest in his wife's pretty, lively maid, and once that interest took shape, Norfolk and his conservative ally, Stephen Gardiner, bishop of Winchester, needed little persuasion to encourage Henry in his pursuit. As soon as the marriage with Anne was declared invalid, Henry married Katherine, on 28 July 1540. He was forty-eight, his bride barely twenty. She was small, plump and vivacious and generally regarded as the most beautiful of his wives, and the king was clearly besotted with her. He lavished presents on her, and for a time felt healthy and young again himself. The new queen received Jane Seymour's former jointure as well as lands that had belonged to Cromwell, Lord Hungerford and the abbot of Reading. Her household ladies were headed by the king's niece, Margaret Douglas, and the queen's grandmother, the duchess of Norfolk.

Although history seemed to have repeated itself, Katherine was not really in the same position as either her cousin Anne or Jane Seymour. They had both been at court for a long period before they caught the eye of the king, and both had close relatives among those near the king. Katherine, in contrast, was much younger, without experience, and with nobody to keep an eye on her. She was not interested in the administration of her estates or the exercise of charity. She was a girl whose neglected childhood, lived in genteel poverty, had ended with a fairy-tale come true. All she was interested in was enjoying herself. For six months all was well, but in March 1541 Henry fell ill from his ulcered leg and feared he might die. Instead of the devoted husband he became a fractious invalid, moody, irritable and hard to please. Katherine lacked either the maturity or the instinctive understanding to deal with the situation and reacted like a spoilt child. Although she seems to have got on well with her predecessor, Anne of Cleves, she quarrelled with Princess Mary, four years her senior, and was apparently unable to inspire any liking or loyalty among those who surrounded her at court, which meant she lacked any sensible advice from older women. Her case was similar to that of her cousin Anne in one particular; if she had been pregnant she would have been secure; as it was, she became the target for all those who opposed her uncle and the conservatives. There was, however, little need to plot against her; Katherine was responsible for her own downfall.

At the request of her grandmother, the queen found a post in her household for Francis Dereham as a secretary. Trusting in her support, he behaved arrogantly and boastfully. He did not, however, regain her favours. These were reserved for her cousin Thomas Culpeper, who had become a gentleman of the Privy Chamber. Her only extant letter was written to him after she became queen. Within less than a year of her marriage, Katherine was committing adultery. Their go-between was one of her senior ladies, Anne, Lady Rochford, widow of George Boleyn, who had played a questionable role in the downfall of her husband and sister-in-law. On a royal progress in the late summer of 1541 that the king and court made to the north, the couple were unbelievably reckless. While there is evidence that all three were aware of the danger, they seemed to have lacked any instinct for self-preservation. Meanwhile in London, the Council were told by an informer of the queen's misconduct with Dereham in her youth and when Henry returned to London, Cranmer was given the unpleasant task of breaking the bad news to him. At first he refused to believe it, but when forced by the evidence to accept it, his reaction was predictably harsh. The queen's death was not yet inevitable, especially if she had claimed a precontract to Dereham which would have allowed Henry to claim the marriage invalid, but Katherine refused to see wherein lay her safety and denied that there had ever been a promise between herself and Dereham, preferring to die as queen than live in disgrace. In the meantime, news of the relationship with Culpeper leaked out and all hope for the three of them was lost. Whether or not the queen and Culpeper really loved each other, they both behaved very badly, lying, each trying to blame the other and avoid the consequences of their actions. The duchess of Norfolk, who destroyed papers of Dereham in an attempt to conceal evidence, and several other members of the Howard family were arrested on charges of misprision of treason, which enabled them to be despoiled of large sums of money and goods. The queen was sent to Syon while a bill of attainder was passed against her, which, incidently, made it treason for an unchaste woman to marry the king and misprision of treason for anyone to conceal such unchastity. After her first hysterical attempts to reach the king failed, Katherine pulled herself together and finally confessed her guilt, begging the king not to impute guilt to her entire family. Two days later she and Lady Rochford, who had gone mad under the strain of interrogation, went to the block; Culpeper and Dereham had gone to their deaths earlier. The fall of Katherine Howard contained none of the tragedy or dignity of the end of Anne Boleyn. She was a foolish girl who lacked either the moral sense or common sense to see that behaviour which could be tolerated in the girls' dormitory would be unacceptable in a queen.

The letter that follows is the only extant one of Katherine Howard and is written, as she explains, with some effort on her part. It appears to have been sent in 1541, probably in March or April, about eight months after she became queen. In the débâcle that followed, Katherine claimed that she met Culpeper only to reward his pleadings, while he insisted that the meetings were solely at the bidding of the queen who was 'languishing and dying of love for him'. The evidence, what little there is of it, suggests that the initiative did indeed come from Katherine. The parting phrase

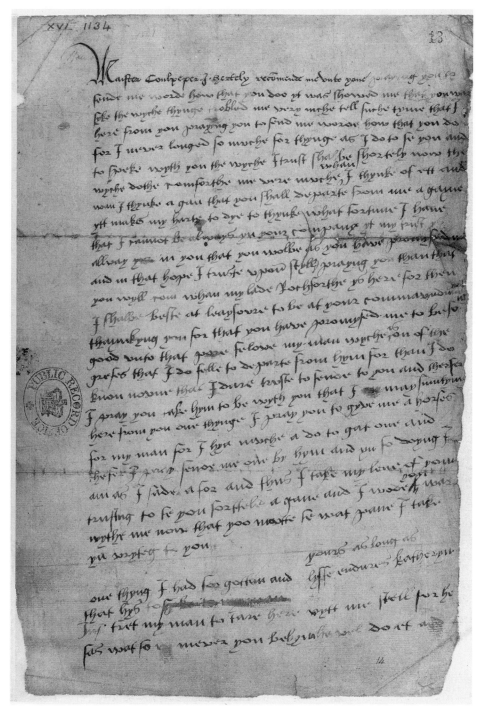

Letter written by Katherine Howard to Thomas Culpeper (PRO SP 1/167, f. 14)

of her letter hardly indicates a queen granting a gracious audience to a suppliant courtier. Lady Rochford, who so successfully arranged the secret meetings, claimed she did so on the queen's explicit instructions. Jane Rochford had retired from court on her husband's death, but returned to serve Katherine as one of the ladies of the privy chamber. Daughter of Henry Parker, Lord Morley, she was the granddaughter on her mother's side of Lady Margaret Beaufort's half-brother and was thus a distant cousin of the king. She was charged with having acted as procuress for the queen and was executed with her.

Katherine Howard, Queen of England, to Thomas Culpeper, 1541

Master Culpeper, I heartily recommend me unto you, praying you to send me word how that you do. It was showed me that you was sick, the which thing troubled me very much till such time that I hear from you praying you to send me word how that you do, for I never longed so much for [a] thing as I do to see you and to speak with you, the which I trust shall be shortly now. The which doth comfortly me very much when I think of it, and when I think again that you shall depart from me again it makes my heart to die to think what fortune I have that I cannot be always in your company. It my trust is always in you that you will be as you have promised me, and in that hope I trust upon still, praying you that you will come when my Lady Rochford is here for then I shall be best at leisure to be at your commandment, thanking you for that you have promised me to be so good unto that poor fellow my man which is one of the griefs that I do feel to depart from him for then I do know no one that I dare trust to send to you, and therefore I pray you take him to be with you that I may sometime hear from you one thing. I pray you to give me a horse for my man for I had much ado to get one and therefore I pray send me one by him and in so doing I am as I said afor, and thus I take my leave of you, trusting to see you shortly again and I would you was with me now that you might see what pain I take in writing to you.
Yours as long as life endures,
Katheryn

One thing I had forgotten and that is to instruct my man to tarry here with me still for he says whatsomever you bid him he will do it.

(PRO SP 1/167, f. 14; Letters and Papers, *xvi, 1134; Lacey Baldwin Smith,* A Tudor Tragedy: the life and times of Catherine Howard *(1961), pp. 168–9.)*

KATHERINE PARR, SIXTH WIFE OF HENRY VIII

Katherine was born about 1513, the daughter of Sir Thomas Parr of Kendal, Master of the Court of Wards and Controller of the Household, and Maud, daughter and heiress of Sir Thomas Green of Boughton. Through the Neville family, Katherine and the king were fourth cousins. Katherine's father died in 1517 and her mother never remarried, but devoted herself to the education and upbringing of Katherine, her brother William, the future marquess of Northampton and sister Anne, later countess of Pembroke. When she was queen, Katherine both wrote and read Latin, was conversant with Greek, and was fluent in French and Italian, but this may have been as much a result of self-education as she grew older than formal education as a child. An early plan to match Katherine with the son and heir of Lord Scrope of Bolton collapsed because of an inability to agree on the financial side of the arrangements, and she married Edward, son of Thomas, Lord Borough of Gainsborough, in about 1529. The marriage was a brief one, for Edward died before 1533, and Katherine was left a youthful, childless widow. Since Lady Parr had also just died and Katherine's sister was still unmarried, Katherine went to reside with her kinswoman, Katherine Neville, widow of Sir Walter Strickland of Sizergh Castle, where examples of her needlework can be seen. We do not know how long she remained a widow, but she was probably still only about twenty when she married, as his third wife, John Neville, Lord Latimer, a much older man with children. Their chief residence was Snape Hall in Yorkshire. Latimer was an ardent supporter of the Church, enough so to become involved with the Pilgrimage of Grace, but not enough to pay the final penalty of such involvement. His wife had influential friends at court, for her sister, now Lady Herbert, was one of Queen Jane's ladies and her uncle, Sir William Parr, was a member of the royal household. It is reasonably certain that by this time Katherine and the king were known to each other. Lord Latimer died late in 1542 or early 1543.

Henry grieved more for the loss of Katherine Howard than for any previous wife and was in no great hurry to look for a replacement. It was to be sixteen months before he married his sixth and last wife. Despite her husband's conservative religious attitude, Lady Latimer seems to have developed moderate Protestant views of her own and in the period after her husband's death received reformers such as Coverdale and the royal protégé, Hugh Latimer, in her house. In a more worldly mode, she was being courted by Thomas Seymour, brother of Queen Jane, a gallant who obviously made considerable headway with the widow of an elderly man, who was possessed of two very comfortable jointures. When the king began to take an interest, however, Katherine is said to have taken it as a sign of God that she use the opportunity to work for the cause of the reformed religion at court. Henry and

Katherine were married at Hampton Court on 12 July 1543, and the king ended his matrimonial adventures with a sixth wife very similar in many ways to his first.

One of Katherine's major achievements as queen was to bring all three of Henry's children together in the royal household for the first time. She reorganized the arrangements for the education of the two younger ones, ensuring that the humanist education that was provided was shared by other, noble children as well as Edward and Elizabeth. She encouraged Mary and Elizabeth to make translations of the works of Erasmus, and herself composed two devotional treatises, *The Prayers stirring the Mind unto Heavenly Meditation*s, printed in 1545, and *The Lamentations of a Sinner,* published after her death. Despite their different theological views, the queen and Princess Mary became close friends; they were of a similar age, and their learning and studies provided a strong mutual interest. In a letter written in French to Katherine, her stepson Prince Edward praised her letters to him both for the beauty of their penmanship and their imagination, and referred also to the kindness of her nature. There is no doubt that all her stepchildren, both Latimer and Tudor, loved her. So too did the king. The devotion of a kind, understanding and intelligent wife, who quickly learned to give him all the adulation he craved, was just what he needed during his last years. In his turn he settled the succession after Edward on any children she might bear him, and when he undertook a voyage to France, formally appointed her queen-regent, with Edward Seymour, earl of Hertford, as her lieutenant. Sir Thomas Wroithesley, writing in a private letter, described her as 'a woman, in my judgement, for certain wisdom and gentleness most meet for his highness; and sure I am his majesty never had a wife more agreeable to his heart than she is.'

The queen's interest in the reformed religion was bound to draw upon her the opprobium of the conservative faction led by Stephen Gardiner, bishop of Winchester. Indeed, even the king, with whom his wife liked to have theological discussions, found her views a little too advanced for him, but while Gardiner could make object lessons of a few lesser reformers, he seemed quite unable to touch the queen. She appointed Miles Coverdale to the office of almoner in her household and her patronage enabled Nicholas Udall to edit his translation of Erasmus's *Paraphrases on the Gospels*, and it was published at the queen's expense. Her connection with Anne Askew, whom she received at court and had been given books by, was used in an attempt to implicate the queen in a charge of heresy or treason, but Anne refused, even under torture, to furnish the material for such a charge. Gardiner, apparently with Henry's approval, moved to draw up articles of heresy against Katherine but, warned of the plot, she forestalled it by abjectly casting herself upon her husband's mercy, submitting humbly to his superior wisdom in all things and declaring that she had only talked theology with him to ease him during his infirmity. Henry's famous response 'And is it even so, sweetheart, and tended

Katherine Parr by W. Scrots, *c.* 1545

your argument to no worse end? Then perfect friends we are now as ever at any time heretofore', leaves open the question of Henry's motive. Was it to teach Katherine a lesson and crush her independence of mind or was the lesson one for Gardiner?

Despite her theological interests, the new queen's nature was by no means all serious. Like most ladies with experience at court, she enjoyed dancing and music and, indeed, had her own consort of Italian musicians. She took to heart the need to dress as became a queen, and seems to have had a passion for shoes; she ordered nearly fifty pairs in one year. She retained her skill in embroidery and spent hours at the work. Much of her time was taken up with physically nursing the king, who refused to allow anyone else to dress his ulcered leg. Katherine, at least, had experience in nursing a sick and elderly husband. Henry died on 28 January 1547. His death was kept secret for three days until the earl of Hertford obtained possession of the person of his nephew, the young king, and produced a patent declaring himself to be Henry's choice for protector of the realm. Katherine had been appointed protector and governor during the king's absence at Boulogne in 1544, but even if she had been the mother of the heir, it was highly unlikely that she would have received such an appointment. In addition to her dower, Henry's will bequeathed her £3,000 in plate and jewels and a further £1,000 in cash. In her brief period of royal widowhood, Katherine resided at her jointure house in Chelsea, where it was easy for a member of the late king's household and of the council of regency to have access to her. Thomas Seymour picked up where he had been forced by the king to break off nearly four years previously. He had made more than one attempt at an advantageous marriage in the intervening period (both Anne of Cleves and Princess Mary had been spoken of in this context), but it was not difficult to convince the queen that he had stayed single for her sake. Katherine was thirty-five years old and had been married to two elderly widowers in succession; she loved Seymour and was only too happy to believe him. They were privately married sometime in May. The young king, fond of his uncle and loving Katherine as a mother, was delighted with the match, but the council, and in particular the bridegroom's elder brother, were furious at Seymour's presumption in not seeking their permission. To testify to their hostility they withheld from Katherine all the jewels presented to her by the late king on the grounds that they were not private property but heirlooms. Relations between the Seymour brothers worsened to the extent that Thomas tried to stir up opposition to Somerset and spoke openly of retaining and leading men.

In her residence at Chelsea both before and after her remarriage, the queen had charge of the young Princess Elizabeth and her cousin, Lady Jane Grey, whose education she was supervising. The notorious stories of Seymour's early morning rompings with Elizabeth were doubtless very upsetting to Katherine in her first pregnancy, but she tactfully withdrew her household to Seymour's residence at Sudeley Castle, leaving Elizabeth in London, and did not allow her feelings to blight either her relations with her stepdaughter or the latter's reputation. Seymour, whose ambitions were directed at replacing his brother as protector, was too powerful to touch while the queen lived, but Katherine died eight days after giving birth to a daughter, on 30 August 1548, and her husband survived her only by six months, executed for treason in seeking to marry Princess Elizabeth and quite possibly attempting to kidnap the king to secure governorship of his person. The queen-dowager was buried in the chapel at Sudeley. Her orphaned daughter, Mary, was sent with her attendants to the household of the queen's friend, the duchess of Suffolk, but died as a small child. Perhaps Katherine's epitaph should be supplied by Henry VIII himself, who, in the preamble to the legacy he makes her in his will, describes her virtues as great love, obedience, chastity of life and wisdom.

In an Anglo-Imperial alliance against France, Henry made his final trip to the continent in the summer of 1544. Conflicting aims between the allies, Henry's determination to take part in the campaign in person despite his poor health, and no clear objective for the large army under the veteran dukes of Norfolk and Suffolk, led to a muddled campaign. By the time Henry arrived, in mid-July, Suffolk's forces were besieging Boulogne and, to the king's delight, took it while he was with them. At the end of September he and a few companions slipped quietly home. During his six-week absence Queen Katherine was appointed to govern the realm with the title of Queen-Regent, with the earl of Hertford as her deputy should she require assistance. When the king set out for France there was considerable anxiety about his health, though in the event his sojourn beside the sea at Boulogne left him in better health and spirits than he had been for years. This anxiety is clearly expressed in Katherine's letter to the council, more muted in those to Henry himself. The latter are very loving and humbly expressed; just the right tone for Henry and an indication of Katherine's skill in handling her husband. They are also practical. The campaign was an extremely expensive one and cost Henry, not the estimated £250,000, but nearer £650,000. One of the tasks of the queen-regent and council at home was to ensure that a steady supply of cash arrived safely in Calais, and in the fourth letter Katherine took advantage of a courier's departure to enclose a note to her husband.

One of the reasons for the attack on France was to discourage French aid to Scotland, where Henry was trying to ensure that supporters of a match between his son and the infant queen, Mary, were in control of the government, hence Katherine's decision to inform the king immediately of the capture of the Scottish ship with its crucial cargo of letters. The dowager referred to in that letter is, of course, James V's widow, Mary of Guise, whose family was the most powerful in France. Two of the letters refer specifically to Henry's children, for the first time all united in the royal household in a family atmosphere for which their stepmother was wholly responsible.

Katherine Parr, Queen of England, to Henry VIII (July 1544)

. . . Although the distance of time and account of days neither is long nor many of your majesty's absence, yet the want of your presence, so much desired and beloved by me, maketh me that I cannot quietly pleasure in anything until I hear from your majesty. The time, therefore, seemeth to me very long, with a great desire to know how your highness hath done since your departing hence, whose prosperity and health I prefer and desire more than mine own. And whereas I know your majesty's absence is never without great need, yet love and affection compel me to desire your presence.

Again, the same zeal and affection force me to be best content with that which is your will and pleasure. Thus love maketh me in all things to set apart mine own convenience and pleasure, and to embrace most joyfully his will and pleasure whom I love. God, the knower of secrets, can judge these words not to be written only with ink, but most truly impressed on the heart. Much more I omit, lest it be thought I go about to praise myself, or crave a thank; which thing to do I mind nothing less, but a plain, simple relation of the love and zeal I bear your majesty, proceeding from the abundance of the heart. Wherein I must confess I desire no commendation, having such just occasion to do the same.

I make like account with your majesty as I do with God for his benefits and gifts heaped upon me daily, acknowledging myself a great debtor to him, not being able to recompense the least of his benefits; in which state I am certain and sure to die, yet I hope in His gracious acceptation of my goodwill. Even such confidence have I in your majesty's gentleness, knowing myself never to have done my duty as were requisite and meet for such a noble prince, at whose hands I have found and received so much love and goodness, that with words I cannot express it. Lest I should be too tedious to your majesty, I finish this my scribbled letter, committing you to the governance of the Lord with long and prosperous life here, and after this life to enjoy the kingdom of his elect.

From Greenwich, by your majesty's humble and obedient servant, Katherine the Queen.

(Strype's Memoirs, *reprinted Strickland, vol. ii, p. 419.*)

Katherine Parr, Queen-Regent of England, to the Council with the King, 25 July 1544

Katherine the Queen

Right trusty and well-beloved cousins, we greet you well. Letting you wit that having received your letters of the 23rd of this present, we have by the same had singular comfort, as well to perceive thereby the state of health my lord the king's majesty was in at that present, as also the good beginning of success of his grace's affairs there; for your joyful news whereof we give unto you our right hearty thanks. And forasmuch as, touching the other contents of your said letters, we have presently written at length unto my said lord, the king's majesty, we forbear to repeat the same unto you, not doubting but that his highness will communicate the same unto you accordingly. Given under our signet at my said lord the king's majesty's honour of Hampton Court, the 25th day of July, the 36th year of his majesty's most noble reign.

(PRO SP 1/190, f. 156. Wood, vol. iii, letter lxxix.)

Katherine Parr, Queen of England, to Henry VIII, 31 July 1544

Pleaseth it your majesty to be advertised, this afternoon were brought to me letters from your majesty's lieutenant of the north, declaring the apprehension of a Scottish ship by certain fishermen of Rye, and in the same certain Frenchmen and Scots, being sent with divers letters and credence towards the French king and others in France. And because I thought this taking of them, with the interception of the said letters, to be of much importance for the advancement of your majesty's affairs, ordained (I doubt not) of God, as well to the intent your highness might thereby certainly understand the crafty dealing and juggling of that nation, as also mete with the same after such sort as to your high wisdom shall be thought most convenient; I have presently sent such of the letters as, upon the view of the same, appeared of most importance unto your majesty. There are a great number of other letters to the French king and others, both from the dowager [Mary of Guise] and others, but they are either of the same effect that these be which I have sent unto your majesty, or general letters only for credence. My lords of your majesty's council have sent to have certain of the chief, both of the Scots and Frenchmen, sent up, upon whose examination your majesty shall be further advertised with diligence.

My lord prince and the rest of your majesty's children are all, thanks be to God, in very good health. And thus with my most humble commendations unto your majesty,

I pray Almighty God have the same in His most blessed keeping. From your majesty's honour of Hampton Court, the last day of July, the 36th year of your majesty's most noble reign.

Your grace's most humble loving wife and servant, Katherine the Queen.

(PRO SP 1/190, f. 221. Wood, vol. iii, letter lxxx.)

Katherine Parr, Queen of England, to Henry VIII, 25 August 1544

Pleaseth it your majesty to be advertised, albeit I had at this present none occurents of importance to be signified unto your highness, your realm being, thanks be to Almighty God, in very good order and quiet; yet forasmuch as Richard Higham is at this time dispatched hence unto your majesty with a mass of £30,000, I thought it my duty to advertise your majesty of the sending of the same; praying Almighty God to send your majesty continuance of health and most prosperous success in all your highness' most noble enterprises. My lord prince and the rest of your majesty's children be in very good health. And thus, with my most humble commendations unto your majesty, I pray Almighty God have the same in his most blessed keeping. From your majesty's honour of Hampton Court, the 25th of August, the 36th year of your majesty's most noble reign.

Your majesty's most humble loving wife and servant, Katherine the Queen.

(PRO SP 1/190, f. 166. Wood, vol. iii, letter lxxxi.)

There is no doubt of the affection all three of Henry's children felt for his last wife. Katherine's letter to Mary printed here shows a loving and sincere concern for her, and Mary's gift of a purse, almost certainly in some part her own handiwork, indicates her feelings for Katherine. The two were much of an age, the queen only three or four years older than the princess and their scholarly interests gave them much in common despite the queen's support of the reformed religion. To their shared love of music the queen specifically testifies in her letter. The work to which she refers was Mary's work in translating Erasmus's *Paraphrase on the Gospel of St John*, a task which the queen had encouraged her to undertake. Francis Mallet, who helped Mary, was promoted by her when she became queen, to the deanery of Lincoln; only her death prevented his elevation to the bishopric of Salisbury. The translation was eventually published under the name of Nicholas Udall, master of Eton, at Katherine's expense. Udall pays tribute to the princess's work in his preface. Mary's work was cut short by her illness, hence Katherine's concern. After her father's marriage to Katherine, Mary had lived mainly at court in the queen's company, but at the time the letter was written, Katherine was staying at her manor of Hanworth, Middlesex.

Katherine Parr, Queen of England, to Princess Mary, 20 September 1544

Although, most noble and dearest lady, there are many reasons that easily induce my writing to you at this time, yet nothing so greatly moves me thereto as my concern for your health; which, as I hope it is very good, so am I greatly desirous to be assured thereof.

Wherefor, I despatch to you this messenger, who will be (I judge) most acceptable to you, not only from his skill in music, in which you, I am well aware, take as much delight as myself, but also because, having long sojourned with me, he can give the most certain information of my whole estate and health. And, in truth, I have had it in mind before this to have made a journey to you and salute you in person; but all things do not correspond with my will. Now, however, I hope this winter, and that ere long, that, being nearer, we shall meet; than which, I assure you, nothing can be to me more agreeable, and more to my heart's desire.

Now since, as I have heard, the finishing touch (as far as the translation is concerned) is given by Mallet to Erasmus's work upon John, and nought now remains but that proper care and vigilance should be taken in revising, I entreat you to send over to me this very excellent and useful work, now amended by Mallet, or some of your people, that it may be committed to the press in due time; and farther, to signify whether you wish it to go forth to the world (most auspiciously) under your name, or as the production of an unknown writer. To which work you will, in my opinion, do a real injury, if you refuse to let it go down to posterity under the auspices of your own name, since you have undertaken so much labour in accurately translating it for the great good of the public, and would have undertaken still greater (as is well known) if the health of your body had permitted.

And, since all the world knows that you have toiled and laboured much in this business, I do not see why you should repudiate that praise which all men justly confer on you. However, I leave this whole matter to your discretion, and, whatever resolution you may adopt, that will meet my fullest approbation.

For the purse, which you have sent me as a present, I return you great thanks. I pray God, the greatest and best of beings, that He deign to bless you uninterruptedly with true and unalloyed happiness. May you long fare well in him. From Hanworth, 20th of September,
Most devotedly and lovingly yours, Katherine the Queen.

(Cotton MS Vespasian, F III, art. 35, fol. 29, Latin. Wood, vol. iii, letter lxxxiv.)

Henry's financial straits after the expensive expedition to France in 1544 led him to virtual bankruptcy. He was forced to debase the coinage and extract forced loans and heavy subsidies from his reluctant subjects. The act of 1545, which abolished the chantries, gave the king the power to dissolve any institution at either of the universities and seize its possessions. He had never shown himself a friend to education, and the University of Cambridge, recognizing both the severity of the threat and the queen's devotion to learning, wrote in desperation to Katherine, imploring her protection. The following letter is her reply.

Katherine Parr, Queen of England, to the University of Cambridge, 26 February 1546

You show me how agreeable it is to me, being in this worldly estate, not only for mine own part to be studious, but also a maintainer and cherisher of the learned state, bearing me in hand [insisting] that I am endowed and perfected with those qualities which ought to be in a person of my station. Truly this your discreet and politic document I as thankfully accept as you desire that I should embrace it. And forasmuch (as I do hear) all kind of learning doth flourish among you in this age as it did amongst the Greeks at Athens long ago, I desire you all not so to hunger for the exquisite knowledge of profane learning, that it may be thought that the Greek university was but transposed or now in England revived, forgetting our Christianity, since their excellency did only attain to moral and natural things; but rather, I gently exhort you to study and apply those doctrines as means and apt degrees to the attaining and setting forth Christ's reverent and sacred doctrine; for this Latin lesson I am taught to say of St Paul, Non me pudet evangelii, to the setting forth whereof (I trust) universally in all your vocations and ministries you will apply, and conform your sundry gifts, arts and studies in such end and sort, that Cambridge may be accounted rather an university of divine philosophy than of natural and moral, as Athens was. Upon the confidence of which your accomplishment of my expectation, zeal and request, I (according to your desires) have attempted my lord the king for the establishment of your livelihood and possessions, in which (notwithstanding his majesty's property and interest, through the consent of the high court of parliament), his highness being such a patron to good learning doth tender you so much, that he would rather advance learning and erect new occasion thereof than confound your ancient and godly institutions; so that such learning may hereafter ascribe her very original whole conversation to our sovereign lord the king, her only defence and worthy ornament, the prosperous estate and princely government of whom long to preserve, I doubt not but every one of you will in the daily invocation call upon Him, who alone and only, can dispose to every creature.

Scribbled with the rude hand of her, that prayeth to the Lord and immortal God to send you all prosperous success in holy learning and knowledge. From my lord the king's majesty's manor of Greenwich, the 16th Feb.

(Corpus Christi Coll. MS 206. Strickland, vol. ii, p. 427.)

It might have been possible to believe in Sir Thomas Seymour's romantic devotion to Katherine Parr during the years she was his sovereign's wife, if it were not for the fact that he proposed marriage to her stepdaughter, Elizabeth, before he addressed the widowed queen. The letter Elizabeth wrote declining his proposal is quoted in Wood (vol. iii, letter lxxxviii), where she expresses surprise that anyone should imagine she could think of marriage so soon after the death of her father, and that she would need at least two years to mourn his loss. Despite the refusal the letter is a friendly one, but the letter that follows, to her sister Mary, displays her shock and horror at Seymour's hasty marriage to Katherine. She says nothing of the proposal to herself, of course, but talks only of the dishonour done to their father's memory.

Katherine's own feelings for Seymour are clearly expressed in her letters, which are candid and honest. She had loved him before her elevation to the throne and she still did so. The queen's brother Herbert was her sister Anne's husband, later to be earl of Pembroke. Seymour's marriage plans were not favoured by his powerful elder brother, the earl of Hertford, nor by Hertford's wife, who heartily disliked the idea of her brother-in-law's wife taking precedence over her at court. Their hostility to the queen is shown in the withholding of the late king's bequest to her of jewels and in the matter of Fausterne, to which she refers. The park of Fostern in Wootton Basset, Wiltshire, was part of her dower lands; Hertford (or duke of Somerset, as he became) was determined to obtain a lease of it for a man named Long, and with the authority of his office, obtained from the king the reversion of many of the queen's dower lands and had Long admitted as tenant despite the queen's wish to retain it in her own hands, even instructing her own chancellor to draw up the lease. It was an incredible affront; even the king would not have behaved so cavalierly over his wife's own lands. In a scene between them, Katherine reported to her lover, she had been made 'a little warm. It was fortunate we were so much distant, for I suppose else I should have bitten him.' Lady Suffolk, to whom the queen refers, was a very close friend. She was Frances Willoughby, daughter of Katherine of Aragon's devoted lady-in-waiting, Maria de Salinas, and was the last wife of the king's brother-in-law, Charles Brandon, duke of Suffolk.

Of all the royal letters in this volume, those of Katherine Parr are the most informal, the most expressive of her real emotions and the most accessible to twentieth-century readers.

Katherine Parr, Queen-Dowager, to Thomas Seymour, Lord Sudeley (1547)

My Lord,

I send you my most humble and hearty commendations, being desirous to know how you have done since I saw you. I pray you be not offended with me, in that I send sooner to you than I said I would, for my promise was but once in a fortnight.

Howbeit the time is well abbreviated, by what means I know not, except weeks be shorter at Chelsea than in other places.

My lord, your brother, hath deferred answering such requests as I made to him till his coming hither, which he saith shall be immediately after the term. This is not the first promise I have received of his coming, and yet unperformed. I think my lady hath taught him that lesson, for it is her custom to promise many comings to her friends, and to perform none. I trust in greater matters she is more circumspect. And thus, my lord, I make my end, bidding you most heartily farewell, wishing you the good I would myself. From Chelsea.

PS. I would not have you think that this mine honest goodwill towards you to proceed of any sudden motion of passion; for, as truly as God is God, my mind was fully bent, the other time I was at liberty, to marry you before any man I know. Howbeit, God withstood my will therein most vehemently for a time, and, through his grace and goodness, made that possible which seemed to me most impossible; that was, made me renounce utterly mine own will, and to follow his will most willingly. It were long to write all the process of this matter; if I live, I shall declare it to you myself. I can say nothing but as my lady of Suffolk saith, 'God is a marvellous man'.
By her, that is yours to serve and obey during her life, Katherine the Queen.

(Strickland, vol. ii, pp. 445–6.)

Katherine Parr, Queen-Dowager, to Thomas Seymour, Lord Sudeley (1547)

My Lord,

As I gather, by your letter delivered to my brother Herbert, you are in some fear how to frame my lord your brother to speak in your favour, the denial of your request will make his folly more manifest to the world, which will more grieve me than the want of his speaking. I would not wish you to importune for his goodwill if it come not frankly at the first; it shall be sufficient once to require it, and then to cease. I would desire you might obtain the king's letters in your favour, and also the aid and furtherance of the most notable of the council, such as you shall think convenient; which thing obtained, shall be no small shame to your brother and loving sister, in case they do not the like.

My lord, whereas you charge me with a promise, written with mine own hand, to change the two years into two months, I think you have no such plain sentence written with my hand. I know not whether you be a paraphraser or not. If you be learned in that science, it is possible you may of one word make a whole sentence, and yet not at all times alter the true meaning of the writer, as it appeareth by this your exposition upon my writing.

When it shall be your pleasure to repair hither, you must take some pain to come early in the morning, that you may be gone again by seven o'clock; and so I suppose you may come without suspect. I pray you let me have knowledge over-night at what hour you will come that your portress may wait at the gate to the fields for you. And thus, with my most humble and hearty commendations, I take my leave of you for this time, giving you like thanks for your coming to court when I was there. From Chelsea.

PS. I will keep in store, till I speak with you, my lord's large offer for Fausterne, at which time I shall be glad to know your further pleasure therein.

By her that is, and shall be, your true, humble and loving wife during her life, Katherine the Queen.

(Strickland, vol. ii, p. 446.)

Genealogies

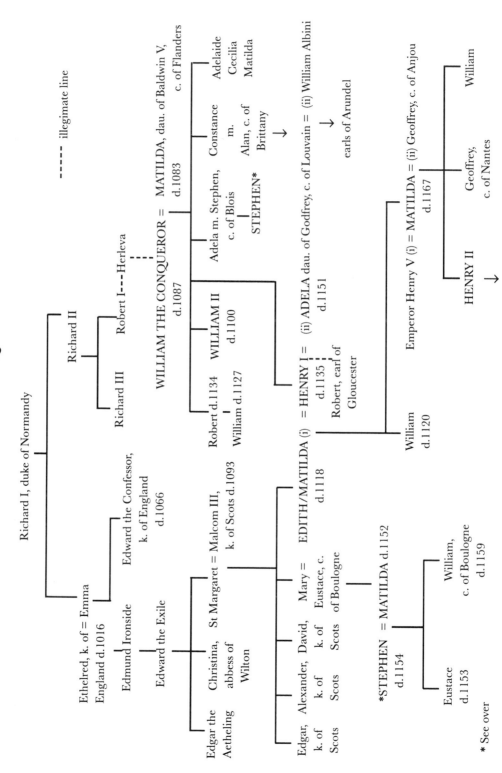

THE NORMAN QUEENS

The Angevin Queens

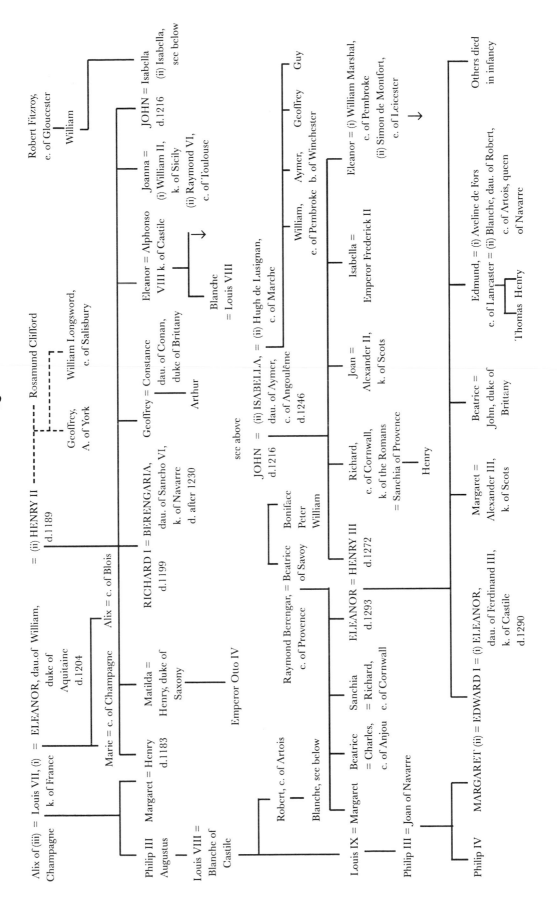

THE PLANTAGENET QUEENS

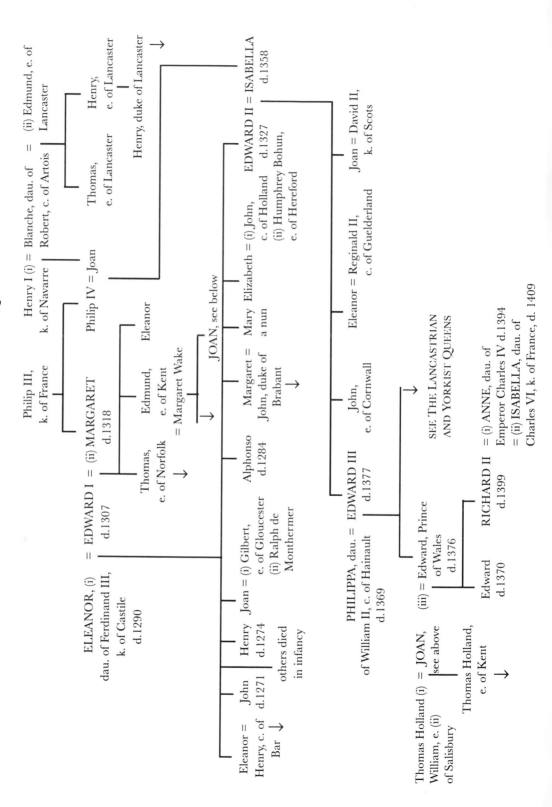

THE LANCASTRIAN AND YORKIST QUEENS

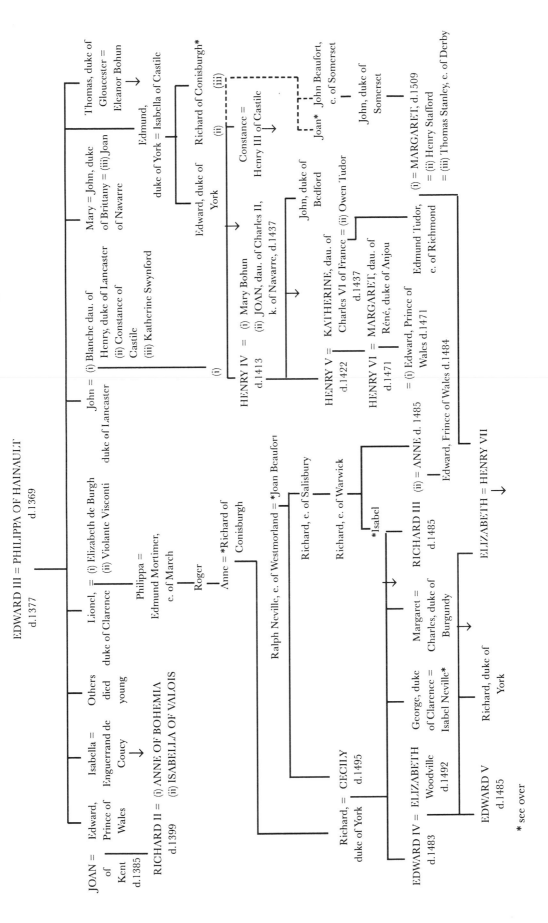

* see over

THE TUDOR QUEENS

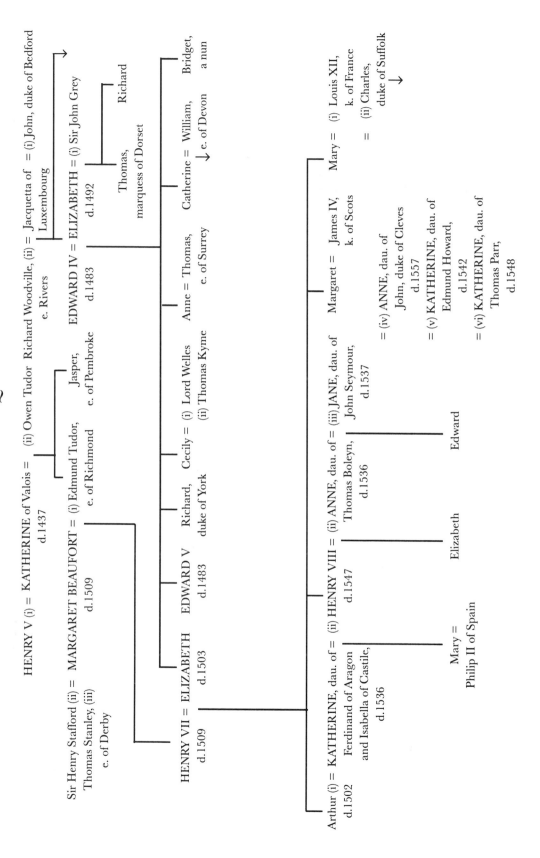

Table of Royal Marriages, 1066–1547

William I, m.?1050–1, **Matilda**, b.?, d.1083, da. of Baldwin V, count of Flanders. Issue:

  Robert, duke of Normandy, b.*c*.1051, d.1134
  William II, b.*c*.1056–60, acc.1087, d.1100
  Henry I, b.1068, acc.1100, d.1135
  Adelaide, d.1073
  Cecilia, abbess of Caen, b.bef.1066, d.1127
  Constance, m.1086, Alan, count of Brittany, d.1090
  Adela, m.1080, Stephen, count of Blois-Chartres, d.1090
  Matilda

William II, unmarried

Henry I, m.(1)1100, **Edith/Matilda**, b.1080, d.1118, da. of Malcolm III (Canmore), king of Scots and St Margaret, sister of Edgar Aetheling and granddaughter of King Edmund Ironside. Issue:

  William, b.1103, d.1120
  Matilda, b.1102, d.1167, m.(1)1114, Emperor Henry V, (2)1128, Geoffrey, count of Anjou. Issue: **Henry II**
    m.(2)1121, **Adela/Adelicia**, b.?, d.1151?, da. of Godfrey VII, count of Louvain. No issue. She married secondly, William d'Albini; issue

Stephen, m.1125, **Matilda**, b.?1103, d.1152, da. and heir of Eustace III, count of Boulogne. Issue:

  Eustace, b.1130–1, d.1153
  William, b.1132–7, d.1159, count of Boulogne
  Baldwin, d. bef.1137
  Mary, d.1182
  Matilda, b.1134, d.bef.1137

Henry II, m.1152, **Eleanor**, b.1122, d.1204, da. and heir of William X, duke of Aquitaine, former wife of Louis VII of France. Issue:

William, b.1153, d.1156
Henry, b.1155, d.1183
Richard I, b.1157, acc.1189, d.1199
Geoffrey, b.1158, d.1186, count of Brittany
John, b.1167, acc.1199, d.1216
Matilda, b.1156, d.1189, m.1168, Henry the Lion, duke of Saxony
Eleanor, b.1161, d.1214, m.1176, Alphonso VIII, king of Castile
Joanna, b.1165, d.1199, m.(1)1177, William II, king of Sicily, (2)1196, Raymond VI, count of Toulouse

Richard I, m.1191, **Berengaria**, b.*c*.1172, d. after 1230, da. of Sancho VI, king of Navarre. No issue

John, m.(1) Isabella, da. of William, earl of Gloucester, divorced 1199. No issue
m.(2)1200 **Isabella**, b.1188, d.1246, da. and heir of Aymer, count of Angoulême. Married secondly Hugh de Lusignan, count of La Marche; issue.
Issue:
Henry III, b.1207, acc.1216, d.1272
Richard, b.1209, d.1272, earl of Cornwall, king of the Romans
Joanna, b.1210, d.1238, m.1221, Alexander II, king of Scots
Isabella, b.1214, d.1241, m.1235, Emperor Frederick II
Eleanor, b.1215, d.1275, m.(1) William Marshal, earl of Pembroke (2) Simon de Montfort, earl of Leicester

Henry III, m.1236, **Eleanor**, b.*c*.1220, d.1293, da. of Raymond Berengar, count of Provence. Issue:
Edward I, b.1239, acc.1272, d.1307
Edmund 'Crouchback', b.1245, d.1296, earl of Lancaster
Margaret, b.1240, d.1275, m.1252, Alexander III, king of Scots
Beatrice, b.1242, d.1275, m.1260, John, duke of Brittany
Other children who died in infancy

Edward I, m.(1) 1254, **Eleanor**, b.*c*.1240, d.1290, da. of Ferdinand III, king of Castile and Leon. Issue:
John, b.1266, d.1271
Henry, b.1267, d.1274
Alphonso, b.1273, d.1284
Edward II, b.1284, acc.1307, d.1327
Eleanor, b.1264, d.1297, m.1293, Henry, count of Bar
Joan, b.1272, d.1307, m.(1)1290 Gilbert, earl of Gloucester, (2)Ralph de

Monthermer

Margaret, b.1275, d.1318, m.1290 John II, duke of Brabant

Mary, b.1278, d.1332, a nun

Elizabeth, b.1282, d.*c*.1316, m.(1)1296, John, count of Holland, (2)Humphrey de Bohun, earl of Hereford

Other children died in infancy

 m.(2) 1299, **Margaret**, b.*c*.1277, d.1318, da. of Philip III of France. Issue:

Thomas 'of Brotherton', b.1300, d.1338, earl of Norfolk

Edmund 'of Woodstock', b.1301, d.1330, earl of Kent

Eleanor, b.1306, d.1311

Edward II, m.1308, **Isabella**, b.1296, d.1358, da. of Philip IV of France. Issue:

 Edward III, b.1312, acc.1327, d.1377

 John 'of Eltham', b.1316, d.1336, earl of Cornwall

 Eleanor, b.1318, d.1355, m.1332, Reginald II, count of Guelderland

 Joan, b.1321, d.1362, m.1328, David II, king of Scots

Edward III, m.**Philippa**, b.*c*.1315, d.1369, da. of William II, count of Hainault, Holland and Zeeland. Issue:

 Edward, b.1330, d.1376, Prince of Wales, m. Joan, da. of Edmund, earl of Kent. Issue:

  Edward, b.1365, d.1370

  Richard II, b.1367, acc.1377, d.1399

 William, b.1336, d.young

 Lionel, b.1338, d.1368, duke of Clarence

 John, b.1340, d.1399, duke of Lancaster, m.(1)Blanche, da. of Henry, duke of Lancaster. Issue:

  Henry IV, b.1366, acc.1399, d.1413

 m.(2) Constance, da. of Pedro, king of Castile. Issue

 m.(3) Katherine Swynford. Issue:

  John Beaufort, earl of Somerset

  Henry, Cardinal Beaufort, bishop of Winchester

  Thomas Beaufort, duke of Exeter

  Joan, m.(2) Ralph Nevill, earl of Westmorland

 Edmund, b.1342, d.1402, duke of York

 Thomas, b.1355, d.1397, duke of Gloucester

 Isabella, b.1332, d.1379, m.1365, Enguerrand de Coucy, earl of Bedford

 Mary, b.1344, d.1362, m.1361, John IV, duke of Brittany

 Margaret, b.1346, d.1361, m.1359 John Hastings, earl of Pembroke

 Other children who died in infancy

Richard II, m.(1)1382, **Anne**, b.1366, d.1394, da. of Emperor Charles IV. No issue

m.(2)1396, **Isabella**, b.1387, d.1410, da. of Charles VI of France. No issue. Married secondly, Charles, duke of Orleans

Henry IV, m.(1)1380/1, Mary, b.*c.*1370, d.1394, da. and co-heir of Humphrey de Bohun, earl of Hereford. Issue:

Henry V, b.1387, acc. 1413, d.1422

Thomas, b.1388, d.1421, duke of Clarence

John, b.1389, d.1435, duke of Bedford

Humphrey, b.1390, d.1447, duke of Gloucester

Blanche, b.1392, d.1409, m.1402, Ludwig of Bavaria, son of Rupert, king of the Romans

Philippa, b.1394, d.1430, m.1406, Eric IX, king of Denmark

m.(2)1403, **Joan**, b.*c.*1373, d.1437, da. of Charles II, king of Navarre, widow of John IV, duke of Brittany. No issue

Henry V, m.1420, **Katherine**, b.1401, d.1437, da. of Charles VI, king of France. Issue:

Henry VI, b.1421, acc.1422, d.1471

Katherine married secondly Owen Tudor. Issue:

Edmund, earl of Richmond, m.Margaret, da. of John Beaufort, duke of Somerset. Issue:

Henry VII, see below

Jasper, earl of Pembroke

Henry VI, m.1445, **Margaret**, b.1429, d.1482, da. of Rene, duke of Anjou. Issue:

Edward, b.1453, d.1471, Prince of Wales, m.1471, Anne, da. and co-heir of Richard Neville, earl of Warwick

Edward IV (b.1442, acc.1461, d.1483, son of Richard, duke of York and Cecily Neville, da. of Ralph, earl of Westmoreland), m.1464, **Elizabeth**, b.*c.*1437, d.1492, da. of Richard Woodville, earl Rivers, widow of Sir John Grey, by whom she had issue. Issue:

Edward V, b.1470, acc.1483, d.1485

Richard, b.1473, d. 1485, duke of York

Elizabeth, b.1466, d.1503, m.1486, **Henry VII**

Mary, b.1467, d.1482

Cecily, b.1469, d.1507, m.(1)1487, John, viscount Welles, m.(2)1504 Thomas Kyme

Anne, b.1475, d.*c*.1511, m.1495, Thomas Howard, later duke of Norfolk

Catherine, b.1479, d.1527, m.1495, Sir William Courtenay

Bridget, b.1480, d.*c*.1513, a nun

Edward V, unmarried

Richard III (b.1452, acc.1483, d.1485, brother of Edward IV), m.1472, **Anne** da. and co-heir of Richard Neville, earl of Warwick, widow of Edward, Prince of Wales. Issue:

Edward, b.1473, d.1484, Prince of Wales

Henry VII (b.1457, acc.1485, d.1509), m.1486, **Elizabeth**, da. of Edward IV. Issue:

Arthur, b.1486, d.1502, Prince of Wales, m.1501, Katherine, da. of Ferdinand, king of Aragon and Isabella, queen of Castile

Henry VIII, b.1491, acc.1509, d.1547

Margaret, b.1489, d.1541, m.1503, James IV, king of Scotland

Mary, b.1496, d.1533, m.(1)1514, Louis XII, king of France, m.(2)1515, Charles Brandon, duke of Suffolk

Henry VIII, m.(1)1509, **Katherine**, b.1485, d.1536, da. of Ferdinand, king of Aragon and Isabella of Castile; marriage annulled 1533. Issue:

Mary, b.1516, acc.1553, d.1558

m.(2)1533, **Anne**, b.?1501, d.1536, da. of Sir Thomas Boleyn; executed. Issue:

Elizabeth, b.1533, acc.1558, d.1603

m.(3)1536, **Jane**, b.?1509, d.1537, da. of Sir John Seymour. Issue:

Edward VI, 1537, acc.1547, d.1553

m.(4)1540, **Anne**, b.1515, d.1557, da. of John, duke of Cleves and Juliers; marriage annulled 1540

m.(5)1540, **Katherine**, b.?1521, d.1542, da. of Edmund Howard

m.(6)1543, **Katherine**, b.1512, d.1548, da. of Sir Thomas Parr, widow of John, Lord Latimer. Married secondly, Sir Thomas Seymour

Sources

Unpublished letters are from collections in the Public Record Office and British Library. They are reproduced by permission of the Controller of Her Majesty's Stationery Office. Each letter is given its document reference. Where the current document references of printed letters are known, they are also given.

The printed references of previously published letters are to the following works:

Ellis, H., *Original Letters Illustrative of English History*, 1st series. 3 vols. 1825.

Foedera, Conventiones, Literae. . . et Acta Publica, Thomas Rymer (ed.). 20 vols. 1704–35.

Leti, G., *La Vie d'Elizabeth Reine d'Angleterre*. Amsterdam, 1714.

Letters and Papers, Foreign and Domestic, of the Reign of Henry VIII. J.S. Brewer *et al.* (ed.). 1862–1932.

Mattingly, G., *Catherine of Aragon*. 1942.

Monro, C. (ed.), *Letters of Queen Margaret of Anjou, Bishop Beckington and Others*. Camden Society, Vol. 86. 1863.

Moriarty, C., *The Voice of the Middle Ages in Personal Letters, 1100–1500*. 1989.

Paston Letters, J. Gairdner (ed.). 6 vols. 1904, reprinted 1983.

Shirley, W.W. (ed.), *Royal and Other Historical Letters Illustrative of the Reign of Henry III*. 2 vols. 1866.

Smith, L.B., *A Tudor Tragedy: The Life and Times of Catherine Howard*. 1961.

Stevenson, J., (ed.), *Documents Illustrative of the History of Scotland*, Vol. 1. 1870.

Strickland, A., *Lives of the Queens of England from the Norman Conquest*. 6 vols. 1864.

Tanquerey, F.J., *Recueil de Lettres Anglo-Françaises, 1265–1399*. Paris, 1916.

Wood, M.A.E. (ed.), *Letters of Royal and Illustrious Ladies of Great Britain*. 3 vols. 1846.

Select Bibliography

The Norman Queens

Barlow, F., *William Rufus*. 1983.

Brooke, C., *The Saxon and Norman Kings*. 1963.

Chibnall, M.,*The Empress Matilda*, 1991.

Davis, R.H.C., *King Stephen*. 1967.

Douglas, D.C., *William the Conqueror*. 1964.

Gesta Stephani, K.R. Potter (ed.). 1955.

Given-Wilson, C., and Curteis, A., *The Royal Bastards of Medieval England*. 1984.

Le Patourel, J., 'The Norman succession, 995–1135', *English Historical Review*, cccxxxix (1971), pp. 225–50.

Midmer, R., *English Medieval Monasteries, 1066–1540*. 1979.

Pain, N., *Empress Matilda*. 1978.

Power, E., *Medieval English Nunneries*. 1922.

Southern, R.W., 'The place of Henry I in English history', *Proceedings of the British Academy*, xlviii (1962), pp. 127–56.

Stafford, P., *Queens, Concubines and Dowagers: The King's Wife in the Early Middle Ages*. 1983.

White, G.H., 'The household of the Norman kings', *Transactions of the Royal Historical Society*, 4th series, xxx (1948), pp. 127–55.

The Angevin Queens

Brieger, P., *English Art, 1216–1307*. 1957.

Brown, E.A.R., 'Eleanor as Parent, Queen and Duchess', in *Eleanor of Aquitaine: Patron and Politician*, W.W. Kibler (ed.). Austin, Texas, 1977.

Brundage, J.A., *Richard Lionheart*. 1974.

Gillingham, J., *Richard the Lionheart*. 1978.

Gillingham, J., 'Richard I and Berengaria of Navarre', *Bulletin of the Institute of Historical Research*, liii (1980), pp. 157–73.

Hallam, E., 'Bérèngere de Navarre', *La Province du Maine*, 93 (Le Mans, 1991), pp. 225–37.

Harvey, J., *The Plantagenets*. 1948.

Howell, M., 'The Resources of Eleanor of Provence as Queen Consort', *English Historical Review*, cii (1987), pp. 372–93.

Johnstone, H., 'Poor relief in the royal households of the thirteenth century', *Speculum*, iv (1929), pp. 149–67.

Johnstone, H., 'The Queen's Household', in *Chapters in the Administrative History of England*, T.F. Tout (ed.), Vol. v, 1937.

Kelly, A., *Eleanor of Aquitaine and the Four Kings*. 1950.

Painter, S., and Cazel, F.A., 'The Marriage of Isabella of Angoulême', *English Historical Review*, lxiii (1948), pp. 83–9.

Pernoud, R., *Eleanor of Aquitaine*, P. Wiles (trans.), 1967.

Powicke, F.M., *Henry III and the Lord Edward*. 2 vols. 1947.

Richardson, H.G., 'Letters and Charters of Eleanor of Aquitaine', *English Historical Review*, lxxiv (1959), p. 196.

Ridgeway, H.W., 'Foreign favourites and Henry III's problems of patronage, 1247–1258', *English Historical Review*, civ (1989), pp. 590–610.

Saunders, E.O., *English Art in the Middle Ages*. 1952.

Snellgrove, H.S., *The Lusignans in England, 1247–1258*. 1950.

Warren, W.L., *King John*. 1961.

Warren, W.L., *Henry II*. 1973.

The Plantagenet Queens

Barber, R., *Edward, Prince of Wales and Aquitaine*. 1978.

Blackley, F.D., 'Isabella and the Bishop of Exeter', in *Essays in Medieval History presented to Bertie Wilkinson*. 1968.

Blackley, F.D., and Hermansen, J. (eds), *The Household Book of Queen Isabella of England, 1311–1312*. Alberta, 1971.

Brown, Elizabeth A.R., 'The political repercussions of family ties in the early fourteenth century: the marriage of Edward II of England and Isabelle of France', *Speculum*, 63 (1988), pp. 573–95.

Byerley, B.P., and Byerley, C.R. (eds), *Records of the Wardrobe and Household, 1285–1286*. 1977.

Fryde, N., 'A royal enquiry into abuses: Queen Eleanor's ministers in north east Wales, 1291–1292', *Welsh History Review*, 5 (1970–1).

Fryde, N., *The Tyranny and Fall of Edward II*. 1979.

Galway, M., 'Joan of Kent and the Order of the Garter', *University of Birmingham Historical Journal*, 1 (1947), pp. 15–16.

Given-Wilson, C., *The Royal Household and the King's Affinity, 1360–1413*. 1986.

Harvey, J., *The Black Prince and his Age*. 1973.

Harvey, J., *The Plantagenets*. 1959.

Johnstone, H., 'The County of Ponthieu, 1279–1307', *English Historical Review*, xxix (1914), pp. 435–52.

Johnstone, H., 'The Queen's Exchequer under the three Edwards', in *Historical Essays in Honour of James Tait*, J.G. Edwards, V.H. Galbraith and E.F. Jacob (eds). 1933.

Johnstone, H., 'Isabella, the She-Wolf of France', *History*, new series, xxi (1936).

Johnstone, H., 'The Queen's Household', in *The English Government at Work, 1327–1336*, J.F. Willard and W.A. Morris (eds). Cambridge, Mass., 1940.

McLeod, E., *Charles of Orleans*. 1969.

Mathew, G., *The Court of Richard II*. 1968.

Ormrod, W.M., 'Edward III and his family', *Journal of British Studies*, 26 (1987), pp. 398–422.

Packe, M., *King Edward III*. 1983.

Parsons, D. (ed.), *Eleanor of Castile, 1290–1990: Essays to commemorate the 700th anniversary of her death*. 1991.

Parsons, J.C. (ed.), *The Court and Household of Eleanor of Castile in 1290*. Toronto, 1977.

Prestwich, M., *The Three Edwards*. 1980.

Salzman, L., *Edward I*. 1968.

Steel, A., *Richard II*. 1941.

Suggett, H., 'The use of French in England in the later Middle Ages', *Transactions of the Royal Historical Society*, xxviii (1946), pp. 63–5

Tuchman, B., *A Distant Mirror*. 1978.

The Lancastrian and Yorkist Queens

Bagley, J.J., *Margaret of Anjou, Queen of England*. 1948.

Chrimes, S.B., *Henry VII*. 1972.

Crawford, A., 'The King's Burden? – The Consequences of Royal Marriages in Fifteenth-Century England', in *Patronage, The Crown and The Provinces in Later Medieval England*, R.A. Griffiths (ed.). Gloucester, 1981.

Crawford, A., 'The Piety of Late Medieval English Queens', in *The Church in Pre-Reformation Society: Essays in Honour of F.R.H. Du Boulay*, Caroline Barron and Christopher Harper-Bill (eds). 1985.

Griffiths, R.A., 'Queen Katherine of Valois and a missing statute of the realm', *Law Quarterly Review*, xciii (1977), pp. 248–58.

Griffiths, R.A., *The Reign of Henry VI*. 1981.

Hutchinson, H.F., *Henry V*. 1967.

Kirby, J.L., *Henry IV of England*. 1970.

Lee, P.A., 'Reflections of Power: Margaret of Anjou and the Dark Side of Queenship', *Renaissance Quarterly*, XXXIX, no. 2 (1986), pp. 183–217.

MacGibbon, D., *Elizabeth Woodville*. 1938.

Myers, A.R., 'The captivity of a royal witch: the household accounts of Queen Joan of Navarre, 1419–1421', *Bulletin of the John Rylands Library*, 24 (1940), pp. 264.

Myers, A.R., 'Some household ordinances of Henry VI', *ibid.*, 36 (1953–4), pp. 449–67.

Myers, A.R., 'The household of Margaret of Anjou, 1452–3', ibid., 40 (1957–8) pp. 99–113.

Myers, A.R. (ed.), *The Household of Edward IV: The Black Book and the Ordinance of 1478*. 1958.

Myers, A.R., 'The household of Queen Elizabeth Woodville, 1466–1467', *Bulletin of the John Rylands Library*, 50 (1967–8), pp. 207–15.

Ross, C., *Edward IV*. 1974.Ross, C., *Richard III*. 1981.

Somerville, R., *History of the Duchy of Lancaster*, Vol. 1, *1265–1603*. 1953.

Stevenson, J. (ed.), *Letters and Papers Illustrative of the Wars of the English in France during the Reign of Henry the Sixth, King of England*, Rolls Series, Vol. 2. 1864.

Wolffe, B., *Henry VI*. 1981.

Wylie, J.H., *History of England under Henry the Fourth*. 4 vols. 1884–98.

Wylie, J.H., and Waugh, W.T., *The Reign of Henry V*. 3 vols. 1914–29.

The Tudor Queens

Armstrong, C.A.J., 'The Piety of Cecily, Duchess of York', in *England, France and Burgundy in the Fifteenth Century*. 1983.

Campbell, W. (ed.), *Materials for a History of the Reign of Henry VII*, Rolls Series, 2 vols. 1873–77.

Chrimes, S.B., *Henry VII*. 1972.

Fraser, A., *The Six Wives of Henry VIII*. 1992.

Griffiths, R.A., and Thomas, R.S., *The Making of the Tudor Dynasty*, Gloucester, 1985.

Ives, E., *Anne Boleyn*. 1986.

Jones, M.K., and Underwood, M., *The King's Mother: Lady Margaret Beaufort, Countess of Richmond and Derby*. 1992.

Nicolas, N.H. (ed.), *Privy Purse Expenses of Elizabeth of York*. 1830.

Scarisbrick, J.J., *Henry VIII*. 1968.

Warnicke, R.M., *The Rise and Fall of Anne Boleyn*. 1989.

Picture Credits

The author and publisher would like to acknowledge the following for their kind permission to reproduce photographs: Bibliothèque Nationale, Paris, MS 1AT. 1158 (p. 140), British Library (pp. 24 (seal of Matilda of Scotland), 67 (seal of Eleanor of Provence), 81 (seal of Margaret of France), 92 (seal of Isabella of France), 100 (seal of Philippa of Hainault), 106 (seal of Anne of Bohemia), 180 (signature of Katherine of Aragon), 194, 199 (signature of Jane Seymour)), The Conway Library, Courtauld Institute of Art (p. 56), The Master and Fellows of Corpus Christi College, Cambridge (p. 27), Kunsthistorisches Museum, Vienna (pp. 161, 197), National Portrait Gallery (pp. 183, 213), Public Record Office (pp. 205 (signature of Anne of Cleves), 209, 223 (signature of Katherine Parr)), Residenz Museum, Munich (p. 155), Geoffrey Wheeler (pp. 29 (seal of the Empress Matilda), 33, 45, 49, 71, 77, 84, 95, 103, 110, 116 (signature of Joan of Navarre), 121, 129 (signature of Margaret of Anjou), 131, 136 (signature of Elizabeth Woodville), 143 (signature of Cecily Neville), 146, 152 (signature of Margaret of Beaufort), 155, 158 (signature of Elizabeth of York)). Crown Copyright material in the Public Record Office and British Library is reproduced by permission of the Controller of Her Majesty's Stationery Office.

Index

Note: queens and other members of ruling families are indexed under their Christian names; where a woman's maiden name is given in the text, that is the name under which she is indexed.
